The Negro in the Christian Pulpit

16180.

J. W. Hood

THE

Negro in the Christian Pulpit;

OR, THE

TWO CHARACTERS AND TWO DESTINIES,

AS DELINEATED IN

TWENTY-ONE PRACTICAL SERMONS.

By J. W. HOOD,

Bishop of the A. M. E. Zion Church.

WITH AN APPENDIX,

CONTAINING SPECIMEN SERMONS BY OTHER BISHOPS OF
THE SAME CHURCH.

INTRODUCTION

By Rev. A. G. HAYGOOD, D. D.,

AUTHOR OF "OUR BROTHER IN BLACK."

RALEIGH:
EDWARDS, BROUGHTON & CO., STEAM POWER PRINTERS AND BINDERS.
1884.

THE

Negro in the Christian Pulpit;

OR, THE

TWO CHARACTERS AND TWO DESTINIES,

AS DELINEATED IN

TWENTY-ONE PRACTICAL SERMONS.

By J. W. HOOD,

Bishop of the A. M. E. Zion Church.

WITH AN APPENDIX,

CONTAINING SPECIMEN SERMONS BY OTHER BISHOPS OF
THE SAME CHURCH.

INTRODUCTION

By Rev. A. G. HAYGOOD, D. D.,

AUTHOR OF "OUR BROTHER IN BLACK," &c.

RALEIGH:
EDWARDS, BROUGHTON & CO., STEAM POWER PRINTERS AND BINDERS.
1884.

INTRODUCTION.

At the request of Bishop Hood, I cheerfully write this brief introduction. His long, faithful, able and useful work among his people commend him to the respect and confidence of those who have knowledge of him. In addition to what I have learned of the author of this volume of Sermons from the public prints, I have both from Southern and Northern men of high character the most unreserved expressions of approval. It seems to me that we understand a book better when we know something of the man who wrote it. It is in order to present at this place a few facts concerning the life of the preacher who speaks to us in this volume of Sermons

JAMES WALKER HOOD was born in Kennett township, Chester county, Pennsylvania, May 30, 1831. His father, the Rev. Levi Hood, and his mother, Harriet Hood, were Methodists, and were among the thirteen families that, in 1813, founded a separate colored Methodist church in Wilmington, Delaware. Some years after their marriage and settlement in Wilmington, the parents of the future Bishop moved to a farm nine miles from the city and situated on the line between Delaware and Pennsylvania. Here several of their twelve children were born—among them the subject of this sketch. The farm belonged to Ephraim Jackson. The Jacksons were numerous in that neighborhood and several of the Hood children were brought up in their service. The preacher's father was opposed to " binding " his children to service, as being too much like slavery. But, accepting his word as sufficient, the children were taken on verbal agreements that they should work for "food, clothing and six week's schooling annually till they were sixteen years old." The Jackson, into whose hands James Walker fell, retired from business soon after his semi-apprentice came to his family. The lad was thrown out of employment and, as it turned out, grew up with very limited educational advantages. In Philadelphia and New York the youth spent several of the following years, doing such work as opportunity allowed. He was fortunate enough to escape, during this period, an attempt to kidnap him; he was also brought under religious conviction, and at the age of eleven experienced, as he now believes, a true change of heart. The extravagant pretensions and superstitious conceits of many of his race, with whom he had religious association, had the effect of bringing the young convert into much doubt and spiritual distress God's blessing on the common sense and steadfast piety of his parents delivered him from the plague and peril of this sort of unbelief, and in his eighteenth year, "resting in the doctrine of justification by faith," he found true and lasting peace.

When he was twenty-five years old, he realized his call to preach, and his unfitness for the work upon which he was about to enter. But he was "licensed to preach," and began to do what he could both to preach and to improve himself. These Sermons show that, considering his opportunities, he surpassed many who have had every advantage.

In 1859 he was "received on trial" into the New England Conference of the African Methodist Episcopal Zion

Church. In 1860 he was ordained deacon, and sent as a Missionary to Nova Scotia. In 1862 he returned to the session of his Conference, was ordained Elder, and returned to the Nova Scotia Mission for another year. In 1863 he was stationed in Bridgeport, Connecticut. During this year he was sent to North Carolina " as the first one of his race appointed as a regular Missionary to the freedmen in the South." During the following eighteen years, North Carolina, the southern counties of Virginia, and the northern counties of South Carolina, have been the field of his chief labors. During that time in this field nearly 600 churches have been formed and about 500 church buildings erected

Mr. Hood was elected a Bishop in his Church by the General Conference which met in Charlotte, N. C., in 1872. As one of the "General Superintendents" of his widely extended Church, Bishop Hood has travelled the Continent to and fro. His ability, his eloquence, his zeal and his usefulness, have commanded the respect and confidence of the best people of both races. As one of the members of the Ecumenical Conference that met in London in 1881, Bishop Hood made a lasting impression. These sermons speak for themselves. Their naturalness, their clearness, their force, and their general soundness of doctrine, and wholesomeness of sentiment, commend them to sensible and pious people. I have found them as useful as interesting.

Those who still question whether the negro in this country is capable of education and "uplifting," will modify their opinions when they read these sermons, or else will conclude that their author is a very striking exception to what they assume is a general rule. Bishop Hood entertains many broad and important views as to the wants and duties and future of his people. He believes that their best interests are to be conserved in preserving the race from admixture of other bloods. They should, he thinks, hang together, and he is persuaded that if his people are to succeed permanently and broadly in this country, they must largely "work out their own salvation." Men like Bishop Hood deserve encouragement in their good work. They have a great work to do in the United States. May we not believe that in doing that work they are being trained for the yet greater work of redeeming Africa?

ATTICUS G. HAYGOOD.

EMORY COLLEGE, OXFORD, GA., }
October 16, 1884. }

THE APOLOGY.

And why should there be an apology for publishing a book of sermons? New publications are continually appearing. It is, however, customary to give a reason for the appearance of a new work. There are extraordinary reasons for the appearance of this work:

First. The absolute absence of such a work from the pen of a colored Methodist minister. This class of ministers is numbered by thousands, and their ministry has covered a period of nearly one hundred years. It seems time that a sample of their pulpit deliverances was put in the form of a book for public criticism. A single sermon from some distinguished one of them has occasionally appeared, and more frequently a short sketch, but something more than this seems to be demanded.

Secondly. In the course of studies laid down for our candidates for the ministry, the reading of sermons is included. It seems to me that if we require our young men to read printed sermons, we ought to produce them.

Thirdly. I have been urged, for several years, by the ministers among whom I have labored to publish my sermons.

With a single exception, the sermons herewith presented were written before the title of the book was selected. The harmony, therefore, of a course of sermons written upon a single topic may to not be expected, as they are selections from sermons prepared for ordinary

pulpit effort. This fact will also prepare the reader to expect a more frequent repetition of the same illustration
and scripture quotation than would be expected in a
course of Sermons written for publication. My constant
travels, connected with Episcopal duties, have forbidden
my reading the proof with as much care as I desired. I
notice some errors which were corrected in reading the
proof, but still appear.

On page 22d, line nine, " could " is erroneously repeated ; on page 40, sixth line from the bottom, " state "
should be " change "; on page 56, line eight, " their
friendship " should read : " these friends," same page, 14th
line, should read, " It was mysterious love " ; on page 61,
the first line of poetry should begin with " In," not
" And "; on page 83, line six, " of Luther " should read
" by Luther "; on page 90, seventh line from the bottom,
instead of " those days " it should read " — day
which ", on page 101, ninth line from the bottom,
" trembling " should read " tumbling " ; on page 110, fifth
line from the bottom, " light " should read " life ", on
page 150, after the word " torch," in line seventeen,
" for " should be inserted ; on page 165, sixth line from
the bottom, after speaker; " of " should read " in "; on
page 189, fifth line of poetry, instead of " unfathomless "
it should read " unfathomable." These are some of the
more vexing errors. Critical readers will discover others,
the true reading of which will be apparent at a glance.

I requested contributions from my colleagues, three of
whom furnish a sermon each, and the fourth two sermons. These productions present a rich variety of doctrine, of style and of thought; which add much to the
value of the work.

The introduction by Dr. Haygood is another evidence of the interest which that great philanthropist feels in advancement of the interests of the Black Brother, by which he has placed us under lasting obligations. He has our best thanks. For suggesting the idea of soliciting Dr. Haygood to write the introduction, and for opening correspondence on the subject, I am indebted to Rev. J. C. Price, M. A. I am also indebted to Rev. L. S. Burk-head, D. D. (of the M. E. Church, South), and Hon. A. W. Tourgee of "The Continent," published in New York, for letters to Dr. Haygood, commendatory of myself and work. These, with the Bishops who have furnished sermons, will please accept grateful thanks.

THE AUTHOR.

CONTENTS.

                                                 PAGE.

Introduction—By Rev. A. G. HAYGOOD, D. D., Author of "Our
    Brother in Black," &c., ... 3

The Author's Apology, ... 6

SERMON I.

The Claims of the Gospel Message, ... 9

SERMON II.

Personal Consecration, ... 20

SERMON III.

Exemplified Attachment to Christ and the Reward, ... 33

SERMON IV.

Divine Sonship the Sequence of Wondrous Love, ... 49

SERMON V.

Why was the Rich Man in Torment, ... 61

SERMON VI.

The Marvelous Vitality of the Church, ... 79

SERMON VII.

On Easter, ... 90

SERMON VIII.

Creation's First-born, or the Earliest Symbol of the Gospel, ... 105

SERMON IX.

The Soul's Anchor, ... 122

SERMON X.

The Loss of the Soul, ... 136

SERMON XI.

The Two Characters and Two Destinies, ... 148

SERMON XII.

Man's Natural Disinclination to turn in his Distresses to his Maker, ... 165

SERMON XIII.

The Streams which Gladden God's City, ... 178

SERMON XIV
PAGE

The Perfect Felicity of the Resurrected Saints a Result of Conformity
to the Divine Likeness,-- 190

SERMON XV.

The Doom of the Hypocrit's Hope,----------------------------- 205

SERMON XVI

The Glory Revealed in the Christian Character,------------------ 222

SERMON XVII.

A Desirable Consummation,--- ----------------------------- ------- 236

SERMON XVIII.

Loss of First Love,-- 247

SERMON XIX.

The Helplessness of Human Nature,-----------------------------262

SERMON XX.

The Christian Characteristics,--------------------------------,- 278

SERMON XXI.

David's Root and Offspring, or Venus in the Apocalypse,----------- 290

APPENDIX.

SERMON I.

The Unpardonable Sin, by Bishop J. J. Moore, D D ,------------- 307

SERMON II.

The First Pair Banished, by Bishop J. P. Thompson, M. D.,-------- 315

SERMON III.

The Love of God—Its Objects, Gift and Design, by Bishop Thomas
H. Lomax,--------- ----------,------------------------- 322

SERMON IV.

A Farewell, delivered before the Kentucky Conference by Bishop S. J.
Jones, D. D ,---------------------- ---------------------- 335

AN ADDRESS.

The Good Samaritan, by Bishop S. J. Jones, D. D.,--------------- 353

Electrotypes of Bishops contributing Sermons, in a group,----------- 304

SERMON I.

THE CLAIMS OF THE GOSPEL MESSAGE.

"Therefore we ought to give the more earnest heed to the things that we have heard, lest at any time we should let them slip." Heb. II, 1.

The object of writing the Epistle to the Hebrews seems to have been, to confirm the faith of those who had embraced the Gospel, to prevent them from being drawn away, and apostatizing therefrom, and to convince the unbelieving of the importance of the Gospel message. The apostle, at the opening of his discourse, set forth the fact that the Gospel economy was more excellent than the Jewish, which it was wholly to supersede, and that it was a more complete revelation of the mind and will of God, than he had ever before communicated to man—a revelation which proclaims, in all its richness, fulness and efficiency, the plan of salvation, secured through the suffering of the Son of God, for the perishing millions of the human race.

In the text we are reminded of the attention which the subject demands. Being more excellent and more important than any former message ever sent from God to man, it demands more earnest heed. The apostle desired that his Hebrew brethren should enjoy all the abundant blessings which it affords, and to

this end he urged that they should give it the necessary
attention—that they should grasp, and hang on to the
subject, as one upon which their eternal interests hinged.
He unites himself with them to avoid appearing invidious, or suspicious of any special indifference on their
part. It has been remarked that people are not so ready
to receive exhortations, which they suspect are urged
upon the ground of undeserved blame. He therefore
expressed himself in such a way as to indicate that the
duty urged was of general concern, and not singular to
them ; but because the Son of God, by whom the Father
has sent this great message of mercy to the human race,
is a person so infinitely more excellent and glorious than
any by whom he has ever spoken to man before; because
the message he brings is so vastly more important than
any former message communicated to man, and because
this great and glorious messenger suffered so much to
secure to us the blessings offered in this message, "therefore we ought to give" it "the more earnest heed"; more
than was given to any former message, yea, more than former messages (which were less important) deserved, and
more than we have hitherto given to this. Not being duly
impressed with its importance, we have not, hitherto,
given it the attention we should. Let us, therefore, cease
this indifference and heedlessness, call in the wanderings
of our minds, and turn them to the contemplation of
this great and all important subject of the soul's eternal
salvation, contained in the words spoken by the Son of
God. Such in brief is the sense of the text.

Let us enter into the spirit of the apostle, endeavor to
grasp his theme, and make it our own. There is no sub-

ject of so much importance to us, as this, and hence none
which has so strong a claim upon us. The Gospel offers
to all, who will embrace it, blessings rich, abundant and
eternal.

Our theme is, THE CLAIMS OF THE GOSPEL MESSAGE.
And our thoughts first revert to the grounds upon which
these claims rest. Why ought we to give heed to the
things which we have heard respecting the Gospel message? There are several points from which we may urge
attention to this subject;

I. ITS SOURCE, ORIGIN, AUTHOR.

The message is divine, it is from God. This is the point
at which the apostle begins. Indeed it was necessary for
him to settle this point, else he could not hope to induce
the Hebrews to embrace it. Hence, he starts off with the
following declaration: " God, who at sundry times and in
divers manners spake in time past unto the fathers by the
prophets, hath in these last days spoken unto us by his
Son." Thus he shows that the Gospel message is from
God, the only living and true God, the same who spoke
to the fathers by the prophets, the God of Abraham, of
Moses and Elijah. This was the first great fact to which
the apostle admonished the Hebrews to give heed. He
was not calling upon them to renounce the God of their
fathers, nor to embrace a new religion, but declares that
the same God, who had for ages been revealing his will
unto the fathers at sundry times and in divers manners,
had now at one time, by one whole message, in a more
complete manner, and by a more glorious messenger than
was ever before employed, revealed himself to the sons of
men in a new and living way. It was, therefore, not his

purpose to lead them away from the God of their fathers, but to lead them to him, by his own better way of approach, which he had revealed by his Son. By this we are reminded that as to authority, the Gospel message is fully equal to any former message, and, as we shall see, it is in all other respects superior.

1. *It is superior in its completeness.*

God had never given a complete revelation of his mind and will to man before. He had gradually unfolded his benevolent purposes, but had not fully revealed the mystery of redemption, in any of the messages given by the prophets to the fathers.

The former revelations were given by degrees, a part at a time—"at sundry times." The order and extent of creation was revealed in Adam's time. The general judgment and future rewards and punishments were made known to Enoch. To Adam, it was also made known that victory over the enemy of man should be obtained by the seed of the woman. To Abraham, it was made known that in his seed all the nations of the earth should be blessed. Jacob, looking down the line of the tribe of Judah, saw the promised seed of the woman and of Abraham, as a peaceful prince, to whom should the gathering of the people be. To Moses, it was revealed that Messiah should be a prophet, whose predictions would claim universal attention. To Isaiah and other prophets, many important truths were revealed. Among other visions of Isaiah, he saw the world's Redeemer as a mighty conqueror, coming up from Bozrah, meeting man's enemy, single handed and alone, and vanquishing him, staining his garments with the blood of the vanquished, and exulting in his power to save. Isaiah viewed him, until, by his suffering and triumph, he secured man's redemption, and obtained victory over death. Thus gradually and in parts, had God formerly revealed his mind and will, and the progress, triumph and victory of his kingdom, unto men. Not only had he given his former revelations at sundry times, but in divers manners, by dreams, by visions, by audible voices, and by the appearance of angels. Now the Gospel is God's last message to man, complete in itself, and delivered in all its fulness and completeness, by one messenger; not in dreamsor visions, not in types, shadows or dark sayings, as in the past, but in plain and popular language, which carries conviction to the heart, fills the understanding with knowledge and the heart with hope; not in words of terror, (as that voice which caused Sinai to quake, and filled the Israelites with mortal dread, so that they desired " that God should not speak to them any more,") but with a voice of infinite tenderness, with words that contain eternal life. "Therefore, we ought to give" it "the more earnest heed."

2. *But the apostle refers to the medium through which this message comes to us, the exalted character of him who brings it, the sacrifice he made, and the suffering he endured to obtain man's redemption.*

"By his Son." This is the second point from which he would have us view the importance of the Gospel, namely, that God regarded it so highly, that he would entrust it to no less person than his Son. That which is of little worth, we will intrust to any one; not so with that which we regard as of great value. The necessary conclusion is, that a message which God regarded so highly, must be of infinite importance.

The apostle stops not here, but to heighten our admiration, and to carry our thoughts up to the loftiest summit where we can view the subject in all its grandeur and glory, and have a full realization of its momentous consequences to man, he proceeds to portray the characteristics of the Son of God. " This is he whom he hath appointed heir of all things, by whom he made the worlds." The saints are sometimes called sons of God, but on none of the saints hath he conferred the title of creator, or the honor of universal inheritance or empire. Angels are called sons of God, but " unto which of the angels said he at any time, Thou art art my Son, this day have I begotten thee." " And again, when he bringeth his first begotten into the world, he saith, And let all the angels of God worship him." Heb. i, 5, 6. He is the Son of God in a sense that no other being can claim sonship. All other beings are the work of his fingers, or breath of his nostrils, but the Son is the product of his redeeming love, his first and only begotten Son—his second self, the offspring of his bowels of compassion, the eternal Son, his Son from all eternity, co-equal, co-essential and co-eternal with the Father. He is not only a Son in a sense that no other being can be, but he occupies an honor that no other being has attained to. " To which of the angels said he at any time, Sit thou on my right hand till I make thine enemies thy footstool." Jesus, as the Son of God, has by inheritance a right to sit at God's right hand.

But there was a further fact in connection with this

Gospel message to which the apostle had especially referred, namely, the sacrifice made by the Son of God, to meet all the exigencies of the sinner's case. That man might enjoy the benefits of the Gospel economy, much needed to be done for him. He had lost the power to do anything toward delivering himself, as completely as a man shut up in an iron prison, or in a grave, hence he is said to be dead and buried; therefore he that brought to him the message of mercy, had also to give him power to receive it. Man by disobedience had dishonored God, broken his law, and made himself a transgressor. This separated him from the divine favor, involved him in spiritual death, and condemned him to natural and eternal death. To meet man's condition, and deliver him therefrom, Jesus offered himself a sacrifice. For man's disgraceful conduct, he deserved to be put to shame, and for his transgression to suffer pain; hence Jesus, as his ransom, suffered both shame and agony on the cross. But man also deserved death, and Jesus died for him. Thus Jesus met all the necessities of man's helpless condition, and hence it is written, "the chastisement of our peace was upon him, and by his stripes we are healed." He rendered unto God an acceptable sacrifice, God himself bearing witness to its acceptance by sitting him at his own right hand—"when he had by himself purged our sins, sat down at the right hand of the majesty on high."

> "He ever lives above
> For me to intercede,
> His all redeeming love,
> His precious blood to plead :—
> Forgive him, oh forgive, they cry,
> Nor let the ransomed sinner die."

II. Let us consider THE EXHORTATION.

We are exhorted to give heed, earnest heed, yea "more earnest heed" to the things that we heard respecting the gospel message, and its claims upon us, and thus avoid the danger of letting the things, which make for our peace, slip from us, or, in other words, avoid the danger of loosing our interest in them. Thoughtlessness and heedlessness are most prevalent, and also most dangerous evils. Those misquote God's word, who say, "he that runs may read." They put it wrong end foremost. It should be, "he that reads may run." You must stop and read, and then run. You cannot read while running. Coming to the point at which two roads meet, if you rush on, you are as likely to take the wrong road as the right one, but if you stop and read the direction on the signpost, and thus learn the right way, you may then go forward with all possible speed. That saying, "Be sure you are right, and then go ahead," is a wise one.

The admonitions to take heed are numerous, and are found in almost every part of the sacred volume. Moses thus writes: "Only take heed to thyself, and keep thy soul diligently, lest thou forget the things which thine eyes have seen, and lest they depart from thy heart all the days of thy life." Deut. iv, 9. Again, "Take heed unto yourselves, lest ye forget the covenant of the Lord your God, which he made with you." Verse 23. Solomon admonishes us to ponder the paths of our feet, and Jesus frequently gives this solemn injunction, "He that hath an ear to hear, let him hear." To his disciples, after he had explained the parable of the sower, he said, "Take heed what ye hear," Mark iv, 24; and in another place

he said, "Take heed, therefore, how ye hear." These
passages indicate that inattention to the soul's interests is
a prevalent evil, and that the tendency of the mind to
drift away from the things that pertain to our eternal interests is so strong, that it needs to be held up to them,
as a ship needs to be held up by its helm, in order to
make head against a contrary wind. When the wind is
contrary, but little head is made, if the man at the helm
is careless or neglectful of duty. In our voyage across
time's billows, the wind is always contrary, and nothing
but the most careful attention to duty, the most ceaseless
energy and watchfulness, will enable us to make head.
This steadiness of purpose, energy of soul, unceasing
watchfulness, and constant holding of the mind and attention up to the things which most concern us is, what
so many, even professing christians lack. Many are
wholly thoughtless, heedless and indifferent. They are
warned that they are in the broad road to ruin, that
their way is dark and leads to hell; but they don't take
heed. The charming sound of the Gospel fills their ears,
the wrath and indignation of Almighty God is proclaimed in thunder tones, the brink upon which they
stand is pointed out by the solemn and sorrowful warning voice of faithful ministers, but all to no effect; they
don't take heed; along the downward road they pursue
their dark and woful way. O heedless mortal! we appeal
to you on this first Sabbath morning in the new year.
O stop and think! Give heed and hear, turn to God,
and your souls shall live.

But the text is especially addressed to those who are not
wholly heedless—those who have heard. It is to the

things that we have heard, that we are exhorted to give heed, lest at any time we should let them slip. It is our duty to hold what we hear, but by heedlessness we let go that which we ought to hold on to. In the revised version of the New Testament it is rendered, " Lest haply we drift away from them." The sense is about the same. The idea is, that if the things are not retained, it is our own fault. Mr. Benson thinks "run out" would be a better rendering, that it alludes to a leaky vessel, which lets out the water many ways, which is poured in one way. Preaching is represented as watering men with the word, and receiving the word by faith is represented as drawing water from the wells of salvation. If we do not retain what is poured into us by preaching, and received through faith, we may be charged with letting it run out, or slip from us.

But our attention is called to time. " Lest at any time." Some persons would hold on to and reap the full benefit of what they have heard, if all seasons were favorable. When they have no cross nor vexation, and are enjoying the flood tide of divine blessings, both spiritual and temporal, they run well. But we shall not reach a state here on earth that is free from vexations. Vexations are the natural products of time's soil, and so long as we are creatures of time, we shall be subject to various, changing seasons and circumstances, and therefore in danger of letting the good things we have heard slip from us, or of drifting away from them.

Some drift away under the soft and balmy breezes of worldly prosperity, some are driven by the storms of adversity, some are the subjects of peculiar temptation

God sometimes suffers his people to be severely tried, that they may be confirmed to the Captain of our salvation, who was made perfect by suffering. Jesus himself was led up by the Spirit into the wilderness that he might be tempted by the devil, and no mortal can tell, or even conceive, what he endured during those forty days. We are taught to pray, " Lead us not into temptation." While God tempts no man, yet he leads us in the path of duty, and Satan lays his snares in that very path, and unless we can prevail with the Lord to lead us to duty by some other path, we shall have sore trial. In these trying times many are drawn away from their steadfastness, let their grace leak out, make shipwreck of faith, let slip the things which they have heard, lose all the good effect of the word, and drift away from the truth. Such is the result of heedlessness. This evil effect is sometimes suddenly produced, but more frequently like water from a leaky vessel, the good effect of the word gradually runs out of the soul, till it becomes empty. The only sure preventative against this evil is to take heed. "Therefore we ought to give the more earnest heed to the things which we have heard, lest at any time we should let them slip."

SERMON II.

PERSONAL CONSECRATION.

"And who then is willing to consecrate his service this day unto the Lord ?" 1 Chronicles xxix, 5.

Our text is associated with the effort, which David put forth to induce his people to supply the material necessary for the erection of the Lord's house, which Solomon his son was ordained to erect. It was in David's heart to build this house himself, but it was not God's will that he should. There was no objection, however, to his gathering together such materials as he could, and David was quite content to do such part of the work, as it pleased the Lord that he should do. There are some men who, if they can't do what they choose, won't do anything. Not so with David, he was so deeply interested in the Lord's work, that he was ready to do whatever part God would permit him. Finding that it was not God's pleasure that he should erect the building, nor even know the plan of it, yet being permitted to do so, he went to work, with all his might, to collect the materials ; some of his collections being the most costly, of which that magnificent structure was composed, namely, silver, gold, even the gold of Ophir, and stones most precious. In collecting the materials, he drew both upon his own private resources, and the public resources of his kingdom. Yet all of this he considered not enough, but believed that a work of so much importance should be engaged in by all of the people. He therefore made a personal appeal, in the language of the text, to each individual. He prefaced his appeal with a statement of the grounds upon which it was made:

(1). The youthfulness of his son, whom God had chosen to erect this building. (2). The vastness of the work. (3). The grandeur and glory associated with it. The palace was not for man, but for the Lord God, who was to dwell therein, or be therein represented by a glorious splendor, the bright symbol of his divine presence. It was therefore a work worthy of their best effort, to push it forward. The more rich, costly and abundant their gifts, the more splendid would be the adornment, and the more suitable would be the house for its divine occupant. (4). He referred them to his own example. He had contributed of his most costly and precious possessions, had given the best he had, not for show or any vain or selfish motive, but from love toward's God's house. "Moreover, because I have set my affection to the house of my God, I have of mine own proper good, of gold and silver, which I have given to the house of my God, over and above all that I have prepared for the holy house." When what we do for God springs from love toward him, we may be sure that both our person and work are accepted.

Having presented the grounds, David makes his appeal direct and personal. "Who then is willing to consecrate his service this day unto the Lord?" I repeat, this appeal was direct and personal. It went directly home to each and every one, to whom it was addressed. No one could feel that he was not included, that it did not mean him; but each one must have felt that he was required to respond for himself. There could have been no looking about to see who was referred to, but each must have felt a personal responsibility, that he could could not shirk or shake off.

In like manner, direct and personal, does the text come home to each of us to-day. I wish that each one present would regard the text as a personal appeal to himself. "Who then is willing to consecrate his service this day unto the Lord?" Not merely a little seriousness. which might be produced by a thunder storm, a hurricane, or a sudden death ; not a little amendment of our ways, the breaking off of our viler habits merely; but a consecration is called for—a consecration of our service unto the Lord. Conse-crate is from the Latin *con* and *sacro*, to make or declare sacred, to separate from a common to a sacred purpose, to set apart, to dedicate, to devote to the service and worship of God. It carries with it the idea of perpetuity. He that comes to consecrate his service unto the Lord, should come with his mind fully made up, never to separate himself from the divine service, but to say with the poet,

"The covenant I this moment make,
    I'll ever keep in mind,
I will no more my God forsake,
    Nor cast his word behind."

There is peculiar wickedness attached to the desecra-tion of sacred things, and those who are thus guilty are sure to feel the divine displeasure. The ark of God so plagued the Philistines that they were glad to get rid of it; and Belshazzar was punished with death, for profaning the sacred vessels taken from the temple of the Lord at Jerusalem.

Now we are called upon to consecrate our service unto the Lord; to do it this day. All Scripture appeals are put in the present tense. ' "To-day" and "this day" is the language in which appeals are made. Such is the language of the Psalmist, " To-day if ye will hear his voice," Psa. xcv, 7. And Paul reminds us that this was not merely the language of David, but of the Holy Ghost: " Wherefore as the Holy Ghost saith, To-day if ye will hear his voice." Heb. iii, 7. Joshua thus addressed Israel, " Choose ye this day." Joshua xxiv, 15. Likewise Moses said unto Israel, " See, I have set before thee this day life and good." There is no intimation that another day will be given, or that this offer will ever be made again. The text, it seems to me, has a peculiar force to-day. This is the first Sunday in the new year, and it happens upon the first day of the year. Some of you have no recollection of new year's day falling on the Sabbath before. The periods that elapse between the times that the first of January falls on the Sabbath, are five, six, and eleven years. We have just passed the longest period, which occurs only once in twenty-eight years. Many of us will never see this long period elapse again. Some will never see the first of January come on the Sabbath again. Some will never see another new year's day. Some, perhaps, will never see another day. How solemn the thought! Even before this day is gone we may go to eternity, before this day is closed we may close our eyes in death. How important, then, that we should consecrate our service unto the Lord to-day.

I. Let us notice WHAT THIS CONSECRATION IMPLIES.

It is a complete and entire separation from every other service, and includes a surrender of all our physical and mental powers to God, to serve him with our bodies which are his, to esteem him as the chief good, and to render unto him the adoration of the whole heart.

1. *We must abandon Satan's service entirely.*

Our consecration to God's service will not be complete so long as we do any work for Satan, nor will God accept our service so long as Satan has a share. We cannot serve two masters, and the attempt to do so will prove fatal to our spiritual prospects for the future. We must not only abandon Satan's service, but must live at the greatest possible distance from his dominion. Thousands are ruined by settling too near to the border of Satan's kingdom. They complain that Satan troubles them. They can expect nothing else, while they live so near to him. If you don't want to be troubled by him, you must move further from him. If we live near to Christ, the devil can't harm us. If we are constantly employed in divine service, the devil will have no opportunity to entice us.

2. *We must abandon creed service.*

The sum total of some men's religion is their church and its peculiar forms, ceremonies and doctrines. You would never know that they made any pretense to piety, were it not for their activity in the sanctuary on the Sabbath day. Their zeal would be a good thing, if it was

for God's glory, if it were God's work in which they engage; but it is not. It is not the kingdom of Christ
they are laboring to build up, but a kingdom of their
own fancy. Whether souls are saved or not is not their
concern, but the enlargement of what they are pleased to
style "the church," and the means employed, like Peter's
words, savor more of the things that be of men than the
things of God. There is much more of earth than of
heaven in all their labor and toil; much more of the
wisdom of this world, than of that which cometh from
above, which the apostle tells us, "is first pure, then
peaceable, gentle and easy to be entreated, full of mercy
and good fruits, without partiality and without hypoc-
ricy." James iii, 17.

3. *We must abandon self service.*

We are naturally selfish. Self seeks to be gratified,
to be indulged, to be extoled and exalted. We are self
willed, self opinionated, self conceited. God demands the
sacrifice of self, and reminds us that without it acceptable service to him is impossible. "If any man will come
after me, let him deny himself." Matt. xvi, 24. To sacrifice self requires the greatest possible effort; it is represented as the cutting off of a hand and the plucking out
of an eye. The poet also reminds us how unwilling man
is to make this sacrifice:

> "If self must be denied,
> And sin forsaken quite,
> They'd rather choose the road that's wide,
> And strive to think it's right."

Men persuade themselves that their way is right, because it is congenial to their selfish inclination. Some

mistake self will for divine impulse, and claim to be inspired to do that, to which they are induced by naked selfishness. We have an instance of this in the man who is now on trial for the assassination of President Garfield. He would have us believe that he was led to the commission of that most heinous crime by divine inspiration; and it appears that he had worked himself up into the notion that it was all right, before he could nerve himself to commit the crime. There are thousands of evil deeds of less magnitude, to the commission of which men work themselves up in the same way, and selfishness lies at the root of the evil. We serve self. Be assured that if we would consecrate our service unto the Lord, self must be sacrificed, crucified, die and be buried.

3. *We must abandon our sinful state.*

By nature we are sinners, and we cannot serve God in our sins. The heart, the carnal mind, is enmity against God, is not in subjection to his will, and cannot be, therefore the carnal mind must be removed. The old man and his deeds must be cast out. We must have a new nature. You might as soon expect a stream to run up hill, or a fish to live on dry land, as to expect a sinner to serve God in his sins. Remember the language of Christ to Nicodemus, " Except a man be born again, he cannot see the kingdom of God." If we had not had our natural birth, we would never have seen the light of this world, likewise except we are born into the kingdom of Christ, we can know nothing of it. We must be born into the kingdom of God, in order to live and move and act our part in it, and we need the divine nature to qualify us to render service acceptable to God.

4. Finally, we must make a public entrance upon the divine service.

We must get up boldly and leave the devil's camp, renounce our allegiance to him and publicly declare ourselves the servants of the Lord. Why not? we have served the devil publicly, why not forsake his service openly? Otherwise, Satan may charge us with sneaking away from him. He may claim our service on the ground that we have not given him proper notice that we have quit him. All work for God must be done in his vineyard. To render acceptable service to him, we must unite with those who are in his service.

II. Let us notice THE NATURE OF ACCEPTABLE SERVICE.

1. *It must be voluntary.*

Hence the language of David, "Who is willing?"

Revelation lays great stress on the will. "Whosoever will, let him take the water of life freely." The will is the fountain whence all our moral actions flow. The will determines our course, and is responsible for every act of ours. We may be acted upon against our will, but if we act at all, our will consents. To consecrate our service unto the Lord, therefore, it is only necessary to get the consent of the will. "Who then is willing?" God will not have the service of constraint, he demands the free consent of the will. Inanimate matter is governed by fixed laws, laws that it cannot resist, in connection with which there can be no will but that of him who governs it. The inferior creatures are governed by instinct, but man is a moral free agent, and therefore responsible. He has the power of reflection and the faculty of reason. He can bring matters to the scales of his

judgment and weigh them. He can think and form con-
clusions. He can form resolutions and act upon them.
He is, therefore, morally free and responsible. God declares, " He hath showed thee, O man, what is good ; and
what doth the Lord require of thee but to do justly, love
mercy and walk humbly with thy God?" The right
way is made plain, and if we walk not in it, it is because
we will not.

The fatalist would rob man of his moral free agency,
and make him a mere machine, incapable of doing good
or evil, and hence not responsible. This doctrine would
exclude the necessity, or even the possibility of a judgment. There would be no virtue to reward and no vice
to punish. But God, in his Word, declares that there
will be a judgment, both of the just and the unjust. He
has been reiterating it ever since the days of Enoch, that
men will be judged according to their deeds, and that
whether we are rewarded or punished depends upon our
conduct in this life; that good and evil are set before us,
and that grace is given us to reject the one and choose
the other. Such is the import of the text, " Who then is
willing to consecrate his service unto the Lord this day?"

And this language stands not alone, as we have seen,
but besides the passages we have quoted, the following
are of equal force : " They hated knowledge, and did not
choose the fear of the Lord. * * Therefore, shall they
eat the fruit of their own way, and be filled with their
own devices." Prov. i, 29 and 31.

There are two ways set before the sons of men, and
they are permitted to choose which they will. Our des-
tiny and happiness depend upon our choice. Jesus said

of Mary, she "hath chosen that good part." Fate has not made it hers, but she has made it her choice; she has not possessed it by the force of necessity, but by her own free will. Thank God, He adds, "it shall not be taken from her." It was not forced upon her, and it shall not be forced from her. God will see to it that none shall take us out of his vineyard by violence. We are free to consecrate ourselves unto his service, and free to continue in his service, for none can pluck us out of his hand. Having been made free from sin, we become the servants of God, have our fruit unto holiness, and the end ever-lasting life. All of this is offered to us freely, but we must accept it freely. There are many reasons why we should fly from the road to death, and seek that which leads to life, yet, we are free. A gaping hell, with howling demons, making it hideous with more than ten thousand terrors, awaits the sinner in the road to death, but you are free. You can force your way, if you will, down to that burning lake, over the prayers of a loving mother, a faithful minister, over the blood of a crucified Saviour' and all the means employed to keep you back from the pit. This you can do, because you are morally free.

Heaven with all its glories awaits you at the end of the road to life. There the enraptured host of glorified saints await to welcome you to the blissful regions of God's eternal domain, and to the joys of eternal day. There that darling babe that angels rocked to sleep, is waiting to meet and embrace you, and to fill your ears with such music as heaven alone can afford. All these and untold millions of charms, unknown to mortals here,

await you in the glory world, and invite you there; but
you are free; you can reject them if you will; you can
have them if you will. Who then is willing? Who will
close in with the offered blessings this day? '

2. *This is a pleasant service.*

I am aware of the fact that some professed christians
complain and whine about their troubles and vexations.
They will have it that their lot is a hard one. I am quite
sure that a sinner would find it hard work to serve God
in his sins. Yea, impossible. A hypocrite would make
no better head, and it is possible that there may be some
sincere seekers after the right way, who are so weak and
feeble, that duty may seem a load and worship a task.
But to the sound, healthy christian, the service of God is
really delightful. It must be so, for the true christian
loves the Lord with all his heart, and can it be hard
work to serve one we love with all the heart? Does the
lover find it hard work to serve his spouse? Does the
bridegroom find it hard work to serve his bride? Does
the loving mother find it hard work to serve her helpless
infant? I anticipate the answer, there can be but one.
In all these cases love makes the service delightful, and
the more that can be done, the more happiness there is
afforded.

It is midnight! The cloud hangs heavy and dark.
Heaven's artillery shakes the earth. Lightning flash
chases lightning's flash. Yet, in the midst of this storm
and darkness I see a man leave his bed, dress himself
and prepare to brave the storm. Where goes that man
in the storm and darkness reigning without? Why does

he leave his comfortable bed, and comfortable room, and go forth to grope his way in the dark? He is a loving husband, his wife is suddenly ill, he goes for the doctor who is five miles away, the streams are swollen, bridges are afloat, so that crossing would be dangerous in day light, yet the husband ventures. Love lends speed to his pace, which he slacks not until the desired object is reached. Was it hard work to get that man out of his bed? It would have been hard work to have kept him in it. It would have taken chains, and strong chains, to have held that man back. Why? Because he loved his wife.

Now if we love God with all our heart, it will be our chief delight to serve him. The angels don't find it hard work to serve God, it is their delight. Jesus says: " My yoke is easy, and my burden light" Solomon says, " her ways are ways of pleasantness." If we have on a heavy yoke, it is not the yoke of Jesus; if your way is not pleasant, it is not the way to heaven. There is a kind of good and evil equal bent, more a devil than a saint state, that some get into, and it's a hard road. O get out of it to-day, if any of you have gotten into it; and you may be sure that you have, if you find it hard work to serve God. The truly pious find it joyful work to serve God; hence they sing, " Let the children of Zion be joyful in their king," and again, " Rejoice in the Lord alway, and again I say rejoice."

3. *But this is a profitable service.*

The devil, in his attempt to slander Job, by mistake uttered a very important truth. He said that Job did not serve God " for nought." It is true. The christian does not serve God for nought. He, that serves God has the assurance of an abundant reward. Godliness, says the apostle, is profitable. The sinner toils in vain, and labors all his day to reap eternal woe. But he that serves God is assured of an inheritance with the saints. God grant you grace to " consecrate your service unto the Lord this day."

SERMON III.

EXEMPLIFIED ATTACHMENT TO CHRIST AND THE REWARD.

"Behold, we have forsaken all, and followed thee; what shall we have therefore?" Matt. xix, 27.

I have thought, that, if the advantages which christianity offers to its votaries, were sufficient to overcome Peter's extreme selfishness, and induce him to forsake all and follow Christ, there is no good reason why any other heart should not yield to its influences. Selfishness was one of the most prominent features in Peter's nature: to this our attention is directed on several occasions. First, at his call. On other occasions, Jesus simply said," Follow me," and was obeyed. I am not certain that Peter would have left his nets, if nothing more than this had been said to him. Knowing his natural selfishness, Jesus added the promise : "I will make you fishers of men. And they straightway left their nets and followed him." Matt. iv, 19, 20. Andrew, it is true, was with him, but it is my notion that it was to meet and overcome Peter's selfishness, that the promise was added in this case, which we find in no other. The second occasion was that on which Jesus began to show his disciples, how he must go unto

2

Jerusalem, and suffer many things of the elders, chief
priests and scribes, and be killed, and be raised again the
third day. Matt. xvi, 21. Here Peter's selfishness over-
leaped all bounds, so that he took Jesus and began to
rebuke him, saying, " Be it far from thee, Lord : this shall
not be unto thee." For this, he received the most severe
rebuke that ever a disciple of Jesus received from his
master, "Get thee behind me, Satan : thou art an offence
unto me: for thou savourest not the things that be of
God, but those that be of men." Matt. xvi, 23. The
third occasion was that of the transfiguration, on which
Peter, having got into a good place, wanted to build and
stay. He held a commission to gather the lost sheep
who were perishing in the valley, yet he was so filled
with thoughts of his own comfort, that he was ready to
let them perish in the valley, if he could but continue to
enjoy the rapture of the mount of divine glory. These
passages most clearly indicate that Peter was naturally
a most selfish man ; and would not have embraced the
religion of Jesus, had he not had the best reason to believe
that it was most advantageous to do so. Nor was a mind
like his likely to be deceived ; he was never satisfied with
a cursory view of a matter, but sought to fully inform
himself. When he, with John, came to the sepulchre on
the third morning, John outrunning Peter, reached the
tomb first, and simply stooped down and looked in ; but
Peter, coming a little later, went in and carefully exam
ined the grave clothing. John xx, 5, 6. This same desire to know it all, appears also in the text.

If, however, there is any selfishness exhibited in the
text, it is a commendable selfishness. In this he is not

rebuked, nor is there any hint that his interrogatory
savors of any thing not commendable. So far from this,
Jesus gave a full and complete answer to the question
propounded. An answer that seemed to allay all anxiety,
even in Peter's mind.

We conclude, therefore, that it is quite in accord with
the divine will, that we should consider the benefits of
religion; ' that we are encouraged to inquire and act
upon a well matured judgment And, blessed be God!
the religion of Jesus will bear the most careful scrutiny,
the most rigid examination, and when subjected to the
severest ordeal, every grain of it will stand as pure gold;
and confirm the apostle's declaration, that godliness is
profitable unto all things, not only for the life to come,
but also for this life. Genuine attachment to Christ,
secures blessings, rich, abounding and eternal.

I. But the text leads us TO CONTEMPLATE THE NATURE
OF ACCEPTABLE ATTACHMENT TO CHRIST.

It is exclusive and self-denying The language of the
text grew out of the refusal of a wealthy young man to
give up his earthly possessions, as a prerequisite to his
possessing treasures in heaven. I don't understand that
he was required to sell his property and scatter all of his
money without care. He was simply required to exchange
his property for money, that he might have it in a con-
venient shape to give as occasion required. I don't think
that there is much virtue in giving thoughtlessly. It is
our duty to see to it that our gifts are bestowed where
they will do good. This young man was unwilling to
trust the Lord, which is the fruitful source of disobedience,
and, at least, one great reason why there are not more

genuine, wholesouled christians. A confidential reliance upon God enables us to turn loose the things which are seen and to lay hold of those things which are not seen.

All systems of religion are connected with sacrifice. The worshippers of Moloch caused their children to pass through the fire. As a test of Abraham's faith and obedience, he was required to give up his son, the son through whom the promised seed should come. I do not believe that this young man would have been any more re-quired to render himself penniless, than Abraham was to render himself childless. If he had shown his willingness to obey, Jesus, no doubt, would have said, "it's enough." The consent of the will is what he demands. An entire surrender of soul and body to him, a sacrifice of self. The Jewish economy was connected with many sacrifices. The blood of beasts, and of birds, the burnt offerings, the sin offerings, the wave offerings, and many others.

Jesus, by the sacrifice of himself, has superseded the necessity of these. Neither the blood of beasts, nor human beings, is required under the christian dispensa-tion. And yet there is a sacrifice required. I repeat, a sacrifice of self, self-will, self-indulgence, self-gratification, self exaltation, self-conceit, and self-adoration must be sacrificed. We must sacrifice everything that hinders a full reliance upon the divine promise. This sacrifice is not made without pain to the natural man; to make it does violence to the carnal inclinations. It is represented as the plucking out of an eye, or the amputation of a member. But who would not sooner lose an eye, hand or foot, than to lose the whole body.

This young man who had kept the whole law, so far

as he had learned it, up to that time, asks: "What lack
I yet?" Only one more test was required, and he would
have been perfect, namely, a sacrifice of his property.
When he heard that saying, he went away sorrowful; for
he had great possessions, in which, it seems, he had more
confidence than he had in the promised possession.
None who forsook Jesus ever went away happy.

Jesus said unto his disciples: "How hardly shall they
that have riches, enter into the kingdom of. God—it
is easier for a camel to go through the eye of a needle,
than for a rich man to enter into the kingdom of God,"
that is, if he trusts in his riches. The disciples, in their
astonishment, asked, who then can be saved.

Men have tried to whittle away this passage, and try
to make it appear that Christ did not mean what he said.
The trouble is, they overlook what he did say, and try to
fix up a plausible meaning in accordance with their own
shortsightedness. If we read enough of God's word to
understand it, we won't have any need to exhibit any
such bungling attempts at fixing it up; it is already fixed.
We have been told that Jesus did not mean a needle's
eye, but a gate in Jerusalem, called by that name. This,
seems to me to be far fetched. I have never been able to
accept it. Whatever he meant was something impossi-
blé with man. The doctors seem to have overlooked this
fact, and try to get up a possibility: hence they manage
to get their camel through their needle's eye, after getting
him down on his knees, and his burden off his back.
This interpretation finely illustrates the importance of
humility, but humility was not just the point that Christ
was illustrating at that time. He was showing the folly

of trusting in riches, and the impossibility of any one getting to heaven, who trusted in riches, or who, like this man, had more confidence in riches than he had in Christ. The record in St. Mark makes it clear that stress was laid upon the *trust*. "Children, how hard it is for them that trust in riches, to enter into the kingdom of God." Mark x, 24. While all things are possible with God, all things are not consistent, nor in accord with the established order of his government. It would be inconsistent for God to lie, to deny himself, or to change the arrangement of his own plan of salvation. He could take a camel through a needle's eye, with more consistency and less difficulty, than he could take a man to heaven, who had more confidence in his own possessions than in God's goodness. The camel and needle being irrational creatures, he could do what he would with them, without coming in conflict with any of his own laws or purposes. To send a camel through a needle's eye would simply be to work a miracle. But man is a moral free agent. God himself has devised the plan of salvation, which includes trust in him; and, whosoever will go to heaven in that way, enters, and he only. This plan includes a willingness to renounce all things for Christ's sake. This man was not willing to do that. It includes a faith to let go the things we see and grasp those things which are not seen. This man had no such faith, and it appears that the love of riches deceived him and kept him from it. Jesus had announced that to be his disciple a man must deny himself. This man was unwilling to do that. I think, therefore, while with God all things are possible, it must be clear to any thoughtful mind, that there are

almost insurmountable difficulties in the way of taking
a man to heaven, who won't give up his trust in riches.
God would have to get him in on some new plan, not
contemplated in his own plan of salvation. The mediator
of the new covenant made no arrangement for any except
those that embrace the plan proposed. It must be equally
clear, that there would be no such difficulties for him to
overcome in getting a camel through a needle's eye.
He, to whom all things are possible, could easily pass a
camel through a needle's eye.

The language of Jesus and of Peter indicates that the
disciples understood that he required a willingness to
give up all things, if necessary, to do service for him.
Peter answered: "Behold, we have forsaken all and
followed thee; what shall we have therefore?" And the
answer which follows indicates the same: "Verily, I
say unto you, That ye which have followed me, in the
regeneration when the Son of man shall sit on the throne
of his glory, ye also shall sit upon twelve thrones, judging the twelve tribes of Israel. And every one that hath
forsaken houses, or brethren, or sisters, or father, or
mother, or wife, or children, or lands, for my name's sake,
shall receive a hundredfold, and shall inherit everlasting
life." If this does not show that Christ demands a total
surrender of all things, then words are useless to convey
ideas.

To be a follower of Jesus, we must be willing to endure any pain for conscience's sake. Christianity, or at
least the form of it, has become so popular that it is very
seldom that we have to resist unto blood, striving against
sin; and yet many have not counted their lives dear, if

spent in the vindication of the truth, and if they were thereby able to finish their course with joy.

To be followers of Jesus, we must leave our sinful state. We were shapen in iniquity and born in sin. We are by nature heirs of death. We have no good in us, are corrupt and alienated from God, without hope and without God in the world. No amendment will help our case. Our old nature cannot be purified. We must be formed anew. We must be killed and made alive again. There must be a complete transformation, a complete coming out of our old nature, and the entering into a new. Like Abraham, we must cross the flood and come out of of Chaldea, and like Ruth we must leave the land of our nativity. We must be changed from nature to grace; must " put off the old man with his corrupt deeds, and put on the new man, which is renewed in knowledge, after the image of him that created him." We must die unto sin and be raised again unto righteousness; or, in the language of Jesus, we " must be born again," not naturally, as Nicodemus supposed. A second natural birth, nay, a thousand natural births would not help our case. That which is born of the flesh is flesh, no matter how often so born. We must be born of the Spirit, to become spiritual. "That which is born of the Spirit is spirit." A natural figure is taken to represent a spiritual state. The change is one that no man can explain to the natural understanding. Jesus would not undertake to explain it, except by the natural figures he employed, and great fool would I be should I attempt it. It would be folly to expect an unborn child to understand the things of this world, and equal folly to expect one not

born of the Spirit to understand spiritual things.   Much
ignorance prevails respecting scriptural doctrines, because
we fail to realize that many expressions are figurative.
The figure is not the fact, it is only a way of representing
the fact. A natural birth in this case is not the change
which must take place, but a way of representing it, and
yet falls as far short of the thing represented, as the picture of a man falls short of being a man, or the shadow
falls short of being the substance.   A good picture bears
some resemblance to its original, and likewise this figure
bears some resemblance to the fact, but we must bear in
mind that it is not the fact.   If Nicodemus had been
mindful of this, he would not have asked: "Can a man
enter a second time into his mother's womb and be
born?" he would not have persisted in his demand for
an explanation, "How can these things be?"   We need
not expect a change visible to the eye of sense.   It is not
seen except in its effect.   "The wind bloweth where it
listeth."   No man has ever seen the wind, no more can
you see God's Spirit.   You see light matter flying before
the wind, houses blown down, trees torn up by the roots,
and the ocean's billows lashed to fury, but you don't see
the power effecting it.   We likewise see wonderful changes
effected in human nature.   A persecuting Saul of Tarsus
becomes the most abundant laborer in the vineyard of
the despised Nazarene.   A vile, degraded, miserable,
poor, blind and naked sinner is transformed, clothed with
garments of righteousness, and occupies a place among
the saints; the drunkard leaves his cups, the gambler
burns up his cards; he that delighted in vulgar jargon
for song, or low sentimentalism, has learned the music of

Zion ; the swearer prays, and the maniac sits at the feet of Jesus, clothed and in his right mind. We see all this accomplished, but not the operation of the Spirit in working the wonderful change. By our spiritual birth we are brought out of our natural state. We leave the City of Destruction and come out of spiritual Egypt. We are no more, strangers, aliens, nor outcasts, but are fellow-citizens with all the saints.

But to follow Jesus, we must leave our former associates. We cannot be the companions of worldlings and the friends of Jesus. The influence of the world is chilling. " Blessed is he that walketh not in the counsel of the ungodly, nor standeth in the way of sinners, nor sitteth in the seat of the scornful." I cannot understand how it is that one delivered from spiritual death, should deliberately return, but such is the case; and I have noticed that association with the dead leads to death. In other words, association with sinners leads those who have been delivered, back into sin. Two years ago when we were trying to ratify an act prohibiting the sale of intoxicating drinks, there were many professed christians who took counsel of rumsellers in preference to that of God's own chosen ministers, yea, they took up their stand with them, and to day they are sitting in the seat of the scornful. To grow in grace, to maintain the divine favor, to be truly followers of the meek and lowly Jesus, we must choose the people of God as our companions. Not the theatre nor ball-room, but the assembly of the saints must, be our delight. Those people who find it too warm or too cold to go to church, but not too unpleasant to go to places of amusement, are not following Jesus closely.

But we must abandon our way of living. Our sinful

habits must be forsaken. There is no better evidence of
a change of heart than a change in our conduct—our manner of life. "If ye know that he is righteous, ye know
that every one also that doeth righteousness is begotten
of him." The life is the best evidence of our spiritual
state. To be a follower of Jesus we must forsake all sin.
"Behold, we have left all." This was literally true
of the apostles; they had literally left all. James
and John were in the boat with their father, mending
their nets; but at the command of Jesus they left their
nets with their father, and followed him. Levi was sitting at the receipt of custom; but at the command of
Jesus he left that lucrative employment, and engaged in
gathering revenue for heaven's treasury. Peter and Andrew were fishing; but at the call of Jesus they took up
the Gospel net, and went fishing for the souls of men.
And thus, they had been employed from the day that
they were called. This is still required of the ministry;
they have no business with secular employments, except
in a case like Paul's, in which it may be necessary to
show a little independence. But it is not meant that the
mass of mankind shall thus give up their lawful and
necessary business engagements, and yet they must to-
tally abandon the world as the object of their affection and
trust, and must forsake all sin. "Whosoever is born of
God doth not commit sin ; for his seed remaineth in him."
We know that seed will produce its own. If therefore
the seed of righteousness is sown in the heart, and it produces anything, it will be righteousness. If sinful
words, tempers and actions appear, after a profession

of righteousness, we have good reason to fear that such professors are mistaken. The chains of habit are strong, and it sometimes requires very great effort to break them; yet I have seen some very complete revolutions. The gambler, drunken and profane, have forsaken all at once so completely, that the thought of indulging in either would cause a shudder. It is those who don't see any need of so much strictness, who make a compromise with sin, and live a slack-twisted christian life, that are not able to overcome their wicked habits and needless self indulgences. By a determined effort, with divine assistance, we can wholly overcome long standing wicked habits, and follow Jesus fully.

"Behold, we have forsaken all and followed thee." We must find the paths he trod, and walk therein. It is the path of humility. He humbled himself. It is the path of purity; there was no guile in his mouth. He has given us a perfect example and requires that we shall work by the pattern he has given us.

II. But the text leads us to consider THE REWARD OF ATTACHMENT TO CHRIST.

"What shall we have, therefore?" Dominion, honor and glory, are among the things that are promised. "Shall sit upon twelve thrones judging the twelve tribes of Israel." This idea seems to be borrowed from the reign of Solomon, in whose time the kingdom of Israel reached the zenith of its glory. Solomon enjoyed a peaceful reign over the twelve tribes of Israel. The grandeur of his throne and the glory of his kingdom exceeded any thing ever seen on earth. We are told that the great

Ethiopian queen heard, in her far-off country, of the fame of Solomon, and came to see his wisdom as displayed in his kingdom; and when she came, she was unutterably astonished, and declared that all that she had heard was true, but that the half had not been told her; that his glory far exceeded the fame thereof. This exceeding grand earthly kingdom is taken by the Savior to represent the glory of his saints above. But their glory shall be twelve times greater; they are not only to judge twelve tribes, but are to sit upon twelve thrones, each representing twelve tribes, making a hundred and forty-four tribes. But twelve is a figurative number; it signifies completeness, or perfection, and indicates that the glory of the saints will lack nothing; that they shall be possessed of all their hearts' desire. This figure reminds us of the dignity of the christian character; that it far exceeds any thing that earth affords.

1. *There is dignity of birth.*

Men are wont to boast of high birth and of their lineage. The Jews boasted of their descent from Abraham. "The first families of Virginia" is proverbial. Well, the christian is born high—born of God, born from above, born of the Spirit, born of incorruptible seed. No honor that earthly descent can confer can be compared with what is meant by these expressions. The saints are sons of God, children of the heavenly king, the divine progeny.

2. *Then wealth affords dignity, and the children of the kingdom are rich.*

They are born rich. "Ye," says the apostle, "are begotten unto an inheritance incorruptible, undefiled, and that fadeth not away." An incorruptible inheritance is not vouchsafed to the children of this world, nor have we any unfading portion here. All is fading here; the trees, which in the spring and early summer appear so flourishing and gay in their green dress, with beautiful, yellow, white, red, blue and purple spots, appear in autumn ragged, and in winter naked; the flower faded, the leaf withered, dried, and fallen to the ground; and thus giving to thoughtless mortals the sad and solemn lesson, that we soon, like them, must wither and decay; that all our earthly possessions will likewise fade, and that we have no enduring riches here. But those who forsake all these sublunary things and follow Jesus, are assured of riches that are fadeless, incorruptible and eternal.

3. *There is dignity of association also.*

It is regarded as a great and desirable honor to enjoy the association of wealthy, noble, great and good people. I have known persons who were utterly wretched because they were not admitted into what was regarded as the best society. Those who leave all and follow Jesus, rank and associate with the first and noblest of all created beings. Paul in Hebrews xii, 22, 23, 24, expresses the dignity of association to which the followers of Jesus have come, as follows: "But ye are come unto mount Sion, and unto the city of the living God, the heavenly Jerusalem, and to an innumerable company of angels, to the general assembly and church of the firstborn, which are written in heaven, and to God the Judge of all, and to the spirits of just men made perfect, and to Jesus the mediator of the new covenant." All earthly social circles dwindle into insignificance, into nothing, in comparison with this celestial array of divine majesty, eternal honor, infinite dignity, unlimited power, incomprehensible grace and beauty, matchless worth, immutable grandeur, unfading glory, and innumerable multitude of charming associates, with whom the followers of Jesus shall assemble; not to mingle for a moment merely, or just long enough to learn that the anticipated cupful of blessing is never realized, as is the case with earthly pleasures, every sip of which is mixed with poison, and within every sugar-coat, a pill, most bitter: but there we shall drink in the divine presence from a cup full of unmixed joy.

"What shall we have?" A hundred fold for each and every loss we have sustained as a follower of Jesus here. For the land we have forsaken, we shall have unlimited area; for the houses we have left, we shall have innumerable mansions; for the friends we have lost, we shall enjoy the association of the whole of the blissful inhabitants of heaven. But we shall have everlasting life, which includes victory over death; for the last enemy that shall be destroyed is death. We shall be strengthened to meet this last enemy. Many have feared the conflict, have trembled at the thought of it, and yet have been astonished at the ease with which they got the victory at the trying hour. It is our duty to make all possible preparation for death, to be ever on our watch looking for the coming of the Lord daily, and yet I never expect to feel just like dying till death comes. Then, if faithful till then, we are assured of victory. We shall not shrink back from, nor fear the approach of, the grim monster, but shall welcome his approach, and

> " Dying, find our latest foe
> Under our feet at last."

This will end the conflict, and then we shall grasp the victor's wreath, and seize and wear the victor's crown, and with the victor's palm in hand, raise the triumphant shout, "O death, where is thy sting? O grave, where is thy victory?"

SERMON IV.

DIVINE SONSHIP THE SEQUENCES OF WON-
DROUS LOVE.

" Behold, what manner of love the Father hath bestowed upon
us, that we should be called the sons of God; therefore the world
knoweth us nót, because it knew him not. Beloved, now are we
the sons of God, and it doth not yet appear what we shall be,
but we know that, when he shall appear, we shall be like him;
for we shall see him as he is. And every man that hath this hope
in him purifieth himself, even as he is pure." 1 John iii, 1—3.

The text directs our attention to the love of God, as exhibited in the results of that redemption, by which guilty
and wretched sinners are delivered from the thraldom of
sin, and the penalty of God's violated law, restored to the
divine favor, and brought into the enjoyment of all the
blessings of divine sonship.

"Behold, what manner of love." What love, both in
kind and degree! The text suggests the idea of amazement, and well it may, for it is love surpassing far the
love of all beneath. In kind, it is most tender. When
we consider our natural depravity and worthlessness,
when we consider our ungratefulness, and what vile and
rebellious sinners we have been, we may well be amazed
at the divine display of that more than fatherly tender-

ness, which, disregarding our vileness and rebellion, adopts us as his own dear children, and puts within us a spirit which cries, " Abba, Father." It is love of the highest degree. The love that adopts a poor, friendless orphan, and gives him a home, a parent's affection and care, is the highest degree of love that mortal beings can exhibit to the friendless. It is love far surpassing this that God is constantly presenting to the astonished gaze of both angels and men. To this astonishing exhibition the apostle invites our attention. " Behold, what manner of love!" Let us notice,

I. WHAT DIVINE SONSHIP IMPLIES.

Men are wont to boast of their lineage, the royal ancestors, or noble stock from which they are descendants. But from what ancestry can come such honor as divine sonship implies? Earthly honors, titles, distinctions, connections and inheritances, are valueless in comparison to what is implied in divine sonship. To be called sons of God implies,

1. *A transformation.*

By nature, we are children of the wicked one, sons of Belial; aliens, strangers, outcasts, without hope and without God in the world. This is the natural condition of the whole of Adam's posterity. To become sons of God, our nature must be transformed. The image which Satan has fixed upon our nature must be defaced, the heart of enmity must be taken away, and the carnal mind removed. The apostles speak of this transformation under various terms. It is called passing from death unto life, a resurrection from the dead, the washing of regeneration, and being born again. We frequently call it con-

version, and, it includes all that this word embraces—
change of feelings, change of front, change of state. We
are brought out of darkness into the marvelous light of
the gospel. The rebellion and stubbornness of the will is
removed, and it cheerfully bends in submission to the
divine will. The pollution is removed from the affections, and they are made pure. The guilt is removed
from our conscience, and its burden no longer distresses
us.

2. It implies *the abandonment of the world as the object of
our affection.*

"If any man love the world, the love of the Father is
not in him." "The world knoweth us not, because it
knew him not." We have nothing in common with the
world. Our aspirations, habits of life, manner of conversation, objects of pursuit, sources of pleasure, hopes and
fears are all different. But in nothing, is this difference
more conspicuous than in the objects of our affection, and
the more complete our sanctification, the more marked
will this difference appear. We are thus admonished,
"Be not conformed to this world, but be ye transformed."
Let your transformation be complete. There is no better
mark or evidence of our real state than the objects of our
affections." "Where your treasure is, there will your
yeart be also." If our hearts are set upon the world, it
is evident that the world is our treasure, our trust,
our hope, our all, and that we are not sons of God. If
the frivolities of earth charm and delight us more than
the solid and important concerns of the soul and eternity,
it is evident that we are essentially worldly.

. The sons of God have set their affections on the things

which are above. Secret communion with God, a devotional spirit, a love for the assembling of the saints, attachment to the house of God, a delightful attention to all the exercises of the sanctuary, and a reverential regard and longing for its privileges, are all distinguishing characteristics of the sons of God. They are in the world, but not of it; they are passing through it, and making all needed use of it, but they realize that it is not their home; hence, their hearts are not set upon it. With the eye fixed upon the better land, they sing,

> "Yonder's my house, my portion fair,
> My treasure and my heart are there,
> And my abiding home."

3. It implies *that we have the spirit of Christ.*

"If any man have not the spirit of Christ, he is none of his." "Hereby know we that we dwell in him, and he in us, because he hath given us his spirit." By "spirit" we understand motive, that by which we are actuated. The Savior applied it to that, in his disciples which induced them to ask, if they should burn up the Samaritans with fire from heaven. He replied, "Ye know not what manner of spirit ye are of." He intimated that they were actuated by a wrong spirit, that it was not the vindication of his offended dignity that they were seeking, but the gratification of their own malice. They hated the Samaritans, and therefore were glad of an opportunity to vent their spite. This was not the spirit of Christ. He could never have redeemed the world with such a spirit. "Fury was not in him;" he prayed for his enemies, those who set at naught and sold him, pierced and nailed him to the tree, even for them he prayed, "Father, forgive them, they know not what they do." A meek and lowly, tender, kind and forgiving spirit, were constantly manifested in him. If we are the sons of God, we have the same spirit.

4. It implies *participation in all the divine blessings.*

For if we are sons, we are heirs, joint heirs with Christ of "an inheritance incorruptible, undefiled, and that fadeth not away." This inheritance includes all temporal needs. "No good thing will he withhold from them that walk uprightly." Having committed our all to him, we may rest assured-that he will keep what we have committed to his care It includes a constant supply of needed grace. Without this, our spiritual life could not be maintained. The great enemy would overcome us. Jesus reminded Peter that Satan had desired to have him, that he might sift him as wheat, but he had prayed for him. Peter warned the christians of his time, that their enemy, the devil, was going about seeking what soul he might devour. All this indicates that there is a fearful influence, constantly employed to separate us from our relationship to the Father, to draw us away from God. Indeed, we do not need to look into the Bible to see this, we have only to consult our own feelings. We shall find in our every-day experience temptations and inclinations to evil. We shall have them while we remain in this probationary state. No amount of piety can exempt us from them. It is the devil's business to tempt, a business to which his nature impels him, a business in which he will continue to engage so long as God permits him. We need not, therefore, expect exemption from temptation, nor need we desire it. We can get along as well with, as without temptation, if we will, for in the time of the most severe temptation, if we will listen, we will hear Jesus say, "My grace is sufficient for thee," "be not afraid, it is I." It is not, therefore, exemption from temptation that we need, but the grace of God to sustain us under temptation, and this we can have, in all its overflowing abundance, sufficient for all our need, both for living and for dying.

II. Notice THE MEDIUM THROUGH WHICH THIS TITLE IS OBTAINED, AND THE CONSEQUENT BLESSINGS SECURED.

The love of God. "Behold, what manner of love." Love moved God to give his only begotten Son to die for the redemption of the world.

> What wondrous love is this,
> How passing great, beyond degree,
> That God should give his only Son
> To bleed and die for me.

Of all wonders, the love of God in Christ is the sum total. When it reached its culminating point, in his death upon the cross, angels, struck with wonder, gazed upon the scene, nature stood aghast, the rocks asunder rent, the sun withdrew his beams, and in darkness veiled the earth. The love of God in Christ constitutes the song of the ransomed millions, who move in shining ranks, and, sweeping through the gates of the new Jerusalem, gather beneath the bows of the tree of life, and cease not to sing that enrapturing song, " Unto him that loved us, and washed us from our sins in his own blood, and hath made us kings and priests unto God and his Father, to him be glory and dominion forever and ever." The apostle rejoiced in this theme, " He loved me and gave himself for me." " Behold, what manner of love."

1. It was *disinterested love.*

It was love springing from pure generosity, and bestowed upon objects who were wholly unworthy of it; love flowing from the inexhaustible fulness of divine benevolence; love reaching as deep as the sinner's guilt, and extending to every child of man. " Herein is love, not that we loved God, but that he loved us, and sent his Son into the world to be a propitiation for our sins." 1 John iv, 10. We were not in a state in which favor could be expected, but the opposite. If we had loved and obeyed him, we might have expected love from him, but so far from this, we hated him without a cause, and did not even desire his favor. In this is the nature of divine love displayed, as writes the great apostle, " God commendeth his love toward us, in that, while we were yet sinners, Christ died for us." Romans v, 8. The extent of human love is reached when a man lays down his life for his friend. So He, that knoweth the heart of man, hath declared, " Greater love hath no man than this, that a man lay down his life for his friends." John xv, 13. A few instances are recorded in which men have laid down their lives for their friends, yet this has very seldom occurred, and its occurrence marks the purest friendship and highest benevolence of which the human heart is capable. The apostle thus refers to the rarity of such benevolence : " For scarcely for a righteous man will one die : yet, peradventure, for a good man some would even dare to die." The friendship between Jonathan and David was so strong that one would, probably, have been willing to die for the other. Then we have the case of Damon and Pythias. Damon had been condemned to death. Promising to return at the hour appointed for his execution, he got permission from the tyrant Dionysius to go and settle his affairs, Pythias becoming his surety. He returned just in time to save his friend from being executed in his stead. The tyrant was so struck with the fidelity of their friendship that he remitted the punishment and desired to share their friendship. The sacrifice that Pythias was willing to make, was for his friend, and this, I repeat, is the extent of human love. But the love of Christ goes beyond this, he died for his enemies.

2. *It was a mysterious love.*

Wondrous, incomprehensible love! it constituted the great mystery that the angels desired to look into. Yea, passing by all the wonders of creation, the holy and happy, bright and intelligent host of heaven become the students of the cross, and exhaust the force of their celestial powers in the attempt to sound the depth of redeeming love—the love of God to man. Why such love to sinners, to beings so entirely unworthy and worthless? God did not need us, his happiness was complete without us. He could have sent us all to the world of woe. He could have blotted us out of existence, and created beings every way more worthy in sufficient numbers to have filled every throne in heaven. Why, then, such love to sinners? Simply because he delights in mercy. He is "The Lord God, merciful and gracious, longsuffering, and abundant in goodness and truth, keeping mercy for thousands, and forgiving iniquity, transgression and sin.".

Exodus xxxiv, 6. Isaiah tells us that the Lord "will wait, that he may be gracious unto you, * * that he may have mercy upon you." Isaiah xxx, 18. What a grand idea of divine goodness! He keeps mercy, and waits, not to pour out his wrath upon the guilty, but to see a motion in the sinner's heart, indicating his willingness to receive mercy. He waits and watches for a sympathetic cord in the sinner's heart, that he can touch and melt his hardness into love. O sinner! he waits on you to-day, he waits to see in you a desire for his favor and love.

> "Has waited long, is waiting still,
>   You treat no other friend so ill."

3. *It is all victorious love.*

It overcame all obstacles in the way of man's redemption. The enmity of the human heart, the malice of the devil, and the terrors of death and hell.

> "Sink down, ye separating hills,
> Let sin and death remove ;
> 'Tis love that drives my chariot wheels,
> And death must yield to love."

Love was the moving power in the Father's breast when he exclaimed, "Deliver him from going down to the pit; I have found a ransom." And this his only begotten Son, the darling of his bosom, the Father gave in sacrifice for the sins of the world. It was love that moved the Son to respond to the Father's merciful inclination, "Lo, I come; in the volume of the book it is written of me, I delight to do thy will, O my God: yea, thy law is within my heart." Psa. xl, 7, 8. Im-

3

pelled by a burden of redeeming love, he left those bright regions of glory and bliss to dwell in human flesh.

> " O for this love, let rocks and hills
> Their lasting silence break, ·
> And all harmonious human tongues
> The Saviour's praises speak."

But mortal tongues can never speak his matchless worth, nor can they give the praises due Jehovah's love. Words are inadequate, language utterly fails to meet the demands of the divine theme; earth has no song, nor songster, sufficient to do it justice, hence the poet leaves earth and draws his requisition upon heavens's store:

> " Angels, assist our mighty joys,
> Strike all your harps of gold;
> But when you raise your highest notes,
> His love can ne'er be told."

Love led him to endure a forty days' fast and temptation in the wilderness; over the valleys and mountains of Judea on errands of mercy, through hunger, scorn and reproach, and at last to the judgment hall, to Pilate's bar, and to the cross! Here, amid untold and incomprehensible agonies, he expiated the sins of the world, satisfied all the demands of justice, and made it possible for God to be just and yet the justifier of the ungodly. Only the lost soul in torment will ever know what agony Jesus bore, and God forbid that any one who hears me this day shall ever know or feel such pain as he endured. You may expect to feel something of pain in conviction and conversion. The great change will hardly be effected without pain; it is not well for us that it should be, as our experience will be all the brighter, by reason of the pain endured. Thousands are weak and puny because their experience has not been more vivid. You should not, however, be discouraged if your winter has passed, and your spring ushered in, you will know it by the budding of holy desires, by the putting forth of the flowers of love, even though the March winds failed to blow. The warmth of Christian love in the heart is the best evidence of summer in the soul.

III. Now let us glance at the BENEFITS OF DIVINE WORSHIP.

1. *We have the divine favor and love.*

And his favor is life, his loving kindness better than life. The present portion of the sons of God is princely and abundant, but the future will fill all our soul's desire. We are not permitted to know just what we shall be in the future state. " It doth not yet appear what we shall be." But we have this much revealed, that we shall be like him, and it is intimated that this likeness shall result from beholding him; hence, the apostle adds, " For we shall see him as he is." Our bodies shall be raised in the likeness of his glorious body, and our souls shall be filled with all the fullness of divine knowledge.

Finally, *there are the duties involved in divine sonship.*

" Every one that hath this hope in him purifieth himself even as he is pure." Purity of thought, heart, soul and life is the best evidence of divine sonship, and also necessary to divine acceptance.

How bright and beautiful young people bud and bloom forth into manhood and womanhood—fair as the first rose that bloomed in Eden ; the joy of their parents, inspiring hope that they will become examples to society,

gems in the church, and useful to humanity.   But, alas!
how soon all our expectations are blasted, and our hope
faded.   Impure thoughts arise out of impure hearts; impure actions follow; and the result is, a shipwreck of
good character, and the loss of happiness and hope.

Forget all that I have said in this discourse, if you will,
but don't forget the words of the apostle, "Every one
that hath this hope in him, purifieth himself even as he
is pure."   To the same effect are the words of Jesus,
"Blessed are the pure in heart, for they shall see God."
To have, to retain this hope, we must be pure.

SERMON V.

WHY WAS THE RICH MAN IN TORMENT?

" But Abraham said, Son, remember that thou in thy lifetime receivedst thy good things, and likewise Lazarus evil things; but now he is comforted, and thou art tormented." Luke xvi, 25.

Our text is a part of the only conversation we have any account of, between a spirit in hell and a spirit in heaven. The picture presented is that of the condition of the souls of two beings, who were once mortal and dwelt upon earth; one vastly rich, the other miserably poor. One fared sumptuously every day, the other begged crumbs at the rich man's gate. Both died, and after death found them selves in circumstances the opposite of what they were on earth. The rich man lifted up his eyes in torments, the beggar was lodged in Abraham's bosom. The poet thus describes the variety of scenery in the two states:

> "And what confusion earth appears,
> God's dearest children bathed in tears,
> While they, who heaven and earth deride,
> Riot in luxury and pride.
> But, patient, let my soul attend,
> And, e'er I censure, view the end :
> That end, how different ! Who can tell
> The wide extremes of heaven and hell ?
> See the red flames around him twine,

Who did in gold and purple shine,
Nor can his tongue one drop obtain,
To allay the anguish of his pain.
· While round the saint, so poor below,
Full rivers of salvation flow,
On Abram's breast he leans his head,
And banquets on celestial bread."

The rich man desired that Lazarus should be sent to dip the tip of his finger in water and cool his tongue. Our text is the response. The doctors differ as to whether this is a statement of facts, or a mere parable. Mere opinion is all that any one can give, and under the circumstances, mine would naturally be expected. I incline to the opinion that the characters are real. I will simply give one reason, viz: the fact that Jesus did not give the rich man's name. I suppose that people in his day were much like they are now. With us, it matters not how a man lived, if we speak of him after he is dead, we are expected to put him in heaven; and if we are not prepared to do that, we had best not speak of him at all in the presence of those who loved him.

Now, the care that Jesus took to avoid giving unnecessary offence, would suggest that in speaking of a man in torment, who had lived and been highly respected in Jerusalem, he would withhold his name. This is just what he did in the case before us, while the name of the man who had gone to heaven is given. If we regard it as a mere parable, this difference cannot well be accounted for. But if we regard the discourse as a narration of facts, the reason for the difference is obvious.

It is not at all necessary, however, to any purpose of mine, on the present occasion, to view it in this light. It matters not which way we understand the passage, the doctrine, the lesson taught, is the same. If a history, it is a statement of what has been; if a parable, it is a picture of what may be. It is, at least, a picture of possibilities. It sets forth the fact that a man may be in the enjoyment of the very fat of the land, esteemed and honored by his neighbors, and regarded as among the very best on earth, and yet die and go to the world of woe.

Taking into consideration this whole narrative, or parable, (whichever we understand it to be,) as recorded from the nineteenth verse to the end of the chapter, I want us to think on this important question: *Why was this man in torment?* Perhaps you will say, "*I never thought about that before.*" If so, I think it is time you had. Jesus certainly meant that we should think about it, or he would not have taken such pains to tell us about it. But I have a special reason why I want this question to engage our thoughts; it is this: there are so many people who don't think they are in any danger of torment, because they don't consider themselves great sinners; hence, when urged to flee the wrath to come, they ask, "Why? what harm have I done? I don't think I am a great sinner; I am honest, I pay all my just debts, (and I suspect they have forgotten their greatest debt, what they owe to their Maker,) I don't swear, nor gamble, I don't rob any one, I am not a drunkard, extortioner, nor libertine." Well, suppose you are not guilty of any of these things. Suppose you are what the world calls a good, honest, upright man, or, to go a step further, suppose you have done no harm, as many are wont to say, will that free you from condemnation? Take the twenty-

fifth chapter of Matthew, and you will find three classes
of characters that were condemned, neither of which had
done any harm.   One had failed to take oil in their vessels, but what harm was that?   Another had not improved his talent, but what harm was there in that?   he
had not asked his lord to loan him the money, and he
was careful to return just what he received.   The third
had not exercised themselves in acts of mercy, such as
feeding the hungry, clothing the naked, &c.   The complaint against them was, not that they had done harm,
but that they had done nothing; and for this they were
condemned.   Then, if you are prepared to show that you
have done nothing, that will be your condemnation.   You
will be judged out of your own mouth, and condemned
by your own testimony.   We did not come here to do
nothing.

Coming back to the text, we ask, what harm had this
man done?   Whom had he injured?   I know it is the
custom to load him down with a great many crimes.   I
think it is Dr. Clark, who remarks, " That men do this,
it seems, to justify the Almighty in sending him to torment."   God does not need any such help at our hands.
We spoil his word by our bungling attempts to improve
it.   In some Bibles, the words " the rich glutton " are
written over this chapter.   Who dare write such a head-
ing there?   There is no warrant for assuming that this
man was a glutton.   Jesus does not tell us that he was a
glutton.   He undertook to tell us what there was in this
man's case; he had the ability to do it, and I claim that
he told us whatever there was of any importance to
us.   He says nothing about gluttony.   The nearest he

comes to it is the statement that he had a daily sumptuous repast—plentiful, rich, costly and splendid; well prepared and splendidly served by well trained servants. But I doubt whether any of his entertainments amounted to twenty-two covers, as did an entertainment given by our Secretary of State a few days ago. Might we not with equal propriety call our distinguished Secretary a glutton?

Men have treated this passage as though the object of it was to show that a very wicked man went to torment. This fact is set forth in many passages, but the one before us is not one of them. That the notoriously wicked will be banished from the divine presence, is a fact generally recognized by those who take the Bible as their guide. But the passage before us goes furthert: i teaches us that not only those who are notoriously wicked, but others, who are very differently estimated by the human standard, will also be banished from the divine presence. Here we see a man in torment, against whom nothing of a notoriously wicked character can be alleged. He was what the world would call a splendid specimen of humanity; a grand, good fellow; a gentleman of the first order. Why, then, was he in torment?

Well, we are told that he was rich; but is that a good reason for his being sent to torment? If so, there are thousands who cannot hope to get to heaven. There are thousands who are rich, and thousands more who want to be, and I suspect it is as bad to want riches as to have them. It is not money, but the love of it, that is said to be the root of all evil.

He also dressed well—" was clothed in purple and fine

linen." But was this a sufficient reason for sending him to torment? If so, what will become of the people of this generation? This might well be called the dressy age. When in London, a few weeks ago, I attended a reception given by the Lord Mayor, at which there was a large attendance both of English and American ladies, principally the wives, sisters and daughters of Methodist ministers. Among them I saw ladies who were not satisfied with the amount of dry goods they could carry on their backs, but had a lot beside, trailing on the floor, so that there was constant danger of getting one's feet tangled in their trails. A correspondent, describing one of the grand receptions at Washington City, would not think his work complete, if he failed to mention the style of dress in which the guests appeared, and a lady would make herself notorious by appearing in a plain dress. Nor is the desire for fine, costly, and extravagant dress confined to those in high life; we meet it everywhere, in all our walks. The desire is almost universal, and the indulgence is limited only by the want of means. What, then, will become of us, if this man was sent to torment for wearing fine and costly dress?

We have already mentioned the fact that he fared sumptuously, but in this he was not an exception, as all who feel able to do so, enter largely into the enjoyment of the good things that God has provided for us. And there is no hint that anything beyond this was indulged in at this man's table. I have no idea that there were four or more different wine glasses, for a corresponding number of different kinds of wine at each plate, as I have seen on the tables of professing christians. Certainly no such bachanalian exhibitions, as are witnessed at both private and public dinners in many of our cities, was witnessed at this man's feasts. Why, then, was he in torment?

It has been said that he was so mean and stingy that he would not allow Lazarus to have the crumbs that fell from his table. But there is no warrant for this statement, and a little reflection will make it clear that it is most erroneous. Jesus said that he was laid at the rich man's gate, and was desiring the crumbs. You see the desire continued; if he had been denied the crumbs or cold pieces, he would not have been continually laid there until the dogs become so well acquainted with him as to have compassion on him, and to do him those services which men neglected. Then it must be remembered, that that man was rich, that he had a daily feast, and would therefore not want the cold pieces returned to his own table. His appetite would only take that which was fresh. There are many crumbs which fall from the table of such persons; often much more than the servants can make use of, and whether the balance goes to the dogs or beggars, is a matter about which the wealthy don't concern themselves. There seems to be an intimation here that this beggar and the dogs were companions, and fared alike. The fact that the rich man suffered this beggar to lay at his gate, where he could receive little donations from his wealthy neighbors, as they passed in and out, may be mentioned to his credit. There are some men so mean and cruel-hearted that they would not have suffered him to lay there. The fact that he knew him as soon as he saw him in Abraham's bosom, indicates that he was quite well acquainted with that

countenance, and leads us to conclude that he had frequently seen this man at his gate. Moreover, Lazarus is
selected before all others in heaven, as the person most
likely to be willing to do him the desired kindness. Can
we account for this on the supposition that he had treated
Lazarus rudely? On the contrary supposition, we can
imagine the rich man, on beholding Lazarus, saying:
" Why, yonder is Lazarus, that used to lay at my gate
and receive the crumbs from my table. Surely if he can
help me out of this misery, he will do it." Every çir-
cumstance in the case points to the fact, and irresistibly
leads us to the conclusion, that he received the crumbs.
It may be said that the rich man might have done a little better than that for this beggar. Rich as he was, he
might have done as the Shunamite woman did for Elisha,
he might have made a little chamber on the wall for him,
and had a bed and stool and candlestick put therein.
See 2 Kings iv, 10. Yes, he might have done this, and
we are assured that he would not have lost his reward.
But there are thousands who don't put themselves to that
much trouble to provide for poor beggars, especially when
they are loathsome by reason of many sores, as this man
was.

After the study of years, I have not been able to see
much difference between this man and the mass of
wealthy worldlings : the difference is all in his favor. Indeed, there are many professed christians whose outward
life is not better than his. Are they numbered with the
people of God ? So was he. He addressed Abraham as
" Father," and Abraham acknowledged the relationship
by responding, " Son." He belonged to the favored race,

and enjoyed their dispensation of grace. Why, then, was he in torment?

I think we shall find the answer in the words of our text. Abraham mentions two facts; the first of which includes the reason for his being in torments, and the second, in addition thereto, gives the reason why he must remain there. "Son, remember that thou in thy life time receivedst thy good things. * * And beside all this, between us and you there is a great gulf fixed."

"Thou in thy life time receivedst thy good things." That which he esteemed good he had received. As a moral free agent, he had made his choice, which did not include heaven. He was admonished as to the better part, but did not regard the admonition. He thought he knew better than his Maker what was good for him. Such is the infirmity of human nature, that man sets up his judgment against that of his Maker. This man was urged to lay up for himself treasure in heaven, but he chose rather to lay it up on earth. He chose the things of this world as his portion, and pronounced them good. They were his good things, good in his estimation, and he had received them in his life time. He had made no choice, no provision, no arrangement for the hereafter. No sensible man can expect to have that which he has rejected, and refused or thrown away. Now, in a word, this man was in torments, simply and solely because he failed to prepare for heaven. He allowed the things of this world to so fully engage his attention, that thoughts of the more important concerns of the soul were excluded; and hence the night was upon him before his work, for which the day was given him, had been begun.

His *time* was out, before the work, for which *time* was
given, was commenced. How many here to-day are
copying his example? All who do, will cry in vain for
relief, when lifting up their eyes in the world of woe. O
my dear, dying friends, listen to the voice of mercy.

> " Now God invites, how blessed the day,
>   How sweet the Gospel's charming sound ;
> Come, sinners, haste, O haste away,
>   While yet a pardoning God is found."

But possibly some of you have listened to the sophis-
tries of latter-day skeptics, who are too good natured to
believe in future punishment. We may punish men for
their crimes, to maintain the majesty of the law and the
safety of society, but God, the sovereign of worlds, may
not. Is it quite safe to trust to this? Would it not be
better to be on the safe side? Even skeptics admit that
genuine religion is a good thing, yea, even the best of all
things. " Their rock is not like our rock, even our enemies themselves being judges."

What do we know, or can we know respecting these
matters, except by what is revealed? We don't know
much about this world, except what we have gathered
from the hints that have come out through divine revelation. Much is said of science, but scientists are indebted
to revelation for every useful thing they have learned.
Certainly, on the subject before us, we can know nothing except what we learn from revelation.

What, then, are the statements of revelation? We need
only mention a few: " The wicked shall be turned into
hell, with all the nations that forget God." Psa. ix, 17.
" Upon the wicked he shall rain snares, fire and brim-

stone and a horrible tempest, this shall be the portion of their cup." Psa. xi, 6. "It is better for thee to enter into life with one eye, rather than having two eyes, to be cast into hell fire." Matt. xviii, 9. If there is no place of punishment, what do these passages mean? The skeptic will tell you that the hell referred to is the grave; that hell is translated from a Greek word which means the grave. I admit that it sometimes is, but not always. Our English word "hell" is translated from three different words. But I do not propose to attempt any thing like a learned argument. I think there is a better way. It would require a knowledge of the originals to enable each to appreciate a learned argument. We don't need a knowledge of the Greek and Hebrew, nor much of the English: it only needs a little good, hard, common sense, to enable us to see that hell is mentioned in connections in which the grave cannot be meant. Take Luke xii, 4, 5: "Be not afraid of them that kill the body, and after that have no more that they can do. But I will forewarn you whom ye shall fear: Fear him, which after he hath killed hath power to cast into hell; yea, I say unto you, Fear him." Does the Son of God thus solemnly warn us against the grave digger, or the man who puts the body in the grave? Is it the disposition of the body after death that concerns us most of all things? Are we to stand in mortal dread of those who put the body in the grave? If hell means no more than the grave, this must be the meaning. Can any man with common sense believe it? But it is said that the rich man lifted up his eyes, being in torments. Then, it is a place of torments. We are also told that there is "weeping and wailing

and gnashing of teeth." Are these torments in the grave?
Have you ever heard a wail coming up from the silent
tomb? Where is your graveyard? Let us visit that
solemn place. Let us listen all day, all night, if you
will. Is any sound heard? In the grave the eye weeps
not, the ear hears not, the heart heaves not,—all is silent
there!

> "The eyes that so seldom were closed,
>   By sorrow forbidden to sleep;
> Now wrapped in their silent repose,
>   Have strangely forgotten to weep."

Then the place of torments and of weeping cannot be
the grave. There must be another place, if these passages mean anything. Where is it, O! where? But we
read, that "Their worm dieth not, and the fire is
not quenched." Mark ix, 46. Well, there are worms
in the grave, but I suspect they die. But it is not
worms, but "*their worm.*" What is it? What is the
worm that dieth not? It's the misery that shall prey
upon the lost soul through all eternity. This was mentioned three times by the Son of God in one discourse.
He borrows these words from a prophecy in Isaiah:
"They shall go forth and look upon the carcasses of the
men that have transgressed against me: for their worm
shall not die, neither shall their fire be quenched."
Isaiah lxvi, 24. The picture brought to our view here
is the carnage of a battle-field—the carcasses of the slain
eaten by worms; to heighten which the valley of Hin-
nom, in which idolators sacrificed their children to the
god Moloch, is added But the worms which ate the
bodies of the slain eventually died, and the fire which

consumed the flesh of infants went out; but in the place
into which those who transgress against God are consigned, their worm dieth not and the fire is not quenched.
I repeat, where is that place? It cannot be the grave,
for as we have seen, there the worms die, and there is no
fire in the grave. And if the fire mentioned refers to
whatever it is that consumes the body in the grave, then
it certainly means that the soul shall not be consumed
as the body is. But the skeptic will say, these are figures,
pictures, or shadows, only *shadows!* Yea, this is the conclusion to which I arrived at many years ago. Nor am
I indebted to the skeptic for any light on the subject.
This seems to me to be the natural construction to be put
upon all such passages. It is impossible to convey the
idea of invisible things to mortal beings, except by
figures drawn from visible things. I have no idea that
there is a real worm which shall gnaw the soul, or fire
and brimstone that shall burn and torment the flesh in
the future state, or that they shall eat wormwood and
gall, or that actual smoke shall rise from a bottomless
pit. Thus far I agree with the skeptic. I admit that
these are figures, pictures, shadows, "*only shadows*" But
it strikes me that the skeptic has failed to notice the
natural and logical sequence of this admission. A shadow
is the lightest possible part of any thing. If these are
figures, what are the facts that they represent? If pictures, what is the original from which they are drawn?
If shadows, what is that fearful substance which sends
forth such horrible shadows? If you see the shadow of
a man on the wall, you know there is a man there, or
there would be no shadow. Yes, these are "SHADOWS,

only SHADOWS;" and that is what makes them so fearful.
"There their worm dieth not, and the fire is not quenched,"
and that is only the figure. What is the fact it represents?
"The smoke of their torment shall ascend up forever and
ever," and that is only a picture; what is the original
from which it is drawn? "Death and hell shall be
turned into a lake which burneth with fire and brimstone." This is only a shadow; what is the substance?

Well, let us see if we can solve this fearful problem.
What will constitute the torment of the lost soul? I
think it is intimated that memory will be a fruitful
source of torment. Memory, I think, will constitute the
undying worm. Memory will bring back to the mind
all that has passed, no matter how unpleasant. We have
said and done things, which, after a moment's reflection,
we wished had not transpired, and the thought thereof
pained us. But gradually the remembrance of such things
dies away, until entirely forgotten. Now, in the world of
woe, we have reason to believe that memory will bring
back to, and retain in the mind, every unpleasant thing
that ever passed through it. This alone, it seems to me,
would constitute a burden too intolerable to be borne. But
we shall see things then as they are, and realize what we
have lost by the course we pursued, and memory will
bring back to mind the opportunities we have thrown
away, and the golden-moments we have wasted. We shall
remember that we had the privilege of selecting.for ourselves a place among the blessed, where we should have
been eternally happy. Possibly, we shall have to remember that, at some period in our lives, we came very near
to the turning point, were almost persuaded, felt the flame

of love kindling in the soul, but suffered the *propitious moment to pass without seizing it. The remembrance of those things which have been in reach, and yet lost to us forever, because slighted or neglected until the opportunity to seize them passed, I think will constitute a weight of remorse which will sink all who have been favored with Gospel privileges far beneath the Sodomites.

Many will call to remembrance the prayers and pleadings of sainted mothers, the sermons of faithful pastors, and the wooings of the Holy Spirit, all of which were employed in vain. The groans of agony and bloody sweat of Jesus in the garden, and the tragic scene of the suffering and dying Son of God on Calvary, will come back to the mind, and memory will testify that all this was endured for the lost soul. And why lost? Simply because of its own neglect. Yes, its own neglect will sink it down to mourn in endless woe.

A second fruitful source of torment will be the sight of the saints in glory. Yea, the rich man saw Lazarus in Abraham's bosom. It seems impossible to escape the conclusion that those in torment will see the saints in glory. O agony of all agonies, to be in sight of heaven and yet forbade to enter! Looking out from the darkness of black despair into the noontide of heaven's glorious brightness, the soul in torment will see his mother in glory, mingling her songs with those of the saints of all ages, bathing her soul in seas of endless rest, and drinking from the living streams of bliss which burst forth from the throne of God, while he, condemned to endless woe, drinks of the wrath of God poured out without out mixture from the cup of his indignation, and from the lowest regions of the burning pit, tormented souls will see the Lamb that was slain for sinners, and will exclaim:

"Yonder stands the lovely Saviour,
    With the marks of dying love,
O that I had sought his favor
    When I felt his Spirit move:
Doomed, I'm justly,
    For I have against him strove.

All his warnings I have slighted,
    When he daily sought my soul,
If some vows to him I'd plighted,
    Yet for sin I broke the whole:
Golden moments,
    How neglected did they roll."

And turning their eyes toward the shining throng of enraptured saints who stand upon the sea of glass, dressed in robes of snowy whiteness, with crowns of gold upon their heads, and harps within their hands, the souls in torments will continue their woful poetic wail:

"Yonder stand my godly neighbors,
    Who were once despised by me,
They are clad in dazzling splendor,
    Waiting my sad fate to see:
Farewell, neighbors,
    Dismal gulf, I'm bound for thee."

And turning their eyes downward, and surveying the blazing ranks of frightful demons, foaming out their malicious rage, and making hell hideous with their fierce and fearful howls, while still descending the steps which lead to the fiery lake, they will again take up their poetic lamentation:

"Hail, ye ghosts that dwell in darkness,
  Grovelling, rattling of your chains,
  Christ has now pronounced my sentence,
  Here to dwell, in endless pains,
  Down I'm rolling,
  Never to return again.

  Now experience plainly shows me,
  Hell is not a fable thing,
  Though I see my friends in glory,
  Round the throne they ever sing,
  I'm tormented
  By an everlasting sting "

Lastly, we have here the declaration that the state of the tormented is endless. " Beside this, there is a gulf fixed between us and you, so that those who would pass cannot." The thoughts of woe to come will increase the torment. No matter how great our pain here, we have the consolation to feel that it will soon be over, but in torment, the eternal thought will be, wrath to come.

Now, my beloved friends, there are three strong motives presented in the Gospel to win us away from the world and to induce us to become the servants of God, namely : the love of God, the hope of heaven, and the fear of hell. He that takes away either of these, takes away a part of revealed truth and puts himself in danger of losing his part in the book of life and the holy city, Rev. xxii, 19. He that fails to present these three motives, fails to preach a whole gospel.

It has been my endeavor to present these three motives with what force God has given me ability to command. The subject here considered is drawn from the most striking picture of the world of woe that is found on record. If the love of Christ has failed to draw you, and the hope of heaven has failed to interest you, certainly this fearful picture should at least alarm you. If not, then your wound is incurable—your case is hopeless! But I hope better things. The thought of giving you up for lost moves my very soul. O, that I knew what sentence, what line, what word, what syllable would move you. Tell me, my unconverted friend, how shall I win thee? Hast thou a tender spot, a sympathetic cord that I can touch—no, not I, but the Holy Spirit—and melt thy heart into love? Would weeping win thee, I would exhaust the fountain of tears. Oh! repent and believe, turn now to the Lord and seek salvation, and thou shalt be able to fold thy arms and sing praises unto the Lamb that was slain for thee.

SERMON VI.

THE MARVELOUS VITALITY OF THE CHURCH.

"And there appeared a great wonder in heaven ; a woman clothed with the sun, and the moon under her feet, and upon her head a crown of twelve stars : and she being with child cried, travailing in birth, and pained to be delivered. And there appeared another wonder in heaven; and behold a great red dragon, having seven heads and ten horns, and seven crowns upon his heads. And his tail drew the third part of the stars of heaven, and did cast them to the earth: and the dragon stood before the woman which was ready to be delivered, for to devour her child as soon as it was born. And she brought forth a man child, who was to rule all nations with a rod of iron: and her child was caught up unto God, and to his throne. And the woman fled into the wilderness, where she hath a place prepared of God, that they should feed her there a thousand two hundred and threescore days." Rev. xii, 1—6.

Possibly an explanation of the text, at the beginning, will enable us more easily to comprehend the subject. By the woman, brought to view in the text so splendidly adorned, we have a beautiful figurative representation of the Christian Church. By the sun, with which she is clothed, we are reminded that the Church is invested with the rays of the Sun of Righteousness. The moon under her feet, indicates the exalted position of the Church; and also that the moonlight of the Jewish economy is lost in the splendor of the rays of the Sun of Righteousness. The crown of twelve stars upon her head, is a symbol of the lives and labors of holy men, which have adorned the Church in all its ages, especially the twelve apostles. Her travail and pain fitly symbolizes the persecution and suffering through which the Church has passed, while continuing to bring forth sons and daughters unto God. The man child she brought forth was Constantine, the Great. By the great red dragon, which stood before the woman, we understand the persecuting Roman Empire. By the wings which the woman received, we understand the Divine protection.

I am quite sensible of the fact that this vision has received a very different interpretation at the hands of distinguished authors. Some have applied it to Mary and the birth of Jesus. But they forget that prophecy concerns the future. John heard a voice which said, "Come up higher, and I will show thee things which must be hereafter." The birth of Jesus was not a future but a past event, and could not then be the subject of prophecy. Nor could it with propriety be said of Mary, that she was clothed with the sun and the moon under her feet. Neither was she the object of persecution, as was the woman in the text. Nor can the description of the great red dragon be well applied to Herod the Great. But in applying this vision to the Church, every figure will appear to perfection, as we shall see hereafter.

Keeping these points in view, let us notice:

I. THE GRANDEUR AND GLORY OF THE CHRISTIAN CHURCH, as symbolized by the metaphors in the text.

It appeared to John as a great wonder, or sign in heaven We are not to understand that John was in heaven, or that there are really such things in heaven as appeared to him. John was on the Isle of Patmos; yet so enveloped.

and filled with the divine Spirit, and his mind so occupied with the mystery of the triumph of God's kingdom on earth, that he was insensible to all material things. The thoughts of celestial things so filled up his mind that he entirely lost sight of his terrestrial connections and surroundings. The scenes which he beheld were not real, but imaginary: they were pictures, presented to the mind, of coming events. The events symbolized by these pictures were to transpire, successively on earth, through the whole period of time—till God's purpose respecting his church on earth should be accomplished. This succession of events is indicated by the different degrees in which John was enveloped by the Spirit, the different openings he beheld, and by the deepening mystery of the revelation as it proceeds. When the Lord Jesus first appeared to John, he was simply in the Spirit. His meditations were heavenly and divine; his mind was occupied with spiritual things, and he may have been in a state of ecstacy, but not so much as to lose sight of material things. His physical senses were still performing their functions, and conveying to his mind a sense of his material surroundings; he was still sensible of his connection with the isle of Patmos. He was still in a state in which the divine appearance disturbed him—caused him to fear and tremble, and to fall at the feet of him that talked with him. After that, he became still more occupied with the divine vision, until finally he entirely lost sight of earth and of his connection therewith. The celestial scenery presented to his mind absorbed his entire attention. What he was first commanded to write related to the things that then were, viz: the

4

seven churches in Asia, and their condition. After that, he beheld a door open in heaven, and heard the command: "Come up hither, and I will show thee things that must be hereafter." The things to which his attention had been called before, had already transpired, or were then transpiring. But the things symbolized by the pictures as recorded from the fourth chapter onward, were evidently to transpire after the time of the vision. He obeyed the injunction and ascended, not in body, but in spirit. After that, he saw the temple in heaven open, and finally heaven itself was opened. First a door, then the temple, then heaven itself. In each of these openings the mystery deepens; just as our natural vision becomes less distinct in the dim distance—indicating most clearly the great distance into futurity, to which he was permitted to extend his gaze.

Our text is found under the second opening, the opening of the temple. The period in the history of the Church at which the special events here symbolized transpired, was the latter part of the third century. It was then that the Church brought forth a man child, in the person of Constantine the Great. Many snares were laid for his life, but he escaped them all, and ascended the imperial throne. It is called the throne of God, because God made it subservient to his holy purpose respecting his church. Constantine, having embraced Christianity, became a most zealous defender of the christian church and religion. He put a stop to the persecution of christians, and proclaimed that Christianity should be the religion of his empire.

At this point we notice a remarkable coincidence; that,

so soon as the woman brought forth a man child, and he had ascended the throne, she was compelled to flee into the wilderness, where, in obscurity, she was protected of God for twelve hundred and sixty prophetic days—literally speaking, twelve hundred and sixty years—from the time of Constantine till the reformation of Luther. "And she brought forth a man child, who was to rule all nations with a rod of iron: and her child was caught up unto God, and to his throne. And the woman fled into the wilderness, where she hath a place prepared of God, that they should feed her a thousand two hundred and three score days." Why did not this offspring of the woman protect her? He was enthroned; he ruled all nations with a rod of iron; his pleasure was law; and at his fiat she that brought him forth could have dwelt in safety in any part of his vast dominions. Yet, while he is receiving homage from all nations, she must flee from his presence and dwell in obscurity.

We find the explanation of this singular circumstance in the text. He was a "man child." Constantine was not converted to Christianity by the ordinary means of grace. He had so little of the grace of God in the heart, that he was unwilling to be baptized until his last moments, lest he should backslide and be lost. It was the name of Christianity that he embraced, and the form of the christian religion that he protected. It was not so much to secure treasure in heaven that he became a christian, as to secure dominion on earth. He embraced Christianity, because he believed he would thus insure the attainment of the end of his ambition. It is said that, as he marched at the head of his army, he saw, in the clouds the form of a luminous cross, on which were inscribed words which signify "Conquer by this." He went forth and conquered; and the cross being the symbol of the christian religion, he embraced the name—the shadow of that religion. He may have had something of the substance, but he was very far from using divine means to propagate the christian religion. As a "man child," he introduced human means to subjugate the world to the Church—the sword, the glitter of wealth, pomp and splendor, and all other means employed by men to extend and strengthen their dominions.

Before the time of Constantine, all the victories of the Cross were won by the bow of truth. The word of God, or treasure of divine truth, conveyed in earthen vessels, (weak mortals,) had proved the power of God unto salvation to every one that believed it. In an earlier vision, John saw a rider upon a white horse, with a bow, going forth conquering—a picture which most beautifully symbolizes the peaceful and blissful effects of the Gospel triumph. This is God's means of evangelizing the world; but Constantine departed from this divinely appointed method. In his time, it is said that corruptions were introduced into the Christian Church, which did more to destroy genuine religion than all the fires that ever persecution kindled. And from his time till the Reformation, (a period of about twelve hundred and sixty years,) the woman, the true Church, was nourished in the wilderness. During all this period the reign of the beast and the false prophet, (Papacy and Mohammedanism,) the "witnesses prophecied in sackcloth," the truly pious worshipped God in obscurity. The Bible was closed, and true religion was only found among those who worshipped God in secret. The worship in the public assembly was mere form—a mixture of Judaism and Paganism, in the name of Christianity.

We remarked, that in applying this vision to the Christian church, every figure in the text appears to perfection. For instance, the Church is frequently represented by the figure of a woman. In Isaiath lxiv, 1–7, Jehovah is represented as addressing the church, as his spouse, and calling upon her to sing for joy, in contemplation of the multitude of children that should be born unto her. Her Maker declares himself her husband; for a small moment she had been forsaken, but should be remembered with everlasting kindness. The Apostle tells us, Gal. iv, 27, "The Jerusalem that is from above is free, and is the mother of us all." He also says to the Corinthian church: "I have espoused you to one husband, that I may present you as a chaste virgin unto Christ." 2d Cor. xi, 2. In the forty-fifth Psalm the church is referred to as the king's daughter, adorned with gold, and dressed in raiment of needle-work. When to the foregoing we add that the church is spoken of as the "bride, the lamb's wife," it seems impossible to conceive of any other interpretation of the text than that we have given.

We are told that it was the custom with the ancients to represent their societies by the figure of a woman in some peculiar dress, as we find upon some of their coins. On one of the Roman coins a woman is seen standing upon a globe; on another, the crown is ornamented with the moon and stars. The figures in the text are therefore borrowed from the customs of the times in which this book was written, but exceed in grandeur anything before produced.

Mr. Benson remarks: "That to stand amid a glory formed by the beams of the sun, to wear a crown set with the stars of heaven as jewels, and to stand upon a pavement formed by the soft rays of the silvery queen of night, is a scenery more grand and sublime than anything the ancients ever imagined." This was the resplendent view of the Church presented to the gaze of the beloved disciple.

I. Notice, SHE WAS CLOTHED WITH THE SUN.

That is, invested with the rays of the Sun of Righteousness. Solomon, in his Songs, gives us a figurative representation of the Church, much like that in the text we are considering, as follows: "Who is she that looketh forth as the morning, fair as the moon, clear as the sun, and terrible* as an army with banners?" Sol. Songs vi, 10.

In the first dispensation of grace, the gray dawn that broke over the deep darkness produced by sin and the fall, the Church looked forth as the morning. This dawn lasted for many ages. The Sun of Righteousness was expected, but did not make his appearance. Yet by his rays, dimly seen, believing patriarchs were able to find their way to the blissful regions of eternal day. In the second, the Levitical period, she appeared fair as the moon. In the Gospel period, she appears clear as the sun; the dawn is superseded, the moon has gone down, or her rays are lost in the splendor of his from whom she borrowed them, for the Sun of Righteousness has risen with healing in his wings, and goes forth proclaiming, "I am the light of the world: they which sat in darkness

---

*It should be *glorious*.

have seen the light thereof. and to them that were in the valley and the shadow of death, light has sprung up." It was this glorious Gospel light, which shines forth lighting up the dark places of the earth and dispelling the gloom of sin's dark night, which John beheld, appearing as a garment upon the woman, and hence the language of the text, "clothed with the sun."

II. Notice " THE MOON UNDER HER FEET."

There are three respects in which this figure will appear appropriate :

1. *As representing the typical period,* as a basis upon which the Christian dispensation rests. The blessed Saviour frequently referred to the fulfilment of the types, shadows and prophecies, as indispensable to the establishment of Christianity.

2. *As a symbol of Judaism,* the moon may be said to be under her feet. The severest conflicts which the Church had in the early ages of Christianity were with Judaism. Abundant evidence of this may be found in the epistles of the apostles. The Judaizing teachers struggled hard against the establishment of Christianity, but she finally triumphed and put Judaism under her feet.

3. *As representing the exalted position of the Church.* The Church, composed of true believers, rises above all sublunary things. They set their affections on things which are above. "Risen with Christ," their aspirations are heavenward. They rise in the scale of being, mount up as eagles, and dwell on high.

> Born by a new celestial birth,
> They scorn the vanities of earth;
> Their hearts all taken up in love,
> They seek the blissful realms above.

Contemplating the joys already felt, the believer breaks forth in song:

> " I rode on the sky,
> Freely justified, I
> Did not envy Elijah his seat;
> My soul mounted higher
> In a chariot of fire,
> And the moon was under my feet."

III. SHE HAD A CROWN OF TWELVE STARS UPON HER HEAD.

She had no need of stars to give her light when clothed with the sun. These were, therefore, simply ornaments in her crown. These allude to the twelve apostles; but the symbol is not necessarily confined to them. The number twelve is figurative, signifying many; hence, the martyrs and confessors are included; yea, all who let their light shine. Every man, who truly lets his light shine, is an ornament to the Church, a star in her crown; especially those who turn many to righteousness, " they shall shine as stars forever."

IV. Notice HER LABOR AND FRUITFULNESS.

She was travailing in birth. The Church has suffered many persecutions, but has continued to multiply. Her most fruitful seasons have been the times of her severest persecutions. Forty days after the crucifixion of her founder, three thousand were added to her number. And whenever persecutions scattered them abroad, they went forth bearing the light of truth, and sowing the seeds of righteousness, which took root in every soil.

V. Notice HER PLACE OF SAFETY.

She fled on eagle's wings to a place of safety. The wings of the eagle, which is the strongest, and soars the highest of all birds, bear her in triumph to a place of safety, where the everlasting arms are about her, the munition of rocks is her defence, and the shelter of the Eternal Rock protects her from all evil.

> What, though the elements shall melt,
> And stars their orbits leave,
> And nature's pillars be removed,
> And dried up be the seas :
> Yet, 'mid the crash of falling worlds,
> The Church of God shall stand,
> Surrounded by his arms of love :
> Protected by his hand.

God grant each of us a place within her courts.

SERMON VII.

ON EASTER.

"He is not here : for he is risen, as he said. Come, see the place where the Lord lay." Matt. xxviii, 6.

This is the day set apart by the Christian world to celebrate the resurrection of the world's Redeemer.

I fear that in 'our effort to steer clear of Romanism, and too much formalism, we have' fallen into the opposite evil of neglecting some things which are of special importance. In avoiding the superstitions which attach too much importance to days, times and seasons, we seem to have lost sight of those eventful days which rightfully claim our deepest, reverence.

Beside the weekly Sabbaths which we are commanded to keep holy, there are three other days, upon which christians should bestow more than a mere passing notice. These days should be hallowed as Sabbaths, special Sabbaths. The events which transpired upon them deserve to be brought constantly before the mind; and that we may be more deeply impressed with their importance, their annual, return should be made use of, to instruct the ignorant, to call back the thoughtless wanderer, and to encourage and edify true believers. I refer to the birth-day of Jesus (Christmas), the day of his crucifixion (Good Friday), and the day of his resurrection (Easter Sunday). I don't know but I should have made it five days, adding the day of Ascension and the day of Pentecost.' The resurrection, it is true, is celebrated upon every Sabbath, and evidenced by the change of the Sabbath from the seventh to the first day of the Jewish week; nevertheless, I think an annual celebration must be well-pleasing to God, and most beneficial to his people. It does not matter whether we have the precise day or not; it is not the day, but the event, we celebrate. Since, however, he was crucified at the time of the great feast of the Jews, we can hardly be far amiss as respects the day.

But, as already remarked, it is the event with which we have to do—an event, than which nothing could be more wonderful, grand and sublime; nothing so calculated to inspire hope, and give to the believer the assurance of his own resurrection from the death of sin to a life of holiness. "And," says the apostle, "if Christ be not raised, your faith is vain, ye are yet in your sins." 1 Cor. xv, 17. We shall notice,

I. Some of the things necessarily involved in the resurrection of Christ.

Prominently among these we must consider his death and burial as essential to his resurrection. If he did not die, and was not buried, then he could not have risen. The apostle declares that the Gospel he preached embraced these three facts, viz.: the death, burial, and resurrection of Jesus. "For I delivered unto you first of all that which I also received, how that Christ died for our sins, according to the Scriptures: and that he was buried, and that he rose again the third day, according to the Scriptures." I Cor. xv, 3, 4. Following the apostle's example, we must demonstrate his death and burial, as necessary to the resurrection. We refer,

1. *To his arraignment.*

He was arrested, tried, and condemned to die. His trial, it is true, was the most cruel mockery ever exhibited to mortal gaze. He was arrested without a warrant, placed on trial without an indictment, declared innocent by his judge, and yet sentenced to death! When Pilate asked, "What accusation bring ye against this man?" they answered, "If he were not a malefactor, we would not have delivered him up unto thee." Did you ever hear such a response, in any other court, to the demand for a bill of charges against the defendant at the bar? Pilate is required to believe the prisoner guilty, to conclude that he is guilty, to act upon that conclusion, and declare him guilty, and to order his execution, with no other evidence against him, except the fact of his having been arrested by his blood-thirsty enemies and delivered to the judge. He was taken from Pilate to Herod, where the same farce was enacted, and again back to Pilate, who, for the second time, declared that he found no fault in him, and then washed his hands of his blood. Yet, after all, because of the clamor of the multitude, and incited by the priests, scribes, and other rulers, Pilate delivered Jesus to be crucified. The enmity of the Jews pursued him to the cross, and at last prevailed over all the other influences that were operating upon Pilate's mind, and thus he was condemned to die.

2. We behold *his crucifixion.*

This act was performed in the presence of a vast multitude of every class of Jerusalem's inhabitants. The clamor of the Jews, the cries of "Away with him! crucify him," having prevailed with Pilate, and he having delivered him into their hands, they hurried him away to Calvary, to Golgotha, the place of a skull—the place where the bones of criminals lay scattered over the ground. They mocked and insulted him in every possible way; they placed a crown of thorns upon his head, and saluted him, and bowed the knee in mockery; and when they had inflicted every other torture that Jewish malice could contrive, they lifted him up upon a cross, driving great nails through his feet and hands. There he hung for three hours, suffering the most intense agony, and finally expired; gave up the ghost, committing his soul into the hands of his Father. All nature felt the shock, the vail of the temple was rent from top to bottom, the earth quaked, the rocks were rent, and the graves of the saints were opened; (but they could not leave their tombs until Jesus had broken their chains and relieved their bodies from the power of the grave.) When the Roman officer saw and heard these things, he feared greatly, and said, "Truly, this man was the Son of God."

As the following Sabbath was a high day, the Jews besought Pilate that the legs of the criminals might be broken, to hasten their death, that the bodies might be removed. The legs of the criminals which were crucified with him were broken, but when they came to Jesus, they found he was already dead; nevertheless, a soldier pierced his side with a spear, and forthwith came there

out blood and water. His executioners pronounced him
dead, and it was evident to all that he was dead; therefore, the evidence of his death was conclusive. It has
never been denied, and for the very good reason, that it
was so well attested that no one could deny it, with a
hope of being believed.

3. Then *he was also buried.*

Joseph of Arimathea, a rich disciple of Jesus, went to
Pilate and begged the body, and with the assistance of
Nicodemus, John, and a few faithful women, he laid it
in his own new tomb. When the sun went down on that
eventful day, the Son of Man lay silent in the tomb. But
he had said he would rise on the third day. Therefore,
the Jews went to Pilate and desired that the tomb be
made secure until the third day had passed. They were
troubled in mind; they had seen him perform so many
miracles, that they expected him to fulfill this last engagement, and determined to provide against it, if possible. Pilate gave them the desired band of soldiers; the
sepulchre was hewn out of a rock, and the entrance was
closed with a large stone; this was sealed, so that to open
the sepulchre would have been an unlawful act. Every
precaution possible having now been taken, the tomb
was left to the care of the watch, who were responsible
for the safe keeping of the body till after the third day.
To have suffered the body to have been stolen, or to have
left the tomb, by any negligence on their part, would
have rendered each of them liable to the penalty of death.
With such a charge, and the danger of such a penalty
hanging over them, it is not likely that any one would
sleep while on duty. The occurrences of that day, no

doubt, occupied the thoughts of the sentinel on his beat, and was the theme of discourse in the camp. The possibilities of the near future would also constitute food for reflection, as also the character of the incomprehensible being whose body was resting in the tomb. If these did not afford sufficient matter to engross their attention and keep sleep from their eyes, it is impossible to conjecture what would.

II. But let us notice the RESURRECTION AS ATTESTED BY THE DISCOVERIES OF THE THIRD MORNING, AND THE IMMEDIATELY SUCCEEDING DAYS.

1. We have *the empty tomb.*

To this the text directs our attention : " He is not here ; * * Come, see the place where the Lord lay." This was the language of the angel who, seeing the disappointment of the women that came first to the tomb with sweet spices to anoint him, spoke unto them these words of consolation. It appears that the women must have left the tomb on the day of his burial, before the setting of the watch and sealing of the stone, for they were saying among themselves, " Who shall roll us away the stone?" They would hardly have thought of this as their chief difficulty, if they had known that the stone was sealed and guarded. They found, however, every obstacle to their approach to the tomb removed, for the angel, with his wing, had pushed the stone aside, and by the brightness of his countenance, had filled the soldiers with such terror that they, at first, swooned away, and when they had sufficiently recovered, they went in haste to their employers, to tell the wondrous story of the resurrection. Thus it happened that the women found nothing to ob-

struct them in their approach to the tomb; but, on reaching it, they found not the object of their visit. The body
was gone, the tomb was empty. John and Peter, having
heard from the women that he was risen, also came in
haste to the sepulchre, and found the grave clothing and
the napkin, but they found not the body. I presume
there were thousands who visited that empty tomb, but
a thousand witnesses would make no impression upon a
mind that could doubt the testimony of those already
named. Peter and John, and at least three women, viz.,
the two Marys and Joanna, and an angel from heaven,
six in all, or double the number that is required to establish any fact—all these testify to an empty tomb.
That the tomb had given up the sacred charge, there can
be no doubt. What became of it?

The enemies of Jesus were aware that this question
would have to be answered, that the absence of the body
would have to be accounted for, hence they invented and
circulated the ridiculous story, that his disciples stole him
away while the soldiers slept, and bribed the soldiers to
assist them in circulating this report.

No doubt the soldiers had reported the truth to many
on their way, but they were now to contradict themselves
as far as possible, cease to report the truth, and thus
make way for the circulation of the falsehood. The soldiers were promised security from blame or punishment
for the pretended crime of sleeping while on duty, or
negligence in suffering the body to be stolen, and thus
the attempt was made to deceive the world, to prove
Christ an imposter, and his disciples body snatchers. But
let us examine this story by the light of reason;

(1). Is it likely that his disciples, who all forsook a living Saviour, would have the courage to steal his dead body, guarded, as it was, by a band of Roman soldiers, the best in the world? The courage of Peter, which appeared great before Christ was arrested, forsook him when he saw his Master in the hands of his enemies. John was the only one of the eleven who ventured near the cross on the day of his crucifixion, and he alone, if any, was at the burial. There never was a man more completely deserted by his friends than Jesus. Had he not risen, his memory would have perished. What possible use could his disciples have made of his body? A dead Saviour had no charms for them; it grieved them, yea, put them out of patience to hear of his death. Peter rebuked him for speaking of his death, saying, "Be it far from thee, Lord, this shall not be unto thee." Matt. xvi, 23. No, all their interests were centered in a living Saviour: hence, so soon as they found him hopelessly in the hands of his enemies, they forsook him; and during the period that he lay in the grave, they were the most dejected, heart-broken wretches ever beheld. And if he had not risen from the dead, they would have been, of all men, most miserable. Such, in substance, is the language of the apostle, "If in this life only we have hope in Christ, we are of all men most miserable." But if the body was stolen, why was not a reward offered for it? Why were not the apostles arrested? Why were they permitted to declare publicly, without contradiction, his resurrection? This they did in Jerusalem, in the presence of thousands, and they were not contradicted. Why were not the soldiers punished for sleeping on their post, and thus suffering their charge to be taken out of their hands? If the soldiers had been thus guilty, the Jews would have prosecuted them to the bitter end. The very means that the Jews employed to hinder the fulfilment of Christ's predictions respecting his resurrection, proved to be among the best evidences of their fulfilment. The stone, the seal, the watch, are all witnesses of the resurrection: they testify with one voice against the absurdity of the story started by his enemies, that he was stolen while the soldiers slept. These witnesses are unimpeachable. Reason brings them to the bar, and justice, judgment, and truth are stamped upon their testimony, and their united declarations force the conviction of the fact that his disciples had no hand in the removal of the body.

(2): But if the soldiers slept, how could they tell what became of the body, or what took place during that period? Is not infidelity pretty hard pushed when it has to bring sleeping witnesses to the stand? Would any judge in the land take the testimony of a sleeping witness? You see that absurdity is stamped upon the face of this entire story. It is absurd to suppose that the disciples, who forsook a living Saviour, would have the courage to steal his corpse. It is equally absurd to suppose that his enemies, believing such a thing, should have made no effort to recover the body. It is absurd to suppose that the soldiers, to whom were committed such an important trust, could neglect that trust, and not be called to account. I repeat, the whole story bears the stamp of absurdity upon its face; and this absurdity is all that infidelity can offer against the testimony of the believers in a risen Saviour.

2. We remark *that his resurrection is attested by many creditable witnesses.*

Not, however, by those who saw him rise. It was not the will of God that one single human being should have advantage over another in this respect. No mortal being saw him rise. The truth of the resurrection is received by each and every one in the same way, namely, on the testimony of others.

(1). The first witness is the angel. Whether angels saw him rise or not, is an unsettled question with me. Whether by the fact of seeing him rise, or by his absence from the tomb, or by seeing him after his resurrection; it does not matter by what means the knowledge was obtained, the angel first bore testimony to the resurrection. Such is the record of three of the Evangelists. "And the angel answered, and said unto the women, Fear not ye: for I know that ye seek Jesus, which was crucified. He is not here; for he is risen, as he said." Matt. xxviii, 5, 6. "And entering into the sepulchre, they saw a young man sitting on the right side, clothed in a long white garment, and they were affrighted. And he saith unto them, Be not affrighted: ye seek Jesus of Nazareth, which was crucified: he is risen; he is not here." · Mark xvi, 5, 6. In Luke xxiv, 5, 6, we read as the language of the angel, "Why seek ye the living among the dead? He is not here, but is risen." It is seldom that we find a matter recorded by three authors, in so nearly the same language, as is this record. The expression of the angel as recorded by the three Evangelists is in substance the same, and a part of it in exactly the same words, yet there is sufficient

difference in the manner of expression of the passage to
show that one is not copied from the other.

(2). The second witness was Mary. She received the
information of the resurrection from the angel, which
was confirmed to her by Jesus himself, and with her companions she reported this fact to the disciples. Thus the
angel was sent to tell Mary, (not the mother of Jesus, but
Mary Magdalene,) and she was sent to tell the disciples,
and they were sent to tell the world.

Besides his appearance to Mary, on the morning of
his resurrection, he appeared at sundry other times for
the space of forty days. On the day of his resurrection,
as two of the disciples were journeying to a village a few
miles from Jerusalem, it is said that "Jesus himself drew
near and went with them." But they did not know him;
he talked with them by the way, stopped with them at
a village, and made himself known to them in breaking
of bread. See Luke xxiv, 13—31. He appeared on the
night of that same day to the eleven, who were together
in a room with the door closed. Luke xxiv, 36; John
xx, 19—25. On the following Sabbath evening, he assembled with them again, and after that, he showed
himself to them at the sea of Tiberias. See John xx,
26, and xxi, 1—14

Of the witnesses of his resurrection, the Apostle thus
speaks: "And he was seen of Cephas, then of the twelve.
After that he was seen of above five hundred brethren at
once; of whom the greater remain unto this present,
but some are fallen asleep. After that he was seen of
James; then of all the apostles. Last of all, he was seen
of me as one born out of due time." I Cor. xv, 5—8.

After showing that the whole christian fabric rests upon the resurrection, that if Christ be not risen, there is no resurrection, that preaching is useless, and faith vain, he concludes by the bold assertion: " But now is Christ risen from the dead, and become the first fruits of them that slept." I Cor. xv, 20.

III. Let us indulge a few thoughts respecting THE RESURRECTION AS AN ACCOMPLISHED FACT.

1. *It was an event most necessary.*

The resurrection is the keystone of the arch in the plan of salvation. We have already referred to the Apostle's declaration, that without this both preaching and faith are vain, and that ye are yet in your sins. We may add that his triumph was not complete without this. " He must reign till he hath put all enemies under his feet. The last enemy that shall be destroyed is death." I Cor. xv, 25, 26. Therefore, to complete his triumph, he must place his foot upon the neck of this last enemy. He had met the great enemy on other battle fields and conquered. His first great battle is represented as having been fought on the shining plains of glory, beneath the shade of heaven's high dome. There he met the rebel host and sent them trembling over heaven's battlements down to regions of dark despair. His second engagement was in the wilderness, where he met the prince of the powers of disobedience and thrice repulsed him. His third great battle was in the garden ; and his fourth on Calvary. In all, he had been more than conqueror In all of these battles, however, he had appeared as on the defensive. The contest appeared, so to speak, as forced upon him. The field, the time, and the manner of attack, seem all to have been chosen by the enemy. But in this last great conflict, the scene changes: the victor selects the field of battle; he carries the contest into death's do-minions. The choice of weapons are now his, and he appoints his own time: "Tear down this temple, but in three days I will raise it up again." He had pro-claimed victory by the mouth of the prophet, saying: "I will ransom them from the power of the grave; I will redeem them from death: O death, I will be thy plague; O grave, I will be thy destruction." Hos. xiii, 14. He is described in the book of Job as thirsting for the con-flict, impatient to engage the enemy, scenting the battle from afar, swallowing the ground with fierceness and rage, so that the distance between him and his enemy is as nothing. We must remember that this is Jehovah's description of the contest, for it was he that spake to Job, in person, as follows: "Hast thou given the horse strength? Hast thou clothed his neck with thunder? Canst thou make him afraid as a grasshopper? The glory of his nostrils are terrible. He paweth in the valley, and rejoiceth in his strength: he goeth on to meet the armed men. He mocketh at fear, and is not affrighted; neither turneth he back from the sword. The quiver rattleth against him, the glittering spear and the shield. He swalloweth the ground with fierceness and rage: neither believeth that it is the sound of the trum-pet. He saith among the trumpeters, Ha! ha! and he smelleth the battle afar off, the thunder of the cap-tains, and the shouting." Job xxxix, 18—25. With his eye fixed upon this tremendous conflict, and with full assurance of victory, he exclaims: "Now is the judgment of this world, now shall the prince of this world be cast out." Thus, with pressage of victory sitting upon his brow, he enters death's dominions, attacks Satan in his own territory, meets the hosts of the powers of darkness and conquers. He breaks the bands of death, and draws out his sting; bursts wide the grave, and robs it of its victory. Bearing away the gates of death, and standing with his feet upon the neck of his vanquished enemy, he exclaims: "I am he that liveth, and was dead, and behold, I am alive forever more."

2. *The resurrection was necessary to fulfill the types and prophecies of the Old Testament.*

They all represent him as rising. Joseph was brought up out of prison, Daniel out of the lion's den, and Jonah out of the sea. Peter quotes the language of the Psalmist, and shows most conclusively that it was a prediction of the resurrection of Christ. "Thou wilt not leave my soul in hell, nor suffer thine holy one to see corruption." See Acts ii, 25—31. When Jesus fell in with two of the disciples on the day of his resurrection, and they spoke of that event as an astonishing thing, he exclaimed, " O fools, and slow of heart to believe all that the prophets have spoken: ought not Christ to have suffered these things, and to enter into his glory?" Luke xxiv, 13—27.

3. *This grand achievement was surrounded with circumstances of peculiar glory.*

" And behold," says the Evangelist, " there was a great earthquake "—a mighty shaking of the earth. And an angel descended from heaven, whose majestic countenance flashed forth as lightning, and his raiment glittering with a snowy whiteness, the lustre of which no mortal eye could bear, and for fear of him the keepers did shake and became as dead men—that is, they swooned away. When they returned to consciousness, the stone was rolled away, and the tomb was empty. They were there prepared to resist the attempt of mortal beings to remove the body, but they had not contemplated an encounter with an angel, who had power to shake the earth ; therefore, seeing that the tomb was empty, they fled, and reported what had happened.

4. *This was the grandest of all Christ's achievements.*

He exhibited extraordinary power in his former miracles. To raise another was an act of stupendous power, but having, after being delivered unto death, loosed the pains or cords thereof, because it was not possible for them to hold him, he showed himself the Prince of life, the Plague of death, the Spoiler of hell, and the Captain of eternal salvation. In Him, death has lost its terrors, for those who sleep in Jesus will God bring with him. Through Him, we are assured of our own resurrection, which assurance removes the gloom from the grave.

APPLICATION.

Believer, this is your Savior. He has gone to prepare a place for you, that where he is, you may be also.

Sinner, we offer him to you. He died for your sins, and rose again for your justification. Seek him while he may be found, call upon him while he is near.

The grace of God be with you all. Amen.

SERMON VIII.

CREATION'S FIRST BORN, OR THE EARLIEST GOSPEL SYMBOL.

"And God said, Let there be light: and there was light."
Gen. i, 3.

This opening passage, in Jehovah's own account of his own creation, written by the inspired pensman, is a most striking illustration of his divine power. Men have exhausted their best efforts to account for the existence of the things which do appear, in some way different from that recorded in the book divine. Infidel scientists have. set up their theories, one after another, but have failed to produce one that will bear the light of reason, or any favorable comparison with the plain and simple statement of the inspired historian. Nor can they agree upon any theory to which they will stick. In their last great effort they have led us back to protoplasm, and there left us to grope our way in eternal darkness. Can that be considered a high order of intellect, which is willing to lose itself in a little speck of matter? which finds its creator in what can be handled by the creature? Infidels have not made much progress since Isaiah's time, and what motion they have exhibited, is in a retrograde direction, from gold backwards to protoplasm. "They lav-

5

ish gold out of the bag, * * * and hire a goldsmith ; and he maketh it a god: they fall down, yea, they worship. They bear him upon the shoulder, they carry him, and set him in his place, and he standeth." Isaiah xlvi, 6, 7.

It does seem to me that this boasted age of science and research ought to be able to find a god who can move out of his tracks. But excepting the God of the author of the book of Genesis, none can be found who has exhibited less helplessness than the one described by the prophet. In adopting the account of creation, as given by Moses, as our theory, we are not hard pressed to make it appear plausable. When we accept as a fact the statement of revelation, that there is one only living and true God, who is the Creator, the great First Cause of all things, himself uncaused and eternal, we stand at once upon solid ground ; yea, upon a rock, in comparison with which all else is as sand. By this method of solving the mystery of the origin of the material universe, we steer clear of a thousand difficulties that meet us on any other line. You must find bottom some where. You must find a foundation upon which to build any theory you may be inclined to set up. You must get back to first principles, must find a first cause. We find the Intelligent, Eternal, Almighty God to be that First Cause, and our theory is, that he is the author of all things, and we assert that for any other theory you have nothing but conjecture. Is it said that ours is conjecture, we answer, it is supported by what purports to be a divine revelation, and until it can be demonstrated that it is not, we have something better than conjecture. We are not left to wander in the darkness of unsanctified human reason, but bask in the sunbeams of divine truth, revealed in connection with such evidences as leave no room for disbelief or doubt.

The evident and indisputable fact is, that we find ourselves surrounded by a vast creation—how vast, the mind of man is inadequate to conceive. We live in a period, by all accounts, not much less than six thousand years from that in which Jehovah spake and said, "Let there be light;" and yet, in all these years no substantial progress has been made by unassisted human reason in solving the mystery of creation. We are amazed at the small attainments of man in his effort to find the origin of the material universe. Suppose you could collect the knowledge of all the doctors and professors in the land, unless I am mistaken, (and no one can prove that I am,) it would not all amount to what our father Adam knew on the day that he was created. He was made in the image of his Creator, who is the fountain of knowledge. And for what little we do know, we are largely indebted to divine revelation. The key to the knowledge of astronomy seems to have been borrowed from that sublime discourse which God delivered to Job out of the whirlwind, as recorded in chapters thirty-eight to forty-one inclusive of the book of Job.

Who had been able to solve the question, "Whereupon are the foundations of the earth fastened?" Job xxxviii, 6. The ancients had their notions, but we know how ridiculous and absurd many of them were. Who had demonstrated, or even hinted that a line was stretched over the empty place, and the earth hung upon nothing until God declared it. Who, even at this day, can give a satisfac-

tory answer to all the questions propounded in that in-
imitable discourse? On the question, " Canst thou bring
forth Mazzaroth in his season?" much has been written;
but even the learned admit that they do not certainly
know the meaning of the term. And the fact that those
who profess to know, differ, makes it evident that none
know to a certainty. On the question, " Canst thou bind
the sweet influence of Pleiades?" much had been written,
and ages had elapsed before even astronomers had any
idea that that interesting group had any special influence.* Taking a hint, however, from the question propounded by Jehovah, their investigations have led them
to conclude, pretty generally, that Alcyone, the central
star in that group, is the great central sun of all systems,
that all other suns and systems roll around it, and that
it holds the universe in poise. This is truly a sublime
idea; but it is borrowed from the book divine. It was
he whom we call God that gave out the hint, which
turned the astronomer's mind into the line of thought
which led to this conclusion. The hints thrown out in
that wonderful discourse afford themes for thought, and
lessons of instruction sufficient to keep the world's students employed for many ages yet to come, before they
will have learned them all. We commend these hints
to the consideration of skeptics.

We may ask, How shall we account for the fact that
He, whom we acknowledge and adore as God, knew so
much more, over three thousand years ago, than the
wisest know even at this day? If our notion of his be-

---

*What we call the " seven stars," There are only six visible to
the natural eye.

ing, and estimate of his character be correct, the mystery is solved. If we accept the language of the text as our guide, and admit the declaration of divine revelation, that God is the author of all things, our vision becomes clear, every difficulty vanishes. Our soundings are no longer fruitless, our thoughts no longer sink into a bottomless abyss, but fly back until they reach and find a substantial lodgement in the Eternal Source of all things, the Almighty Maker, and are swallowed up in the glory of his divine perfections.

The characteristics that revelation ascribe to him, render him fully competent to be the author of all things. A God of unlimited duration, wisdom and power, could easily accomplish the work of creating all that we behold, yea, infinitely more than we can conceive of; and without such a being, we are left to grope in the darkness of human conjecture, with the feeble taper of superstition, which only tends to make the darkness more visible.

The account of creation found in the book before us, is the only tangible account we have, or can have. What a grand and sublime opening the inspired pensman gives us! There is no labored preface, no apology for writing no introduction; but the stupendous subject bursts forth upon us from the inspired mind, and is at once set forth in all its grandeur and immensity. "In the beginning God created the heaven and the earth." Then follows a statement of the original state of matter: it was "without form and void; and darkness was upon the face of the deep." The Almighty determined to bring this world of ours into being, he stepped forth in the majesty of his might, and brought his creative energies to bear upon the void immense; the latent caloric heard his voice, and to the astonished gaze of the morning stars, light, creation's first born, leaped from the womb of chaos. "God said, Let there be light: and there was light." At his mandate that brightest and most beautiful image of its Almighty Author burst forth into being. Infidel and skeptical philosophers are wont to treat with derision, what they consider a great blunder on the part of the inspired pensman, in representing the creation of light -as taking place before the creation of the sun, moon, and other luminaries. But they betray their own amazing stupidity, in failing to comprehend the fact that he who had the power to create the sun, moon and stars to give light, could as easily have created light independent of them as with them. He is not dependent upon any second cause; his resources are infinite; he doeth what he will in his own way, according to his own pleasure. He is the great fountain of light, and in him is no darkness, but light ineffable and eternal. He could not, therefore, give an exhibition of himself without producing light. And because he is in everything that exists, latent or hidden heat, by which light is produced, exists in all things. Hence the Apostle says he "was the true Light, which lighteth every man that cometh into the world." It shineth, or existeth in the darkness, even though not seen.

I have chosen the text with the view of considering that system by which light and immortality are brought to light in the Gospel. It is Gospel light we wish to illustrate. We can conceive of no symbol of the Gospel more striking than light. I may also remark, that the idea of a resemblance between light and the Gospel is frequently presented in the Scriptures, and the effect of natural light is taken to illustrate that of the Gospel. Thus the great Teacher illustrates it: " The people that sat in darkness saw great light; and to them which sat in the region and shadow of death, light is sprung up." And the evangelical prophet employs this same figure to represent the Gospel day, and the effect of the Gospel light upon this benighted world. " Arise, shine; for the light is come, and the glory of the Lord is risen upon thee. For, behold, the darkness shall cover the earth, and gross darkness the people; but the Lord shall rise upon thee, and his glory shall be seen upon thee. And the Gentiles shall come to thy light, and kings to the brightness of thy rising." Now, the prophet did not mean that the sun, moon and stars should cease to shine, and that natural darkness should prevail, but that there would be a time of gross spiritual darkness, and that over this darkness should the Sun of Righteousness arise and send forth the rays of Gospel light into all the dark places of the earth; and that the Gentiles, yea, even kings of the earth should be lightened by its gentle rays. I need not to remind you that this prophecy has been largely fulfilled in the spread of the Gospel. Paul, in his second epistle to the Corinthians, gives substantially the same illustration: " For God, who commanded the light to shine out of darkness, hath shined in our hearts, to give the light of the knowledge of the glory of God in the face of Jesus Christ."

Now the Gospel resembles light *in its source.*

Light is the offspring of Deity, the product of his infinite wisdom and almighty power. He spake, and it

heard his voice; he commanded, and it came forth. Likewise, is the Gospel the offspring of Deity. The Gospel,
says the apostle, is not "cunningly devised fables": it is
not the invention of human imagination, or the product
of human ingenuity, but it is the glorious Gospel of the
Son of God. It bears his image and reflects his glory in
every line: in it all his attributes shine forth. Here,
mercy and truth meet, righteousness and peace kiss each
other, and wisdom, power and almighty love shine forth
in all their divine splendor.

But the Gospel resembles light *in its design*.

The light makes manifest. By it, we behold things of
which we would ever have remained ignorant without it.
There might be innumerable beauties around us, and
our organs of vision might be in their perfect state, but
without light we could never enjoy the pleasure of beholding them, but should remain ever ignorant of their
existence. Paul, with all his learning, was ignorant of
his natural depravity and the deceitfulness of his heart,
until the Gospel light shone around him, and the scales
of ignorance fell from his eyes. He thought he was offering acceptable service to God, when he was persecuting the saints, and opposing the doctrines of the despised
Nazarene, until the Gospel light revealed to him the
beauty and saving power of the religion of Jesus. This
is the great object of the Gospel—to make manifest; to
throw light into our dark understanding; to point out
our danger, and our refuge; to show us our disease, and
the remedy; to show us the pit into which we are sinking, and the benevolent hand that is stretched out to deliver us. By the Gospel light, we see our sinful state,

our lost and undone condition ; in it we also see our Saviour. It lights up our path from earth to glory; it is a lamp to our feet, and a "light to shine upon the road that leads us to the Lamb." It lights up the valley and shadow of death, throws a divine radiance over the tomb, and bright rays of joy and hope into the dying christian's eye, by which he has strength to exclaim, in the expiring moment:

"Come, welcome death, the end of fear,
Thy terrors I regard no more."

But the Gospel resembles light *in the mildness of its motion.*

There is nothing so mild in its motion as light. All other bodies, when put in rapid motion, are more or less destructive. The stream, when swollen to a flood, sweeps away all before it. The air, which is balmy and health-giving in its quietude, yet, when agitated, it tears up trees by the roots, levels costly structures with the earth, rolls up the waves of the sea, and engulfs majestic ships beneath the swelling billows. We have heard of hurricanes, which have swept away whole trains of cars, including massive locomotives. Not so with light: though it travels at the rate of twelve millions of miles a minute, yet it falls upon the eye with a mildness truly pleasant. So with the Gospel, in which there is neither lightning, nor thunder, nor tempest, nor smoke, and nothing to frighten or drive us away. It simply says, "Come!" "Come unto me, all ye that labor and are heavy laden, and I will give you rest." Matt. xi, 28.

When the law was thundered forth from Sinai, the trembling Israelites moved back from the mount, and besought God not to speak to them any more, except through Moses, in whose voice there was no thunder. The law proclaimed the terrors of the Lord, his wrath and indignation, which those, who obey not his voice, shall feel through the endless ages of eternity. " Cursed is every one that continueth not in all things which are written in the book of the law to do them." " The soul that sinneth, it shall die."

> " When to the law I trembling fled,'
> It poured its curses on my head,
> I no relief could find :
> This fearful truth increased my pain,
> The sinner must;be born again,
> O'erwhelmed my troubled mind.
> Again did Sinai's thunder roll,
> And guilt lay heavy on my soul,
> A vast, oppressive load :
> Alas ! I read and saw it plain,
> The sinner never born again,
> Must drink the wrath of God
> But while I thus in darkness lay,
> Jesus of Nazareth passed that way ;
> I felt his pity move ;
> A sinner, by his justice slain,
> Now by his grace is born again,
> And sings redeeming love.
> To heaven the joyful tidings flew,
> And angels tuned their harps anew,
> And loftier strains did raise,
> All hail ! the Lamb that once was slain,
> Unnumbered millions born again,
> Shall sing thine endless praise."

The Gospel is a message of mercy : it comes to cheer us. Like light, it is all tenderness, mildness, and heayenly softness. It tells us, that "God so loved the world, that he gave his only begotten Son, that whosoever believeth in him should not perish, but have everlasting life;" that "It is a faithful saying, and worthy of all acceptation, that Christ Jesus came into the world to save sinners;" and that "Jesus stood and cried, If any man thirst, let him come unto me, and drink." What gracious words, what heavenly tenderness, what enrapturing mildness! I repeat, there is nothing in the Gospel to frighten us; its light is sent to cheer us. So said the angel, who first proclaimed the Savior's birth: "Fear not: for, behold, I bring you good tidings of great joy, which shall be to all people."

But the Gospel resembles light *in its purity*.

How beautifully transparent is light! There is no foul mixture in it. It may pass over districts infected with disease; but, unlike the air, it inhales no contagious matter; unpolluted, it sweeps on through space, dispensing joy and gladness, but nothing hurtful or unpleasant. The Gospel is likewise pure; it is a system of purity: its purifying influence is called the "washing of regeneration." It removes sin's guilt and pollution, and diffuses purity: it sanctifies and makes holy. It has come in contact with every foul system—heathenism, paganism, Mohammedanism, and all the corrupting influences that have operated against the Christian Church, and yet it is pure. Stripped of the garments in which sectarians have tried to conceal the beauty of many of its passages, it still remains the pure Gospel word, the sincere milk of which gives strength to the bodies and souls of men. It is healing and invigorating.

The Gospel resembles light *in its effect upon our happiness.*

Solomon says, "Truly the light is sweet." It is only those whose "deeds are evil" that "love darkness more than light." To all others, light is more desirable, and conducive to their happiness. See that poor blind man, how timid and doubtful his motion. The sun pours forth his rays; but the unhappy man gropes his way at noon. The beauties of nature surround him, but he knows nothing of their charms. See that poor, benighted traveller, lost in the lonely desert, exposed to the wild beasts of the forest, the hissing serpents, and the howling tempest. See that tempest-tossed mariner, who has lost his reckoning. No star in the heavens, nor lighthouse on the shore, warn him of danger, or cheer him with hope. What joy would light bring to such distressed mortals! Such is the sinner. He is blinded by the god of this world, is in the darkness of his lost state, and in the road to death. He is tempest-tossed upon the billows of his guilty conscience, and exposed to the breakers of divine wrath. He is lost in the wilderness of sin, and is "without God and without hope in the world." To this blind, bewildered, tempest-tossed wretch, the Gospel brings light. It opens his blind eyes, to behold wonderful things in the kingdom of grace. It dispels the gloom of sin's dark night, and ushers in the light of Gospel day. It calms the raging billows, drives away the clouds of despair, raises the star of hope, and brings to view the lighthouse on the shore. The Gospel fills the understanding with the light of knowledge, the conscience with the light of peace, the

heart with the light of joy, and the expectation with the
light of hope.

> " It scatters all the guilty fear,
> And turns the hell to heaven."

Now it is Jehovah's mandate that the Gospel light shall
shine in all the dark corners of the earth. " Go ye into
all the world and preach the Gospel to every creature."

Let us notice THE MEANS BY WHICH THE GOSPEL LIGHT
IS TO BE DIFFUSED.

By the *Church*, which is the visible kingdom of God on
earth, he designs to accomplish his purpose of filling the
world with the light of divine knowledge. In solving
the mystery of the seven candlesticks, in the midst of
which John saw him standing, Jesus said, " The seven
candlesticks which thou sawest are the seven churches."
As the candlestick holds, and thus displays the light, so
does the church.

By the *life and labors of the ministry*. " The seven stars,"
said Jesus, " are the seven angels of the seven churches;"
that is, the ministers, like stars or planets, reflect the
rays they receive from the Sun of Righteousness. It is
their work to diffuse light, as burning luminaries, to
chase away the gloom of hellish night. Their mission
extends to earth's remotest bounds; and they are encouraged by the assurance of the divine presence. " Lo, I am
with you alway, even unto the end of the world." The
ministry is God's great agency in the work of diffusing
Gospel light. He has chosen them as his special instru-
ments, weak and frail, it is true, in themselves, but
mighty through God, in the accomplishment of his pur-

pose, to fill the world with Gospel light. Take a community, sunk in the very depths of darkness, sin and degradation; let a live, whole-soul Gospel minister go among them, and walk out and in before them, and you will soon see a change in that community. The deep darkness will disappear, and light will spring up and continue to shine, so long as the man of God is among them. Gospel light shines forth from a holy membership. It was Christ's command: "Let your light so shine before men, that they may see your good works, and glorify your Father which is in heaven." Brethren, we are to be lights in this benighted land. To each and to every one of us he says, "Let there be light." If we are not letting the light shine, we are not fulfilling our mission.

A few weeks ago in the town of Charlotte, N. C., they held an election to decide whether or not license should be granted to men, to deal out to that community "liquid damnation." At this election, there were a number of persons, who professed to be christians, that voted what they called "the wet ticket"—that is, they voted to license the sale of intoxicating drinks. I heard of one class-leader, who voted the wet ticket. What shall we say of such a leader?- Where is he leading the people to? Certainly, not into the true Gospel light, but into the darkness of intemperance. We would not sit in judgment upon the christian character of our neighbors; but how a man, who supports the whiskey traffic, can imagine himself a christian, is a mystery beyond my comprehension; and as a watchman upon the walls of Zion, I feel in duty bound to warn the people of the evils of the pres-

ent day. I know of no evil so destructive to every interest of both soul and body, so wide in the extent of its
ravages, so exacting in its demands, or so fearful in its
consequences, as the evil of intemperance. We, as a
race, have lately escaped from a bondage most oppressive,
degrading, and evil in its consequences—a system de-
nounced by a great and good man as the "sum of all
villainies." Whatever were the evils of that system, (and
they were never half told), and whatever were the horrors
to the enslaved class, or the curses upon the slaveholder,
yet the victims of that system were in no such evil
case as are the victims of intemperance! These are enslaved, both soul and body. Death released the victims
of our late system of slavery, and we have no doubt that
thousands of them were conveyed by angels to Abraham's
bosom. We have no such hope respecting the victims
of intemperance. Death sinks them deeper. The Apostle reminds us that the drunkard shall not inherit the
kingdom of heaven, and Jesus warns us that there is a
danger of having our hearts overcharged with drunkenness, and that day come upon us unawares. Drunkenness seems not to have been a prevalent evil in his day.
Very little is said of intemperance among the people of
God at that period. No doubt there was drunkenness in
that day, but it was among those who made no profession of righteousness. The wickedness of intemperance
was so generally acknowledged, it was not necessary for
Jesus to say much about it. It is the sin of all sins of
our day. It is the fruitful promoter of every evil under
the sun. Like the grave, it never says enough. Like
hell, it is never satisfied with the number of its victims.

Like the great red dragon that stood before the woman, this monster seems to have been waiting the results of the emancipation proclamation, that it might seize upon the freed people and enslave them again, before they were strong enough to resist its power. Our penitentiaries are filled with its victims; and the auction block has often been surrounded by horses, mules, cows, and all manner of implements of husbandry, the property of one who had a fair start and was doing well, before he fell under the power of the whiskey traffic. The wretchedness and woe so fearfully prevalent, the ragged and half-starved children, the heart broken wives and mothers, the empty school benches, the half-finished churches, the half-supported preachers, and the vast and untold numbers that are crowding the downward road, all go to show how completely this monster has, in many cases, wholly nullified the intended effect of the freedom proclamation. And yet, there are men among us, professing christians too, even ministers, who indulge in the intoxicating cup, and who oppose the efforts that are put forth to remove it from the land. Some even go so far as to threaten to withhold their support from ministers who speak against this evil. The minister who would swerve one hair's breadth from his duty for fear of men, is not worthy of support. They forget that he who opens and no man can shut, has said, " Your water is sure, and your bread shall be given."

> What then is he whose scorn I dread,
>   Whose savage threat makes me afraid,
> A bar-room pimp, to rum a slave,
>   A bubble on the drunken wave,

If we are to wander forty years in this wilderness, I can see no cause for it but intemperance. Now God says, "Let there be light." Let the light of temperance shine in all our dwellings. Let us drive out King Alcohol, and thus make way for the blessed reign of King Emmanuel.

God grant us grace to diffuse light by a holy example, and thus hasten the day when the kingdoms of this world shall become the kingdoms of our God.

SERMON IX.

THE SOUL'S ANCHOR.

"Which hope we have as an anchor of the soul, both sure and steadfast, and which entereth into that within the vail : whither the forerunner is for us entered, even Jesus, made a high priest forever after the order of Melchisedec." Heb. vi, 19.

At the commencement of the chapter, of which our text is a part, the Apostle intimates his purpose of advancing to the consideration of sublimer truths, and exhorts his Hebrew brethren to leave the first principles, and advance with him. He exhorts them to aspire after greater proficiency in the knowledge and practice of Gospel principles, as a means of preventing their backsliding and final apostacy, which would result in their eternal ruin. Verses 1—8. He expresses a hope that they would persevere in the good way on which they had entered, and thus secure the reward of faith and obedience, in the complete salvation of their souls. Verse 9. By pointing to the life and labors of those who had already obtained the promise, he endeavored to urge them on to greater diligence. He would comfort believers with a view of God's goodness, in the engagements he had condescended to enter into, and which he had confirmed by an oath : " Wherein God, willing more abundantly to show unto the heirs of promise the immutability of his counsel, confirmed it by an oath; that by two immutable things, in which it was impossible for God to lie, we might have a strong consolation, who have fled for refuge to lay hold upon the hope set before us." Then follows the text: "Which hope we have." "We," that is, the Apostle and every other believer, who, having been awakened to the sense of a lost and undone condition, have fled to and laid hold of the promises of God, and made them our refuge, or, as the Apostle puts it, are heirs or inheritors of the promises, "have this hope as an anchor of the soul." All we, who conscious of our natural depravity, weakness, guilt and wretchedness, have, for safety from deserved wrath, laid hold upon the promises set forth in the Gospel, have a strong and consoling assurance that our confidence is well placed, and that our refuge is sure. The Apostle mentions two rocks, or solid foundations, upon which our confidence rests, and intimates a third. "That by two immutable things, in which it was impossible for God to lie, we might have a strong consolation." One immutable thing would have been sufficient to have sustained all who would confide in it, but in the inexhaustible abundance of God's goodness, he gives beyond measure. He presses it down in the measure, shakes it together, and then runs it over; yea, more, he doubles and trebles his blessings.

The two immutable things, of which the Apostle speaks, are, first, the promise of God, (and his promise is sure); and second, the oath by which the promise is confirmed, "The oath," says the Apostle, "is the end of strife." It puts an end to all contradiction. That which is sworn to, is regarded as settled, unless there is strong counter-vailing testimony.   And there can be no testimony against the declarations of him that cannot lie, there can be no oath to rebut his; and because he could swear by no greater, he swore by himself.   Therefore, we have as a ground for our hope the promise of God, who cannot lie, and the oath of God, which cannot be broken.   In addition to this, the Apostle mentions the further fact, that Jesus, our forerunner, has entered also within the vail, and there abideth forever a high priest.   A fore-runner is one who goes before to prepare the way for others to follow.   Jesus said to his disciples, "I go to prepare a place for you."   Into this prepared place, he received the penitent thief, whose faith pierced the vail of ignominy which enveloped the crucified Nazarene, and beheld in him the King of saints, and trusted in him as such.   The Apostle here claims him as the fore-runner, who has entered heaven for us.   He has taken possession of heaven, and prepared it for the accommo-dation of his people.   He has prepared a highway lead-ing to it, and has engaged to conduct us safely, and afford the assistance of his grace, to enable us to finish our course, to fight the good fight of faith, and to lay hold upon eternal life.

I. Let us notice THE CHARACTERISTICS OF THE CHRIS-TIAN'S HOPE.

The Apostle calls it the soul's anchor—"Which hope we have as an anchor of the soul."   The anchor is that which, when cast, holds the ship steady amid the storms and keeps it from being blown upon rocks and dashed to pieces, or drifting off with the tide.   There are times when sailing becomes dangerous; when the black tempest sweeps the swelling billows, the boiling surges mix with the clouds, death rides upon the storm, and the mariner fears destruction upon the rocks; the anchor is then his only hope; if it fails him, his ship is lost.

Amid the storms of life, hope is the christian's anchor. When friends all fail and foes all unite; when subjected to cross providences, or strange afflictions; when the enemy comes upon us as with a flood, all things seem to be against us; and, like old Job, we are constrained to cry out in the bitterness of our soul: "Oh! that my grief were thoroughly weighed, and my calamity laid in the balances together; for now it would be heavier than the sand of the sea: therefore my words are swallowed up. For the arrows of the Almighty are within me, the poison whereof drinketh up my spirit: the terrors of God do set themselves in array against me." In such an hour, hope holds the soul steady, and sweetly whispers:

> " Peace, troubled soul, thou needest not fear,
> Thy great deliverer still is near,
> His tender love protects thee still,
> Be calm, and sink into his will."

Thus encouraged, the confiding soul exclaims: "All the days of my appointed time will I wait till my change come."

The Apostle calls this a "sure" hope. It is not every hope that is sure. We read: "The hypocrite's hope shall perish, whose hope shall be cut off, and whose trust shall be a spider's web." But the christian's hope, like David's covenant, is ordered in all things and sure. It is a hope that sustains him in every discouragement in life, and forsakes him not in death—a hope full of immortality and eternal life.

It is "steadfast"—unyielding, unmoved. The violence of the storm can neither break it nor drag it from its moorage. The thunders roar, the lightnings play among the clouds, the winds howl, the waves lash themselves to fury, but the sheet anchor of hope holds on, and safely keeps the soul until the storm of life has passed—

> Till hope in fruition dies,
> And faith is lost in sight.

Finally, the Apostle refers to the celestial anchorage. "It entereth into that within the vail." Within the vail of the temple, which separated the holy from the most holy place, was the ark of the covenant resting upon the mercy seat; the two tables of stone, upon which was the law written by the finger of God; the pot of manna, and Aaron's rod that budded; all of which were over-shadowed by the cherubim, wrought by the hand of a cunning artificer. Into this holy place the high priest entered once a year to offer sacrifice, first for himself, and then for the people. Behind this vail, except that of the high priest, mortal eye was never to look. This *sanctum sanctorum* was a type of heaven, the holiest of all, where God sitteth upon his glorious throne, over which Isaiah beheld the six winged seraphs praising the divine Majesty. Here, Jesus, our forerunner, sits at God's right hand, and from this divine presence the Holy Spirit comes forth to bear witness with our spirits, that we are the children of God. Within this vail our anchor of hope is cast; the divine Triad is our anchorage, and faith is the strong cable that holds us fast. The Son of God offered himself, as a sacrifice for us, the Father accepted the sacrifice, and the Holy Ghost bears witness that we are accepted in the Beloved.

II. Let us consider THE GROUNDS OF THE CHRISTIAN, HOPE.

Keeping in view the Apostle's metaphor, the anchor, we are reminded that to hold a vessel steady in the storm, the anchor must be cast, and must take hold upon good, solid ground. If the ground yields, the anchor will drag, and the ship will be cast upon the fatal breakers. Likewise hope, to sustain us amid the storms of life, must be an active, well-grounded hope. Such is the christian's hope. It is a lively hope. The anchor is not carried as an useless encumbrage on the vessel's deck, but it is there to be employed, to be used, to be cast on good and solid ground. And the anchor of hope should not be cast on the shoals of formality, nor in the deep sea of philosophy, nor amid the rocks of heterodoxy, nor in the quicksands of superstition; but upon the good and solid grounds of intelligent, heartfelt, practical, pure and undefiled religion.

Now, the believer's hope is grounded upon divine benevolence. "God so loved the world that he gave his only begotten Son, that whosoever believeth in him should not perish, but have everlasting life." This was the Apostle's boast, " He loved me and gave himself for me." Surely, the amazing exhibition of divine love, as displayed in the mystery of redemption, affords ground upon which the christian's hope may safely rest, and bid defiance to the tempest's rage.

The believer's hope rests, also, *upon the finished work of Christ.* He has wrought out for us a complete salvation. By his suffering, death and resurrection, he has procured the right and the power to present us without fault before the throne. The sacrifice he offered met all the demands of insulted divine majesty: in him mercy and truth met, righteousness and peace kissed each other; and through him God can be just, and yet the justifier of the ungodly. Divine truth demanded the infliction of the death penalty, as an atonement for the broken law. Divine mercy, in the person of Jesus, by the oblation of himself once offered, rendered full and complete satisfaction for man's disobedience and sin. He said: "I will magnify the law and make it honorable;" I will restore to it all that man's disobedience has taken from it. By man's rebellion, peace had departed from the sons of men, divine indignation was kindled, and wrath was threatened. To appease the divine anger, an atonement made by the nature that had rebelled was required, and it was also required that the atonement should be perfect; but there was not a just man upon earth. Divine mercy, in the person of Jesus, interposed. "A body thou hast prepared me, it will I offer." Dost thou demand obedience? "Lo! I come, in the volume of the book it is written of me, I delight to do thy will, O God; yea, thy law is within my heart I will declare thy righteousness in the great congregation, and thy loving kindness unto the sons of men. By his righteousness he hath justified many; he has reconciled man to his Maker, restored peace to earth, and good will to man. By the sacrifice of himself, he gave glory to God and peace to man, and also a glorious exhibition of his loving kindness and tender mercy. By his death upon the cross, by his resurrection and ascension to glory, he finished his engagements, put an end to the power of sin, made reconciliation for iniquity, brought in an everlasting righteousness, and gave to his ministers the mystery of reconciliation. I repeat, the believer's hope rests upon this finished work of Christ.

But it *rests also upon his mediatorial intercession.* Having offered himself a sacrifice for sin, he entered death's dominion, spoiled principalities and powers, broke the fetters of death, robbed the grave of its victory and death of its sting, ascended to his Father's throne, and ever liveth to make intercession for us. "A priest forever after the order of Melchisedec," not after the order of Aaron, which was changeable, descending from father to son, "because they were not permitted to continue by reason of death," but like that of Melchisedec, his abides in himself. Like Melchisedec, there was none of his line who filled the office before him, and none will succeed him. Like Melchisedec, there was a mystery hanging over both his birth and his death; and yet, like his type, he was born and also died. He did not receive his priesthood by descent like the sons of Aaron, but by an oath like Melchisedec. Hence, the language of the Psalmist, quoted by the apostle: "The Lord hath sworn, and will not repent, Thou art a priest forever." The apostle continues, "By so much was Jesus made a surety of a better testament. And they truly were many priests, because they were not suffered to continue by reason of death: but this man, because he continueth ever, hath an un-

6

changeable priesthood.   Wherefore he is able also to save
them to the uttermost that come unto God by him, seeing he ever liveth to make intercession for them." The
believer's hope rests firmly upon this intercession, and he
is encouraged, with the immortal Charles Wesley, "To
bid his soul arise, shake off its guilty fear, and behold the
bleeding sacrifice in its behalf appear."

> " He ever lives above, for me to intercede,
> His all redeeming love, his precious blood to plead,
> Which blood atoned for all our race,
> And sprinkles now the throne of grace.
>
> Five bleeding wounds he bears, received on Calvary,
> They pour effectual prayers, they strongly speak for me:
> Forgive him, O forgive, they cry,
> Nor let the ransomed sinner die.
>
> The Father hears him pray, his dear anointed one,
> He cannot turn away the presence of his son,
> His Spirit answers to the blood,
> And tells me I am born of God."

Upon this God-blessed assurance of the effectual intercession of our high priest above, the believer's hope rests,
and all the mad billows rage and foam and lash themselves to fury in vain.

> " For still the Christian's bark outrides
> The blustering winds and swelling tides."

He who intercedes for us knows our weakness, the se-
verity of the temptation to which we are exposed, and
also the enmity and subtlety of the enemy of our souls.
He once dwelt in a frail tenement like ours, and was in
all points tempted as we are.   He passed through a fiery
ordeal, a bloody sweat, a painful agony and exceeding

sorrow of soul—"he trod the wine press alone, and of the people there was none to help him;" yet he triumphed through it all and thereby secured for us the blessing of divine favor, and the assurance of divine sympathy.

"Touched by a sympathy within,
He knows our feeble frame ;
He knows what sore temptations mean,
For he has felt the same."

But the believer's hope rests also *upon his own personal experience.* His knowledge of the forgiveness of his sins, his acceptance with God, his justification by faith, the peace he enjoys within, and the sustaining grace by which he is enabled to stand, and maintain the conflict, and after all to stand ; are all connected with a sure hope. Divine love, the finished work of Christ, and mediatorial intercession, will all go for nothing, unless they are connected with a personal experience, a knowledge that the kingdom of God is within us—that he reigns in our hearts. We must have the Spirit of God in us, bearing witness with our spirits that we are the children of God. We must know by God-blessed experience, that we have passed from death unto life—that the old man with his deeds have been cast out—that our nature has been changed and the new creation formed within. We must be able to say with our favorite poet:

"My God is reconciled, his pardoning voice I hear.
He owns me for his child, I can no longer fear;
With confidence, I now draw nigh,
And Father, Abba Father, cry."

To have a sure and steadfast hope, each must know for himself, that these blessings are his. He must have

the witness in himself, must know the time and place of
the shaking of his dungeon, and the falling off of his
chains. A mere hope that he is a christian is not sufficient; he must "*know.*" He must know that the burden
of sin has been removed, that its heavy load has passed
from his back, and that he is no longer oppressed by its
weight. He must know that the gloom, distress and fear
of sin's dark night have been cleared away, and that
they have been superseded by the light of liberty, peace
and joy, which are the fruits of justification by faith.
If we have them not, we cannot have a sure hope of
heaven. The ship, the cable, the anchor cast, are all important, but their utility depends upon their connection.
The kingdom of grace set up in our hearts, is the substantial sea-worthy craft, which alone will convey us
safely across the tempestuous ocean of time; faith is our
strong cable, which must be made fast to the anchor of
hope, cast within the vail; and while this connection is
maintained, we are safe.

"Though by winds and waves we are tossed and driven,
Yet while freighted with grace we are bound for heaven."

Now if we are in deed and in truth believers in Christ
Jesus, if we have made the promise of God our trust, if
we have fled thereto for refuge, if we have laid hold upon
the hope set before us in the Gospel, and are holding on
thereto, we have the strong consolation these blessings
afford, and may unite with the Apostle in appropriating
the language of the text: "Which hope we have as an
anchor of the soul, both sure and steadfast, and which
entereth into that within the vail, whither the forerun-

ner is for us entered, even Jesus, made a high priest for ever after the order of Melchisedec."

Finally, the believer's hope is *grounded upon his longings for home.* These are the Spirit's implanting; they lead us homeward and make us pant for the living streams of bliss.

> "I cannot, I cannot forbear
> These passionate longings for home ;
> O when will my spirit be there,
> O when will the messenger come ?"

He who has his anchor cast within the vail, has his affections set upon things above, where Christ sitteth at the right hand of God—his heart and his flesh crieth out for the living God. His desires go onward and lead him toward his home, and while standing upon some lofty peak, the heavenly breezes bear to his enraptured soul the fragrance of Eden's flowers, and while his eye feasts upon the golden beams of that glorious light which flows through the city of God, he exclaims:

> "Yonder's my house, my portion fair,
> My treasure and my heart are there,
> And my abiding home."

III. But notice THE CONSOLATIONS OF THE CHRISTIAN'S HOPE.

"That by two immutable things in which it was impossible for God to lie, we might have strong consolation." The promises of God, and the oath by which they are confirmed, are consoling; they afford strong consolation. There are many and sore trials through which most of God's people have to pass in this howling wilderness. Afflictions arise from the temptations of the

devil—he will vex, if he can do no more—from the frailty
of our nature, and from our business, social or domestic
cares. Under the burden of these afflictions, distresses
and cares, we are consoled by the hope of future and eternal felicity. We are consoled by the assurance, that "our
light affliction, which is but for a moment, worketh for
us a far more exceeding and eternal weight of glory,
which shall be revealed in us."

We are consoled by the assurance, that whatever our
trials and difficulties, whatever dark nights of sorrow
and affliction, whatever dark paths duty compels us to
pass through, a hand divine is leading us, and will cheer
us, (for he "giveth songs in the night,") and will lead us
safely and with rapture to the city of everlasting habitations.

We are consoled by the assurance, that however we are
buffeted by the enemy, whatever sore conflicts we may
have, whatever wounds we may receive, however hard
pushed we may be, however numerous, or strong, or malicious our enemies, however long the conflict may last—
in a word—whatever the nature of the engagement, we
shall more than conquer through him that loved us and
gave himself for us.

We are consoled by the assurance, that however strange
and unaccountable the dispensations of Providence, yet
all things shall work together for the good of those that
love the Lord, that—

> "Behind a frowning providence,
> He hides a smiling face."

Consoled and strengthened by such invigorating and
soul-stirring assurances, we are enabled, not only to stem

the current ourselves, but also to encourage the weak
ones, and cheer them by our songs.

"Come on, my partners, in distress,
　My comrades through the wilderness,
　　Who still your bodies fill,
　Awhile forget your griefs and fears,
　And look beyond this vale of tears,
　　To that celestial hill.

Beyond the bounds of time and space,
Look forward to that heavenly place,
　The saints secure abode ;
On faith's strong eagle pinions rise,
And force your passage to the skies,
　And scale the mount of God.

Who suffer with our Master here,
They shall before his face appear,
　And by his side sit down;
To patient faith the prize is sure,
And all that to the end endure
　The cross, shall wear the crown."

SERMON X.

THE LOSS OF THE SOUL.

"For what is a man profited, if he shall gain the whole world, and lose his own soul? or what will a man give in exchange for his soul?" Matt. xvi, 26.

Jesus having entered the coast of Cesarea Phillippi, inquired of his disciples as to what were the sayings respecting him, "Whom do men say that I, the Son of man, am?" They answered that there were a variety of sayings respecting him. Some said he was John the Baptist, risen from the dead. This, it is said, was Herod's opinion. I have a notion that Herod hatched this opinion to quiet his conscience. To satisfy his brother Phillip's wife, whom he had unlawfully taken to himself, he had John beheaded. John had rebuked this wicked couple for their unlawful conduct, and the woman planned for his destruction; the king falling in with, and executing her plan, became responsible for the deed. Wicked as he was, he had not quite sold himself to the devil, hence this act of wickedness disturbed his conscience. Therefore, he would find relief in persuading himself that this was John, risen from the dead; as, in that case, he could console himself with the idea that he had not done him much harm, after all. It often happens that men regret

the consequence of their own doings, when it is too late
to undo them; but they foolishly fall back upon the hope
that God may overrule in such a way as to, at least, nul-
lify the effect of their misdoings. Suppose he should?
That won't help their case. No matter what God may
do for his own glory, their sin remains the same, until
they repent. Repentance and faith alone will remove
guilt and give substantial peace of mind. The more excellent way, however, is to do only that which an enlightened conscience, on calm reflection, will justify.

The disciples further told Jesus, that some said he was
"Elijah; and others Jeremias, or one of the prophets."
He then asked, "But whom say ye that I am? And
Simon Peter answered and said, Thou art the Christ, the
Son of the living God." After assuring them that that
profession of faith was the rock upon which his church
should be built, and securely stand, he proceeded to inform them of what should soon transpire respecting himself. "From that time forth began Jesus to show unto
his disciples how that he must go unto Jerusalem, and
suffer many things of the elders and chief priests and
scribes, and be killed, and be raised again the third day."
At this Peter took him and began to rebuke him, saying,
"This shall not be unto thee." But Jesus said, "Get thee
behind me Satan; thou art an offence unto me, for thou
savourest not the things that be of God, but those that
be of men." Peter had learned his christian lessons but
poorly; he had been taught the importance of self-
denial; that it is the basis upon which discipleship
must rest: he, on the contrary, had exhibited selfishness as a most prominent feature in his character, and

which controlled his action ; yea, it was the corner and capstone thereof. He is here taught that this foundation must be dug up, and a new one laid, from which every particle of selfishness must be removed. And for this, the following reason is given : " For whosoever will save his life, shall lose it." He that would save his life by shrinking from his duty, shall lose it. " And whosoever will lose his life for my sake, shall find it." He that, for love to Christ, does his duty regardless of consequences, and thereby loses his life, shall find it again in heaven. He shall find in the end that he has really lost nothing. Then follows the text: " For what is a man profited, if he shall gain the whole world, and lose his own soul ? or what shall a man give in exchange for his soul ?"

To impress them with the importance of the subject, he employs a method with which men engaged in mercantile pursuits are well acquainted, namely, loss and gain. The merchant who does not pay attention to this rule, will be most likely to suffer loss. If he does not see to it that something is gained by all his transactions, he had best close up shop. If he pays more for what he buys, than it will bring when sold, if the outlay is more than the income, it is clearly a losing business ; and if he continues thus, all eventually will be lost. To ascertain the value of any business in which we are engaged, we must consider the entire outlay. If this subtracted from the income, leaves a balance, then it is evident that the business pays. But if the outlay is the larger of the two, he is admonished by the rule that he cannot subtract a larger number from a smaller, that it is a losing business, and if continued failure will be inevitable. The text leads us to apply this rule of profit and loss to the eternal interests of the soul.

I. Let us consider THE IMAGINARY GAIN.

I say imaginary, for it is not real. He that embraces this world, or sublunary things as substantial good, is deceived. Let us suppose a case in which a man goes into the stock market and a picture of great wealth is held up before his eyes, to be the result of making a certain investment. He is carried away by the promise of great riches; he is encouraged by old stock gamblers, and enraptured with the view of the splendid air castles formed in his mind, and is intoxicated with the idea that he will soon be a millionaire. He at once resolves to invest all his available cash. But this does not satisfy his ambition : "Ventures make millionaires as well as merchants," and he feels a desire to sink his bottom dollar in this one great effort. He, therefore, mortgages all his property, raises all he can thus, and invests it, also. Well, he has spent all, and while he awaits the moment at which he is to realize the expected fortune, he buys on credit, and borrows from his neighbors, until his credit is exhausted and he can borrow no more; because his failure to meet his payments promptly, has shaken the confidence of his creditors. He is surprised that those who had always trusted him should be unwilling to make him further advances. He has not realized, as yet, what he expected from his investments, but has no doubt of their soundness and great productiveness in the end. But the conduct of his neighbors renders him unhappy ; he is vexed at the idea of their lack of confidence, and he says to himself, I will wait no longer; I

will sell my stock at what it will bring; I will pay my
debts, lift my mortgages, and if I have not reached the
object of my ambition, I will yet have comfort and ease,
and I will make my neighbors ashamed of the want of
confidence they have shown. Thus musing, he goes into
the stock market to offer his stock for sale; but he there,
to his astonishment, learns that it is not worth a cent.
He has spent all, and lost all. Can you imagine a more
wretched being than that man, when he awakes to the
full sense of his situation? I repeat, he has invested all,
and lost all. He has lost his expectation, his valuable
property, his money, his credit and standing in society—
yea, hope and all is gone. He is poor and penniless with
a helpless family on his hands, a family refined and edu-
cated; but they have learned only the livery of high life,
of labor they know nothing. They have known nothing
of his financial transactions, and consequently nothing
of his financial ruin ; but they must know it. How can
he face that loving wife and those darling children, and
break to them the doleful story of their poverty and dis-
grace? The shock is too great, the shadow of despair
hovers over him—it falls! and reason leaves its throne,
the vacant stare of the lunatic settles upon his countenance, the last sad act, self-destruction, follows, and all is
over: no, not all, he has changed lives, but not states. .
The hell from which he flees, when he cuts his throat
and leaves this world, meets him in another, intensified
a thousand fold.

Such is the wretch, who barters away his soul for the
things of this life, or setting too great value upon them,
pursues them to the neglect of his soul—in the end he

loses all. What if he has gained much? Suppose he
has accumulated wealth, honors, titles, dominion and
glory; has seen many years of prosperity, has flourished
as the green bay tree? Suppose he has gained the world,
ten thousand worlds, if possible, what will it all amount
to in the dying hour, when he is brought to face the stern
realities of eternity? Alas, it won't purchase for him
one poor drop of water to allay the anguish of his pain,
or cool his scortching tongue! It is like the worthless
stock in the hands of a broken gambler; it will yield
him nothing of any value in the dying hour.

But let us consider this imaginary gain a little more
critically in the light of the text.

"If he shall gain the whole world." Then, it is not
certain that the whole world can be obtained, even at
that fearful price. The "if" implies a doubt; but it is
more than doubtful; it is certain that we cannot gain the
whole world. No man ever did gain the whole world;
and if one had it, he would not know what to do with it,
or with himself after he had possessed it. It is said of
Alexander, (sur-named the Great!) that when he supposed he had conquered the world, he sat down and wept
because there were no more worlds to conquer. Alas!
poor man! he was not happy after all, in his fancied
possession of the world. But suppose he did possess the
whole world, what does it avail him now? Where is
Alexander the Great, the mightiest conquerer that ever
led armies to victory—the "He goat" of Daniel's prophecy, that is described as going forth from conquest to
conquest with such rapidity that he touched not the
ground—he who snatched laurels from conquerers and

placed them upon his own brow—who made toys of the crowns of kings, and seized upon the gold of Ophir as his treasure—I repeat, where is Alexander the Great? The world he conquered and seized upon as his own, no longer affords him a home. He has passed away. Let us follow him to that eternity to which he has gone, and ask him to instruct us on the momentous interrogatories of the text. Supposing that he lost his soul, he has now endured the agonies of the lost for more than two thousand years. Suppose we draw aside the curtain, raise the hatches of hell, and getting assurance from the angel Gabriel of a safe return, we descend that dark abode, and inquire of Alexander the Great, " what is a man profited if he shall gain the whole world and lose his own soul?" What, think you, will be his answer? Yonder he sits upon the bosom of a burning lake. His mighty captains, too, are there, companions of his woe. I see no laurels now upon his brow, no crown upon his head, nor sceptre in his hand; neither are there any marks of conquest, nor tokens of victory. He no longer sighs for other worlds to conquer. He looks not like a conqueror, but wears the visage of one that has been conquered. He looks dejected and hopeless. An angry scowl rests upon his brow, woeful sadness fills his eye, and anguish wrings his soul. He is terrible to behold and fearful to approach; but I accost him from a point beyond which Gabriel warns me not to venture. I ask, "Alexander, what is a man profited who gains the whole world, and loses his own soul?" Hark, his answer: "Profit! profit!! there is no such word in hell's vocabulary. It is all loss here— loss, loss, eternal loss!" " What, then, will a man give in exchange for his soul?" To this he answers: "When I was on earth, I was a fool; I grasped at shadows and missed the substance. I thought there was value in crowns and kingdoms—in earthly honors, titles and dominion, but I have learned by sad and woeful experience, that there is but *one* thing of real value to man—that is his SOUL. Go back! go back! and bear from me this solemn message to the sons of men, yet in time: Forget the imaginary value of wealth, honors and titles; forget everything else—*but don't forget that no price set upon the soul can mark its value!* Its value is beyond computation—it is priceless. Disregard this truth if you will; trifle with it, treat it derisively and contemptuously, or break its force upon the mind by sophistry or ridicule; crowd it out by worldly amusements, or whatever the world can offer you—but learn as I have learned, that the one regret that will eternally gnaw as the undying worm, will be the regret that the *soul's value* was not learned in the season of salvation."

II. Let us now consider THE LOSS OF THE SOUL.

What is it? What is the loss sustained by those who, setting too much value upon material things, pursue them to the neglect of the soul's eternal interests, or barter away their souls to obtain them? I repeat, what is the loss of the soul? What mind can solve the fearful problem? I confess my inability to grasp the mighty theme. The mind staggers at the thought of attempting to penetrate the momentous meaning of the five following words: *Eternal loss of the soul.* If there are five words in any language more expressive of all that is to be feared, their sound has never fallen upon my ears.

There are two thoughts involved. First, of "the soul." What is it? It is the life, the product of God's breath. "God breathed into his nostrils the breath of life, and man became a living soul." Elihu tells us that it is the spirit in man which receiveth instruction from the Almighty. The soul in its purity is the divine image, and possesses kinship to Deity; is capable of feeling Jehovah's touch, as a man the touch of his fellow. It is undying in its nature, must eternally exist somewhere; hence its loss cannot mean annihilation. Socrates, who came nearer to the knowledge of the truth than any other heathen philosopher, arrived at this truth from the light of reason. He will most certainly arise in the judgment to the condemnation of many who have refused to walk in the light of revealed truth. Revelation most plainly teaches this truth: "These shall go away into everlasting punishment, but the righteous into life eternal." Yes, we must eternally exist somewhere, but where? "Man dieth and wasteth away, yea, man giveth up the ghost, and where is he?" Such was the cogitation of Job's mind; and the thought equally concerns us. And the language of the poet may well be sung in every land by every tongue:

"Soon as from earth I flee,
What then will become of me?"

This brings us to the second thought referred to, viz., the "soul's loss." What is it to lose the soul? It evidently includes the loss of every kind of pleasure. If the soul is once lost, we shall never know another moment's ease or comfort while eternal ages roll. To lose the soul is to lose whatever of bliss God has reserved for his loved ones. It is to endure whatever of pain God will inflict upon the disobedient. We know nothing of what either is, except by the pictures in which God, by his Spirit, has painted them in the book of revealed truth, and upon the tablets of our hearts. We know by experience something of joy, of grief, and of pain, and by these we may be instructed. We have five avenues through which either comfort or misery are poured into the soul—hearing, seeing, feeling, smelling, and tasting. If we have only so many in the future state, the pictures we have seen of heaven lead us to the thought that the blessings are sufficient in quantity and variety to keep all the avenues continually crowded. The loss of the soul is the loss of all this.

There are in heaven innumerable beauties, such as mortal eyes never saw. It is represented as a four-square city, with gates of pearl, and streets of gold. There are gardens and pleasant walks, and heavenly music most charming to the ear. We love to hear the music of a well-trained choir, but oh! when the music of heaven's songsters bursts upon our ears, mingled with the music of millions of harpers, the sweetest songs of earth will cease to be remembered as music. The pictures of heaven include abundant provision of most delicious fruits, the product of the tree of life, standing upon both sides of the river, which flows out of the life-giving fountain. Then there are fragrant flowers which fill the heavenly atmosphere with a rich perfume, so that every breath inhaled will be pure and sweet. Then, our hearts shall be filled with a fullness of joy unmixed and eternal. The loss of all this is included in the loss of the soul.

Then hell is the opposite of heaven in every thing but

duration. All the faculties, which in heaven form avenues through which pleasure is conveyed to the soul, will, in torment, be the avenues through which wretchedness and woe will be poured into it forever. Instead of heavenly music, will be sounds of agony and woe. Outbursts of angry demons will make hell hideous. Children will be heard cursing their parents, and charging them with their damnation. Then, there will be the wails of lost souls, and these sounds of agony, woe and sorrow, together with the angry outbursts, will be continual and eternal; for they that worship the beast shall never have rest. Then there will be soul-sickening sights, from which the eye can never turn—gastly and horrid forms, "if form that can be called, which neither shape nor form presents, in member, joint or limb." And, from that sink of all filth and corruption, will constantly arise a stench more obnoxious than that emitted from the most filthy cesspool of earth. And from this sickening odor the nostrils can never turn. We sometimes pass by filthy places in large cities, from which we hasten away, holding our breath to avoid the inhalation of unwholesome and unendurable odors; but there will be no getting away from this offensive odor in the world of woe. Unendurable it may seem, but must be endured. And of this there is no cessation—no interval in which an agreeable or wholesome breath is breathed. No, the inhabitants of torment will never enjoy a sweet or pleasant breath. But the pictures by which the meat and drink furnished for the inhabitants of torment are represented, are extremely uninviting—wormwood and gall—a most bitter repast. We are also told that "they shall drink of the wrath of God, which is poured out without mixture in the cup of his ndignation."

And finally, the entire being will be tortured with most excruciating pain—pains such as never racked the moral frame. In Rev. xiv, 10, 11, we find the following: 'The same (the lost) shall be tormented with fire and brimstone in the presence of the holy angels, and in the presence of the Lamb: and the smoke of their torment shall ascend up forever and ever, and they have no rest day nor night." This is only the shadow, what then must be the substance which sends forth such fearful shadows? This is the picture only; what must be that fearful reality from which it is drawn? Deep and dreadful must be that condemnation which requires such fearful figures to represent it.

I repeat, the loss of the soul is the loss of every kind of enjoyment. It is more: it is to feel every kind of misery of which the soul is capable. The loss of the soul shuts out from it every ray of joy, so that it will never feel a moment of peace any more. "What then is a man profited, if he shall gain the whole world, and lose his own soul? or what will a man give in exchange for his soul?"

A proper appreciation of this subject is calculated to induce us to lay the axe at the root of our own selfishness, to unhinge our affections from the things of this world, and hang them on the things that make to our eternal peace.

SERMON XI.

TWO CHARACTERS AND TWO DESTINIES.

"And these shall go away into eternal punishment; but the righteous into life eternal." Matt. xxv, 46.

The words of our text were uttered by the Son of God, the Saviour of the world, and are found in one of his latest discourses—a private discourse delivered to his disciples. He had administered that fearful rebuke to the hypocritical scribes and Pharisees, in the temple, which is recorded in the 23rd chapter of Matthew, in which he intimated that their sins would eventually bring upon them the destruction of their temple and government. He closed with the following lamentation : "O! Jerusalem, Jerusalem, which killeth the prophets, and stoneth them that are sent unto thee ! how oft would I have gathered thy children together, even as a hen gathereth her chickens under her wings, and ye would not! Behold your house is left unto you desolate."

As he passed out from the temple, his disciples called his attention to the grandeur of the buildings, but he said, they should be utterly destroyed, so that not one stone should be left upon another, which should not be thrown down. As he sat upon the Mount of Olives, his disciples came to him privately, and said : " Tell us, when shall these things be? and what shall be the sign of thy coming, and of the end of the world?" After giving them suitable instruction, by which they might escape the horrors of the destruction of Jerusalem, and by attention to which, thousands of christians did escape them, he turned to the consideration of the last question they had propounded—that respecting the general judgment, or the end of all material things—when shall the end come? What he had to say on this subject, begins with this 25th chapter, runs entirely through it and ends in the words of our text. We remark, that he did not answer their question directly. He did not tell them when the end would come. It has not pleased the Lord to tell us when the end will come. That is a secret which he has hid in his own heart; and it is folly for man to attempt to search it out, as God has determined not to reveal it till the time comes. Silly men have attempted to fix the time, but their followers have found their prophecies delusive. In 1848, they had a day fixed, and some went out and sat on the hill sides, but they might have sat there till now, if they had lived so long and been foolish enough, and yet not realized their expectation. Indeed, I cannot see what good a knowledge of the time would do the world. I suppose, if it were reduced to a certainty that the judgment would come to-morrow at twelve o'clock, scores of people would not think of commencing to get ready till half-past eleven; so much is mankind disposed to put off till the last moment that which ought to be attended to first. For this, or some other good reason, God has kept this matter to himself. He tells us that he will come at an unexpected

hour—at midnight, (figuratively,) the hour at which people sleep most soundly. While he did not tell them
when the end would come, he did tell them what would be
the condition of things, in respect to his kingdom, and
the relation of mankind to it. Under three figures, he
presented the human family into two classes. One class
received favor, reward, and eternal enjoyment; the other
disappointment, punishment, shame and everlasting
misery.

First, he described them under the figure of two classes
of virgins, one wise and the other foolish. They all went
forth at night with lamps to meet the bridegroom, but the
foolish neglected to take oil to recruit their lamps. This
was truly foolish, for the time of his coming was not
fixed, and such feasts were often attended at a very late
hour. I may here remark, that the lamps were not such
as we use. It was a lamp, or torch—what we would call
an outdoor, torchlight procession. When I was a boy,
we used to go fire fishing, for which we made a torch of
broken flax—a good bunch of which we wrapped tightly
around the end of a stick, and soaked it well with oil.
This made a good light and burned a long time; but
when the oil was exhausted, our lamps went out and left
us in darkness. To provide against this, we carried a
vessel of oil to recruit them when we had need to do so,
that is, when we intended to stay out till a late hour. As
one of the Evangelists speaks of smoking flax, I am inclined to the opinion that it was a torch of this kind
that was carried by these virgins; if so, it is easy to understand how important the vessel of oil was. During
the delay of the bridegroom, the virgins all fell asleep.

While Jesus delays his coming, many generations of both classes have fallen asleep in death, but he will come, by and by, and awake them. It was at midnight that the virgins were summoned to arise and meet him; and those whose lamps were trimmed and burning, went in to the marriage, but the others were shut out. He next described them under the figure of servants, among whom their lord distributed talents. Some improved them; one did not. Those who improved their talents, represent the practical christian, who works out his own salvation, while God works in him, both to will and to do of his own good pleasure. The other represents the fearful and unbelieving. He brought the talent back, and told his lord that he knew him to be hard to please, and that he was afraid. There are many of those who tell us that they are afraid to make a start, lest the work should be too hard for them, and they should not be able to hold out. O wretched, shameful cowards! Is it manly or womanly to be afraid to undertake what thousands are accomplishing with apparent ease? The want of courage and energy on this man's part consigned him to endless weeping, wailing and gnashing of teeth; and those, who, like him, are afraid to make an effort, in hope for nothing better.

The final representation of the two classes of characters, into which the world is divided, is that which closes with the text. He draws a picture of the Judge of all, seated upon a glorious throne, the nations of the earth assembled before him, the separation line drawn, the character of each declared, and the sentence pronounced. At this point the righteous, astonished at the commendation for good works, inquired when they were performed. "Lord, when saw we thee a hungered, and fed thee? or thirsty, and gave thee drink? When saw we thee a stranger, and took thee in? or naked, and clothed thee? Or when saw we thee sick, or in. prison, and came unto thee?" He answered, "Verily, I say unto you, Inasmuch as ye have done it unto one of the least of these my brethren, ye have done it unto me." Every deed of charity he acknowledges as work acceptable to him. On the other hand, those who were condemed for the neglect of charity, also asked, "Lord, when saw we thee a hungered, or athirst, or a stranger, or naked, or sick, or in prison, and did not minister unto thee?" He answered, "Verily, I say unto you, Inasmuch as ye did it not to one of the least of these, ye did it not to me." To neglect the humblest mortal in his distress, affliction, or want; to disregard the poorest beggar at the gate; to refuse relief to the raggedest urchin in the street—is to slight the Saviour, incur his displeasure, and risk his condemnation.

Then follows the text: "These shall go away into eternal punishment, but the righteous into life eternal." "These," who have no oil in their vessel, (grace in the heart); he, who has not improved his talent, (has not worked out his salvation by repentance, faith, and practical godliness); and "these" who have neglected the demands of charity, shall depart from the divine presence, and abide in perpetual distance; shut out from the marriage supper of the Lamb, forsaken, abandoned, and crying in vain for admission—shall be taken away from the palace, and bound in prison, in outer darkness, where there is weeping and wailing and gnashing of teeth: they

shall be separated from the company of the blessed; feel
the infliction of divine wrath, and the punishment prepared for the devil and his angels.

> "Far on the left with horror stand,
> And doomed to endless woe."

"But the righteous into life eternal." "The righteous."
Those who have the lamp of profession in full blaze—are
letting their light shine, have the oil of grace in their
hearts, go forth in the practice of every duty; are using
the talents which God has given them, embracing every
opportunity to do good, and waiting patiently on the
Lord, who in his own good time will reward them: such
shall have an eternal life, in fulness of joy, and pleasure
in God's glorious presence forever more.   Such, in short,
are the two characters, and the two destinies, as set forth
in the text, and in the discourse of which the text is the
conclusion.

But the fact that there are two characters and two destinies is not alone supported by the passage before us,
but is also taught in many other portions of revealed
truth.   In Proverbs it is written, "The righteous hath
hope in his death, but the hypocrite's hope shall perish."
In the midst of the wickedness, and consequent famine,
oppression and anarchy in Jerusalem, Isaiah delivered
this message: "Say ye to the righteous, that it shall be
well with him: for they shall eat the fruit of their doings.   Woe unto the wicked: it shall be ill with him:
for the reward of his hands shall be given him."   What
can be more reasonable, or just, than that a man should
enjoy the benefits of his own crop?   Here we are assured

7

that if one produces righteousness, he shall enjoy it. If wickedness, he can only expect a reward of wickedness, the natural product of that state. Finally, the Apostle Peter, in his first general epistle, propounds the solemn interrogatory, "If the righteous scarcely be saved, where shall the ungodly and sinner appear?" If those who make it their business to serve God, that they may be accepted of him; and thus manifest their affection for, and confidence in him, and their obedience to his commands, and declare themselves strangers and pilgrims here, are scarcely saved, what shall become of those who, so far from making any effort to please God, are at enmity and in rebellion against him, and treat his offer of mercy with contempt? If his own dear, loving children are scarcely saved, what shall become of those who hate him? Those who

> "Set at naught and sold him,
> Pierced and nailed him to the tree?"

If, in the light of the foregoing passages of Scripture, chosen as illustrations to enforce the theme under consideration, there is one mind that can doubt the truth set forth, to-wit: that there are two distinct characters, as widely different as light and darkness, and that in the future they will occupy states and conditions as different as are their characters, that mind is beyond the reach of reason, and beyond the persuasive power of the Gospel.

But I have good hope that many are so far convinced, that they will follow us prayerfully as we advance in the further illustration of this important truth.

I. Let us consider a little more fully THE TWO CHAR-ACTERS.

Whatever lines men may draw, whether social or sec-tarian ; however men may class themselves as to wealth, lineage, or intellectual development, God regards them only as belonging to one or the other of two classes. Jesus says, "He that is not with me is against me." I said to a young man once, "Are you on the Lord's side?" He answered, "No." "Why?" I further asked, "what has the Lord done to you that you are against him?" "Oh," he said, "I am not against him." This man fan-cied he was occupying a middle ground, and was neutral, but the declaration of Jesus is, that there is no middle ground upon which a single mortal can stand; that the line is sharply drawn, and that each occupies a position on one side or the other, either for Christ or against him. And there is another delusion which Jesus exposes in the same 'passage, viz: the notion that you are doing nothing. Some say, "Though I am not with you, I am not doing anything against you." That is to say, I am not at work on either side. The following words of Jesus knock the props from under this position : "He that gathereth not with me, scattereth abroad" Matt. xii, 30. This passage teaches most clearly that each and every one is either with Christ or against him, and at work on one side or the other. Each one is doing something in the work of gathering to Christ, or scattering from him. There is no neutral ground, and no idlers in this strug-gle between Christ and Beelzebub: all are engaged in the conflict, and each soldier has the mark of his sover-eign, which fixes his character. Those who are with

Christ are righteous, those who are against him are not. Whatever they may think of themselves, or whatever we may think of them, they are not righteous in the eye of Jehovah, as is evident from revelation. And we can know nothing of what is righteousness in the sight of God, except by what he has revealed in his word. We may fix up a righteousness in our own fancy, but it won't amount to anything when we come to stand before God. The Scribes and Pharisees had what they supposed to be a very excellent righteousness. And it must be admitted that it was in many things highly commendable. They fasted twice in a week, had eighty forms of prayer, never entered a house without praying, prayed in the streets and in the market places, paid tithes of all they possessed, were strict in the observance of the written law and the traditions of the elders; so strict were they that there was a generally accepted adage, that if but two persons were saved, one would be a Scribe and the other a Pharisee: and yet Jesus made, to the multitude upon the mount, the astonishing announcement; "Except your righteousness shall exceed the righteousness of the Scribes and Pharisees, ye shall in no case enter into the kingdom of heaven." Bear in mind, it was not their wickedness that he was finding fault with, but their righteousness. It was not the hypocritical Scribes and Pharisees he was finding fault with on this occasion, but the sincere ones. It was not their badness, but their goodness, he was condemning; their goodness was not good enough. We need not to look into the Bible to discover that there are two separate, distinct, and widely different characters in every community of this christian country.

There are those who profess to have passed through a
spiritual change, or transformation, figuratively spoken of
as a new birth, by which they are enabled and obliged to
lead a new life. In consequence of this change, they claim
to enjoy peace with God, and to have a sure hope of a
blessed immortality. Then there are those who make
no such profession, and claim no such hope. The great
majority of those who make this profession, are members
of the christian church, in its various branches; while the
great majority of those who do not make this profession,
are not members of the christian church. There is very
great variety in both of these characters. Among christian professors there are some who are bold, fearless,
strong, active christians; full of good works, of self-sacri-
fice, of love to God, and love to man : you have no room
for doubt that they are, at least, thoroughly in earnest,
think what you may of their wisdom or intellectual balance. Then there are those whose faith is so weak, grace
so small, good works so few, and love so cold, that it
would require a microscope to discover any christian life
in them. Yet, if they really have any faith, any grace,
any genuine good works, any love to God and to the souls
of men, they are on the Lord's side : however young, if
babes only in Christ, they are numbered with the righteous, and are on their way to heaven : however weak,
sickly, or puny, if christians at all, they are on the Lord's
side, and are numbered with the righteous.

It is the transformation, the new birth, which changes
the nature and forms the christian character. It is the
grace of God, poured into the soul, through justifying
faith, which, working by love, purifies the heart, produces

the transformation, and begins the life of righteousness. "By grace are ye saved, through faith, and that not of yourselves, it is the gift of God." Ephes. ii, 8. It is evangelical obedience, and practical godliness which maintains and continues the reign of righteousness in the soul. That there are persons who make such professions, and whose life and labors testify to their honesty, no candid individual will deny. On the other hand there are those who make no such profession: they know nothing of the new birth, for the reason that they have not been born again. An unborn child is not expected to know anything of this world; nor can we expect a person not born of the Spirit to know anything of the spiritual nature. They know nothing of justification by faith, they doubt the reality of such a thing. They know nothing of divine grace as a means of justification, through faith, they have not tasted that the Lord is gracious, and in their notions of the sufficiency of human nature, they can feel no need of grace. They know nothing of the Holy Spirit, or of his sanctifying influences: they have no faith in his operation. They don't hunger and thirst after righteousness, and therefore are not filled. The bread and water of life is spurned; the invitation to the great feast of oxen and fatlings is slighted, and the inviting messengers are put off with vain excuses. The broad way and its many travellers are preferred to the narrow way and the pilgrims journeying therein—who acknowledge themselves strangers and sojourners, as their fathers were; and that they can tarry but a night. They love the world supremely: it is their portion, their trust, their hope, and their all.   Its wealth, its fashions, its titles, its honors, and glory are their good things, in which they trust, and for which they labor.   That this class of characters exist is evident, and that these two classes make up the human family is equally evident, from our daily experience with those around us.

To consider THE CHARACTER OF THE RIGHTEOUS a little more definitely, we may remark,

1. *That it is an imputed righteousness.*

It is the righteousness of Christ, freely offered to all who will accept it " in faith, believing on him who raised up Jesus from the dead, who was delivered for our offences, and raised again for our justification."   Connected with the imputation of Christ's righteousness, is the non-imputation of our own iniquity.   When Christ's righteousness is imputed to us, that which had been crooked in our conduct is not imputed, what was amiss is not held against us, we are treated as though there never had been any wrong in us, but as obedient children, beloved of the Father.   Also, in connection with imputed righteousness is the forgiving of transgression, the putting away, covering or hiding of sin, and the emptying the heart of all its guile.   To transgress is to pass over a boundary, to do what is forbidden.   All have transgressed, and hence all need forgiveness.   Hence, also, it is written, that by the deeds of the law shall no flesh be justified, because in the flesh the law has been violated.   A citizen who has never violated the law is entitled to all the rights of citizenship, but so soon as he becomes a violator, his condition is changed.   Let us suppose that a man has lived in a community for fifty years, as a most upright citizen, with not a stain upon his character; but at the end of his fiftieth year, he breaks open a neighbor's house and steals his goods; is not that man, in the eye of the law, as much deserving of punishment as any other criminal? Has he not spoilt the whole fabric of his fifty years' righteousness? This is the meaning of the passage which asserts that the man who misses the hundredth only, is guilty of the whole. I think we would understand it better, if we should simply say, he is guilty, notwithstanding his former correctness. He has no power to redeem himself; the law holds him for punishment. If the penalty was death, "Even a great ransom could not deliver him." Such was the condition of human nature; righteousness was lost, through disobedience; mankind stood guilty before God, and justice cried for the infliction of the penalty, which was death—temporal, spiritual, and eternal. It was when man was in this condition, in his extremity, that mercy interposed, and God cried, "Deliver him from going down to the pit: I have found a ransom." I have found one who, by his righteousness, hath the right and power to redeem, and to proclaim righteousness in the great congregation, for the law of his God is in his heart. He also hid, covered, or put away sin out of sight. We have no power to put away sin, we must not attempt to hide our sins, and yet they must be hid. This fact was set forth in the type of the scape-goat, over whose head the priest confessed the sins of the people, after which it was led away to a land not inhabited. To put away our sins, and to bring in an everlasting righteousness, Christ, the antitype, appeared. Upon him God laid "the iniquity of us all," and through him the multitude of believers have escaped the consequences of sin, and have been made righteous. With the heavy load of human guilt upon him, he was led away to Calvary, a land not inhabited by the living—to "Golgotha, the place of a skull." Accepting the pardon offered in his blood, our sins are no more remembered against us; and, so long as the divine injunction, "Look not behind thee," is obeyed, they will no more trouble us. The Holy Spirit removes the guile from the soul, bears testimony to the new creation formed within, and gives to the believer a realization of the blessedness spoken of by the Psalmist: "Blessed is he whose transgression is forgiven, whose sin is covered. Blessed is the man unto whom the Lord imputeth not iniquity, and in whose spirit there is no guile." Psa. xxxii, 1, 2.

2. *It is the righteousness of faith.*

"Not of works, lest any man should boast." It is said that Abraham believed God, and his faith was counted unto him for righteousness. We quoted, a while ago, the passage which represents grace as being received through faith. In that passage faith is represented as the medium through which grace is poured into the heart of the believer. We have sometimes illustrated the idea here presented by the New York aqueduct. The people of that city found themselves in want of sweet, fresh water. Now there was an abundance of pure water in the Croton river, which, however, was many miles distant from the city. To overcome this difficulty an aqueduct was built, through which the water is conveyed all that distance, emptied into a great reservoir, and from thence conveyed to all the houses in the city, through pipes prepared for the purpose. Now, it was pure water that they needed, but they could not have had it without the aqueduct. And no more can we have grace without faith. What if there was an abundance of water in the Croton river? It would not have benefited the people; without the aqueduct, its waters would have flowed on in their God-appointed channel. And what if God's grace is abundant? It cannot benefit us except it can reach us, and it can only reach us through faith. If, therefore, we have no faith, we can have no grace. Faith is a confidential reliance upon the divine promises. The Apostle only made a common-sense statement, when he said, " Without faith it is impossible to please God." No man is pleased with you, when you disbelieve his solemn statements. I do not suppose you could vex a man more, in any way, than by showing that you did not believe a word that he said, especially if he was deeply in earnest, and regarded his message as important. How then can God, who can neither trifle nor lie, feel toward one who will not believe him? Faith is what God demands, and when he sees it in us, he imputes it unto us for righteousness.

Finally, *the righteousness which is accepted of God is complete.* It must enter into every fiber of our nature, and run through the warp and woof of our lives. The Apostle speaks of this completed character as a soldier, standing, clothed in his full armor; with salvation for his headpiece, righteousness his breastplate, his loins girded with truth, his hand grasping the sword of the Spirit, his feet shod with the Gospel; and the great shield of faith completely covering him, and protecting him from the poisoned arrows of the devil. It was in this complete

armor that the poet represents the pilgrim standing when
Satan met him.　He was just from the armor-house, too,
and every piece was shining brightly.　Satan eyed him
for a while, and finally thus addressed him :

> "Good morning, brother Pilgrim:
> Pray tell to me your name ?
> And whence it is you are travelling to,
> Likewise from whence you came ?
> Pray, what is that upon your head,
> Which shines so clear and bright?
> Likewise the covering on your breast,
> Which dazzle so my sight?
> What kind of shoes are those you wear,
> On which you boldly stand?
> Likewise that flaming instrument,
> You hold in your right hand ?"

To which the undaunted pilgrim responded :

> "My name!　It is bold pilgrim,
> To Canaan I am bound,
> I'm from the howling wilderness,
> And the enchanted ground.
> With glorious hope upon my head,
> And on my breast a shield,
> With bright sword I mean to fight
> Until I win the field.
> My feet are shod with gospel grace,
> On which I boldly stand;
> I mean to fight until I die,
> And gain fair Canaan's land."

In conclusion, let us spend a few further thoughts upon
the concluding words of the text, "The righteous into
life eternal."　The love of life is deeply seated in human
nature, indeed in all animate nature.　All things love

life, and cling to it. This feeling, no doubt, is divine in
its origin; it is of the hand planting of Deity. But love
this life as we may, we cannot keep it.

> " Our wasting lives grow shorter still,
>   As days and months increase,
>   And every beating pulse we tell,
>   Leaves but the number less."

The withering grass, the falling leaf, the fading flower,
all testify that our days on earth are but a shadow, and
there is none abiding. To the lovers of this world, this
is a gloom-producing truth. Thousands of young people
refuse to permit their thoughts to stoop, linger, and con·
verse with death. With what rapture such persons
would receive the assurance that they should never get
old, and never die. Such an assurance cannot be given
to mortals here; the experience of all ages is against it.
But the righteous have a far better assurance. It is this,
that mortality shall be swallowed up of life, that when this
earthly house of our tabernacle is dissolved, we shall have
a building of God, an house not made with hands; that
this corruptible state shall end, and that a state of incor-
ruption, of immortality, of eternal life, shall succeed it—a
life of undisturbed peace, of uninterrupted enjoyment, of
unclouded and unending day, of unmixed blessedness, of
endless delights.

> Give joy, come grief, give ease or pain,
>   Take life or friends away,
> But we shall find them all again
>   In that eternal day.

SERMON XII.

MAN'S NATURAL DISINCLINATION TO TURN IN HIS DISTRESS TO HIS MAKER.

" By reason of the multitude of oppressions they make the oppressed to cry : they cry out by reason of the arm of the mighty.
But none saith, Where is God my maker, who giveth songs in the
night ; who teacheth us more than the beasts of the earth, and
maketh us wiser than the fowls of heaven ?" Job xxxv, 9—11.

I know of no history more replete with sublime sentences than this truly wonderful book contains. So tran-
scendently wondrous are the scenes which are brought
to view in rapid succession, that many have been inclined
to set the whole book down as an allegory. I think there
is no necessity for such a conclusion : fact is stronger
than fiction, and what the human mind is capable of
imagining, God is much more than capable of bringing
to pass.

There are several interesting characters brought to view
in this book, but none more so, I think, than Elihu, the
speaker of the text. He is the last actor brought upon
the stage : he does not close the scene, but he plays his
part among the closing exercises. He seems to be a puzzle to many learned commentators. Who was he? is the
question upon which much thought has been spent. A
very sensible writer remarks : " He was the son of Barachel

the Buzite, of the kindred of Ram. Neither Scripture nor history tells us more respecting him, and to push our inquiry further, is timply a waste of time to no purpose." All beyond this is mere conjecture. He appears to have been a man of fine talents, and of great candor. He was much younger than either Job or his three friends. According to the custom of that age, his youthfulness kept him from taking any part in the controversy, until his seniors had, by their silence, indicated that they had exhausted their store of arguments, and had nothing further to say. The silent attention he had given to their discourses was of much benefit to him, and gave him decided advantages, as he was thereby enabled to discern the weak points on both sides, and to profit by the strong ones. Notwithstanding he was younger than they, he was prepared to rebuke them all. This he did, however, in a fair and most respectful manner.

It is remarkable that, though God rebuked Job for his rashness of speech, and declared that his wrath was kindled against his three friends, yet (unless his first remark, " Who is this that darkeneth counsel with words without knowledge?" can be so considered,) he does not utter a word of rebuke to Elihu. The words of the Almighty seem to be addressed to Job, and not to Elihu. "Then the Lord answered Job."

I have long held to the opinion that Elihu was the writer of this truly interesting history ; and notwithstanding the many arguments that I have read to the contrary, and especially the plausible and forcible arguments of Mr. Barnes in his introduction to the book of Job, yet I have not given up my opinion. Like others, mine is

only an opinion, and one that the limits of a sermon is
too short to discuss, yet I think it a well founded opinion. He certainly had all the advantages necessary to
the performance of the work. He was a silent listener
to, and I think the recorder of, the discourses of Job and
his three friends. He was, no doubt, acquainted with
both the former and latter history of Job's life. Seventeen discourses had been prepared and delivered in his
hearing, during which time he said nothing and did nothing, unless, as I suppose, he was taking notes, or record-
ing the discourses. Mr. Barnes doubts Elihu's ability,
and remarks that in the discussion he advances but one
idea. That is true; but that idea was nearer to the point
than any other that had been advanced: it was an idea that
nearly solved the question at issue. But I would call the
attention of the learned to Job xxxii, 15—17. To whom
was Elihu speaking, when he said, " They were amazed,"
&c ? verse 15. Certainly not to Job or his three friends.
Hardly to by-standers, I should think, for they would not
need thus to be informed. To whom, then, if not to those
who should read the book or history he was writing ?
To whom was he speaking, when he said, " When I had
waited, (for they spoke not, but stood still, and answered
no more,) I said, I will answer also my part; I also will
shew you mine opinion "?   Twenty years ago I first carefully observed these verses, and I thought I had found
the author of the book of Job ; and I have seen nothing
since to change my opinion.

   In the chapter in which our text is found, Elihu criti-
cises Job's rashness of speech: " Thinkest thou this to
be right, that thou saidst, My righteousness is more than

God's?" Verse 2. Job had not said this in so many words, but his expression was capable of this construction. He had insisted upon his own righteousness, and yet charged God with multiplying his wounds without cause. Chapter x, 17. Thus it would be inferred that he was more righteous than God. Indeed, God himself intimates the same complaint: " Wilt thou disannul my judgment? Wilt thou condemn me, that thou mayest be righteous?" Chapter xl, 8.

Under severe trials, we need to be especially careful not to so express ourselves as to appear to impeach the goodness of God. Elihu reminds Job of the infinite distance between God and himself, and that neither his righteousness nor his wickedness could affect the Almighty: his conduct might benefit or injure mortal beings, but not the Great Immortal. Then follows the text, in which it is declared that the great reason why men do not find consolation under affliction, is because they do not apply to the right source. If Elihu meant to apply this to Job's case, he was certainly wide of the mark ; yet, applied to mankind in general, his declaration is entirely correct. "They cry out by reason of the arm of the mighty." They cry, but not to the Lord. "None sayeth, Where is God my maker?" God alone can give relief to those in trouble, but men will not apply to him. In him is light, elsewhere is darkness; in him is life, without him is death. In him is joy and peace, out of him is endless woe. God says, "O Israel, thou hast destroyed thyself; but in me is thine help." Yet, men go to dream-books, fortun-tellers, and everywhere else, rather than to

the only source of consolation.   " None sayeth, Where is
God my maker, who giveth songs in the night?"

I. Notice THAT MORTAL BEINGS ARE SUBJECT TO SEA-
SONS OF DARKNESS.

" Nights," seasons of distress, sorrow, wretchedness and
woe.   These are common to humanity: few are exempt
from distress of some kind.

1. They arise often *from the oppression of the mighty.*

Those who are in power, or those who are so situated that they can oppress or afflict others.   " The arm of
the mighty."   Those who are strong or mighty, and who
are thus able to oppress such as they choose to render
the victims of their malice or covetousness.   The disposition in man to oppress his fellowman seems to be of
long standing, and deep-seated.   Cain appears upon history's page as the progenitor of the long line of oppres-
sors, and Abel as the first victim of persecution unto
death.   Since their time, the lines of the oppressed and
the oppressor have run parallel.   On the one side, the
head, heart, and hands have been engaged. in the invention and employment of means of oppression.   On the
other side, the head is dizzy with pain, the heart with
anguish wrung, and bleeding at every pore; and the
hands with fetters torn.

Of the seasons of darkness and distress through which
mortal beings have been called to pass, the history of
Joseph forms a most striking illustration.   What a night
that ancient servant of God was caused to pass through !
How long and dark !   Torn away from a happy home,
deprived of a loving father's affectionate care, sold into
bondage in a strange land, falsely accused of a most hein-

ous crime, and finally lodged in prison with no prospect
but an ignominious death; and all this by reason of the
arm of the mighty. He was the victim of the oppressor's
scorn and hate.

The history of Israel in Egypt, in Babylon, and elsewhere in captivity; indeed, the history of the world, on
almost every page, is full of illustrations of the text. This
world from its infancy has presented a vast " *Valley of
Baca*," in which the tears of the oppressed have been
poured out in streams. Look at Micaiah imprisoned in
the days of Ahab, Jeremiah in the pit, Daniel in the lion's
den, Paul and Silas in Phillippi's prison, Peter, and many
others, suffering martyrdom, and you behold a most melancholy picture of the victims of oppression and the arm
of the mighty.

2. Then *there are nights, or seasons of darkness, which
come upon men from natural causes.*

There are seasons of disease, sickness, and bereavement,
which are common to man, from which few are exempt.
"Peter's wife's mother lay sick of a fever;" the centu-
rion's servant is sick; the daughter of Jairus is dying; at
Bethesda a multitude of sick people are assembled; the
widow of Nain follows her son to the tomb, and Lazarus
has "lain in the grave four days already." But why
need we select instances from Holy Writ? Where is
there a family that disease has passed by? Who has
not lost a friend? And there are few who have never
been sick.

3. Then *there are nights of strange providences.*

There are unaccountable afflictions through which
many are called to pass. Such were the afflictions of

Job: these followed one another in rapid succession. The sound of the voice of one messenger had hardly ceased to fill the ears of Job, when the feet of the second were heard, and a third, and a fourth came, each bringing a more heart-rending message than the former—the last bringing the doleful tidings of the terrible death of all his children. But his distress did not end here: he was afflicted in his own person with a most loathsome disease; his wife, instead of trying to comfort him, gave him the most wicked counsel—"Curse God and die;" and to fill his cup of bitterness to the brim, his confidential friends became his accusers, and charged him with hypocrisy. What a long and dark night was his!

We have seen persons strangely afflicted—one trouble has followed another, until they have been brought to the lowest depths of grief. Strange diseases, too, have been the lot of some—diseases that have baffled the skill of the best physicians, who, for weeks, months, and even years, have labored in vain to find their seat and effect a cure. These seasons of darkness and distress extort a -cry from the afflicted.

II. This brings us to consider THE NATURAL DISINCLINATION OF MANKIND TO TURN TO HIS MAKER IN TIME OF DISTRESS.

"None sayeth, Where is God my maker, who giveth songs in the night?" The mind of man does not naturally turn to God. Without the aid of divine revelation, he knows not God. The most enlightened mind knows not God, except by supernatural agencies.

1. We notice that *distressed human nature turns to self, and*

that self-sufficiency and self-conceit are predominant feelings in the human heart.

It is the nature of man to exhaust all the resources in himself before he turns to any other source. Men love to boast of what they are, what they have done, and what they can do. Listen at the boasting of the king of Babylon: "The king spake, and said, Is this not great Babylon, that I have built for the house of the kingdom by the might of my power, and for the honor of my majesty?" Daniel iv, 30. Now this haughty uplifting of self keeps the soul from God, hence Christ declares the renunciation of selfishness to be essential to discipleship. "If any man will come after me, let him deny himself." It is said of the proud Pharisee, that he stood by himself and prayed, and thanked God for his own goodness: "Lord, I thank thee that I am not as other men are." He was so full of himself, that he forgot what he went up to the temple for. Instead of praying for needed grace and blessings, he occupied his devotional hour in telling God how much better he was than his neighbors. The result was he failed to obtain a blessing, for the very-good reason that he had not sought one. He had gotten into the habit of calling on the name of God like thousands of others, who think not upon the sacred name they are taking in vain, but self really crowded the Lord out of his mind.

2. *Distressed human nature turns to its fellow.*

When self fails him, man turns next to his fellowman. Hence, we have the Magi, witches and wizzards of ancient times, and the astrologers and fortune-tellers of

every grade of the present.   In ancient times even mon-
archs consulted those who had familiar spirits; that is,
those who professed to talk with the dead.   We well remember what a hold spiritualism had upon many a few
years ago; and there are thousands now who depend
upon dream-books and fortune-tellers, for almost everything they want to know—especially, if they have afflictions that they cannot account for.   They seek relief, but
not from the Lord, who invites us to bring our burdens
to him.   The whole system of soothsaying grew out of
this inclination in man to turn to his fellowman, when
burdened with unaccountable distresses.   The cunning
and crafty learned to practice upon and make money out
of the superstitions of the ignorant and credulous. What
a fearful hold these have upon the human mind; how
they keep the mind from God.   Men have even turned
to devils.   Isaiah tells of some *who had made a league with
hell and a covenant with death.*   It thus appears that man
turns everywhere but to his Maker for solace in affliction.
This Elihu gives as the reason why relief is not found:
" None sayeth, Where is God my maker?"

III. Let us notice THE ATTRIBUTES ELIHU ASCRIBES TO
THE ALMIGHTY, TO WHOM MEN REFUSE TO BRING THEIR
BURDENS.

"God, my maker, who giveth songs in the night."
"God," the supreme Being, the infinite and eternal Spirit,
the Sovereign of the universe.   "My maker."   He that
formed me of the dust, breathed into my nostrils the
breath of life, and made me a living soul.   The great
First Cause of all things, himself uncaused and eternal;
the Creator, who gave me an upright form and a reason-

able mind, and thus distinguished me from the rest of the animal creation; making me, indeed, liable to sorrow, but capable of possessing and enjoying the endless bliss of which He himself is the fountain.

1. *Elihu refers to God as man's Maker.*

The Author of our being. This idea includes wisdom and might, for I am "fearfully and wonderfully made." It also supposes his pre-existence; he that created all things that had a creation, must himself have had an eternal existence. He was before all things which had a beginning, or was brought into being. He alone inhabiteth eternity, he is the Ancient of days. He existed in himself and by himself, before time was, before the wheels of nature were set in motion; before the north was stretched out over the empty place, and the earth was hung upon nothing; before the pillars of nature were hewn out, or the corner stone of earth's foundation was laid; before the Master's trestle-board received the impression of creation's plan; before the blue canopy, decked with shining orbs, was stretched out; before the void immense in astonishment awoke at the sound of Jehovah's hammer, beating crude matter into form, or chaos felt the pang that pierced her when light, creation's first born, leaped from her womb;

> "Before the hills in order stood,
> Or earth received her frame,
> From everlasting thou art God,
> To endless years the same."

The mind staggers at the thought of attempting to trace this eternal, unsearchable Being back through the unsurveyed regions, into that eternity where he conceals himself with curtains too thick for mortal thoughts to pierce. We shall not attempt it. But we rejoice to behold his wisdom as displayed in his works. Job says, "He is wise in heart"; Elihu says, "He is mighty in wisdom"; and the Psalmist says, "The heavens declare his glory, the firmanent sheweth his handywork."

But nowhere is his wisdom more fully displayed than in the constitution of man. A minute description of the human body alone would afford much more than enough material for a sermon, to say nothing of the soul, which constitutes the real man. Solomon, however, in the 12th chapter of Ecclesiastes, gives an interesting synoptical description of those parts of the human structure, which most sensibly mark the approach of dissolution and decay —careful attention to which will serve to illustrate the display of divine wisdom in the formation of the human body. "The keepers of the house"—the shoulders, arms, and hands, the principal means of subsistence and protection. "The strong men"—the back, thighs, and legs, in which the main strength of the body consists. "The grinders" —the teeth, which grind the food. "The lookers out of the windows"—the eyes, the lids of which, like window-shutters, are either open or closed. "The doors"—or lips through which the food passes into the throat. "The streets"—which lead to the stomach. "The daughters of music"—the vocal organs, which are exercised in making music. "The silver cord"—the spinal column which goes down the backbone, having a white and silvery appearance. "The golden bowl"—the brain, which has a yellow and golden appearance, and formed in shape like a bowl. "The fountain"—the right ventricle of the heart, which is understood to be the spring or fountain of life. "The pitcher"—the great vein which carries the blood to the "fountain." "The cistern"—the left ventricle of the heart. "The wheel"—the great artery which receives the blood from the "cistern," and distributes it throughout the body, fitly called the "wheel," because it is the grand circulating medium. When it ceases to perform its wonted functions, the lamp of life goes out, and the dust returns to the earth as it was. The study of this fearfully and wonderfully wrought structure, in connection with divine revelation, and under the influence of the Holy Spirit, necessarily forms within the mind a desire to know more of him who formed it, and should produce faith in, and reliance upon, him.

2. *But to his benevolence are our thoughts especially directed.* "He giveth songs in the night." He is the God, or source, of all consolation. He succors the distressed, banishes fear, chases away the gloom of night, and gives peace to the troubled breast. "He giveth songs." Freely, without money and without price, it is his pleasure to give. "In the night." In the season of darkness through which many are called to pass, those who take their troubles to him, will enjoy a full realization of this truth. It is the experience of all who have carried their burdened souls to him, they have received songs, yea, songs for joy. He gives songs when they can be obtained from no other source. "When mother forsakes me, if ever, then will God care for me." "Songs in the night." He not only made me capable of enjoying happiness, but if I will apply to him, when in distress ever so deep, or however dark the season may be, he will not only relieve

me of my distress, but he will fill my soul with melody, and put songs into my mouth. Or, as the Psalmist has it, will "compass me with songs of deliverance."—will give me songs in the night. What can be more cheering than the sound of a choir of sweet singers breaking upon the ear at the midnight hour! There might have been fear and trembling, anguish and wretchedness of soul, but the songs would dispel the gloom, and drive away the fear. Such is the relief that God gives to those who apply to him in their night of sin, ignorance, or calamity.

SERMON XIII.

THE STREAMS WHICH GLADDEN GOD'S CITY.

"There is a river, the streams whereof shall make glad the city of God." Psalms xlvi, 4.

In this Psalm, we have an expression of the confidence which the church has in God. The Psalmist declares what God is to the church: "God is our refuge and strength, a very present help in trouble." Therefore, we have no need to fear: no matter what changes or calamities there may be, we are safe. Though there should be a removal of the earth, and carrying away of the mountains, by such a swelling of the waters as was seen at the deluge, yet, the true people of God should still enjoy a situation so highly favored, so completely encompassed by the everlasting arms, that no evil could approach them. While the inhabitants of the earth may be destroyed by the unusual swelling of the waters, yet that river, which supplies the inhabitants of God's city, shall flow on in its usual peaceful way, unrippled and undisturbed. Though all other waters may be agitated and swollen, until the rivers are lost in the general upheaval, yet there is one river which is not agitated by the flood, its streams pour out the wonted supply—not foaming with madness, nor angered by the storm, but clear and calm as usual. Hence,

"Its streams make glad the city of God. Such, in short, is the declaration of the text; the obvious meaning of which is, that it matters not what troubles there be in the world, the Church, the body of believers in Christ Jesus, shall still enjoy abundant peace, consolation, joy, and gladness.

I. We notice the city designated—"THE CITY OF GOD."

Not his invisible, celestial metropolis; not his holy habitation on high, where he dwells in uncreated light, and receives homage from the six-winged seraphs, which continually surround his throne with anthems of praise; but his visible city, the city of his saints on earth: the Church, in its universal aspect, composed of all who have repented, and truly believe. "The city of God, the holy place of the tabernacle of the Most High." His earthly abode, his terrestial residence. Every true believer is a tabernacle of the Most High, in which he dwells, is honored, loved and praised. "Know ye not," says the Apostle, "that ye are the temple of the living God, and that his Spirit dwelleth in you?" 1 Cor. iii, 16. And again, "What! know ye not that your body is the temple of the Holy Ghost, which is in you?" 1 Cor. vi, 19. And again, "For ye are the temple of the living God; as God said, I will dwell in them, and walk in them." Jesus pronounces a blessing upon those servants who are found watching when their Lord cometh, that openeth the door immediately when he knocketh." Luke xii, 36, 37. To John on Patmos, he said, "Behold, I stand at the door, and knock: if any man hear my voice and open the door, I will come in to him." Rev. iii, 20. These and other passages represent the heart of the believer as the habitation of God; and the church, or association of believers; the bulk, body, or collection of these divine dwellings, or tabernacles, constitute the city of God, his earthly metropolis, the centre of his grandeur and glory—the place where his light shines forth, and his perfections are visibly displayed. The Church, then, is fitly styled " the city of God," because it is composed of divine habitations. The Apostle speaks of christian believers as fellow citizens with the saints, fitly framed together, and built up for a habitation of God. " Now, therefore, ye are no more strangers and foreigners, but fellow citizens with the saints, and of the household of God ; and are built upon the foundation of the apostles and prophets, Jesus Christ himself being the chief corner stone, in whom all the building fitly framed together, groweth up into a holy temple in the Lord, in whom ye also are built together for a habitation of God through the Spirit." Ephesians ii, 19—22. It may fitly be called " the city of God," because he is the chief ruler. Paul tells us that he is the chief Shepherd and Bishop of souls. John saw him with a crown, and again with many crowns upon his head. He introduced himself to Joshua as the " Captain of the Lord's host." Paul says, " He is the head of the body, of the church, who is the beginning, the first born from the dead, that in all things he might have the pre-eminence." And again, " And hath put all things under his feet, and gave him to be head over all things to the church." The church also reflects and displays the divine glory : it is a city whose light emanates from him : its inhabitants walk in his light, and show forth his glory.

II. Notice THE RIVER MENTIONED—THE STREAMS OF WHICH GLADDEN GOD'S CITY.

By this we understand the Gospel dispensation. The Gospel is called glad tidings, tidings which produce joy, a message of reconciliation. "With joy shall ye draw water from the wells of salvation." "I will pour water upon him that is thirsty, and floods upon the dry ground." "Ho! every one that thirsteth, come ye to the waters." "And let him that is athirst come. And whosoever will, let him take of the water of life freely." All these beautiful passages, with many others like them, evidently refer to the Gospel, and chime in with the music to which the Psalmist's harp was tuned, when he expressed the language of the text.

1. *The Gospel, like a river, cleanses thoroughly all who are subjected to its power, without losing any of its cleansing efficacy.*

The flowing of a river keeps its waters pure; thousands may wash, and yet a pure stream is flowing. Likewise, the Gospel removes all impurity, and washes away all pollution. Its cleansing process is called the washing of regeneration, and the renewing of the Holy Ghost. It is said that "Christ gave himself for the Church, that he might sanctify and cleanse it, with the washing of water by the word; that is, the Gospel word." The evangelical prophet utters these soul-cheering words: "Though your sins be like scarlet, they shall be white as snow; though they be red like crimson, they shall be as wool." The Gospel cleanses thoroughly, and still retains its cleansing power undiminished. Though millions of filthy mortals have plunged into its crystal waters and been washed.

yet those waters are clear, sweet, and pure as ever; and when millions more have washed their stains away, its waters still will be pure. Like the water of a river, the Gospel removes the poison as well as the pollution of sin. A most sure cure for the bite of a venomous reptile, is to stand in a flowing stream, and keep the wound open, and the blood flowing freely. The poison will soon thus run out, and be washed away. Sinners are bitten by that old serpent, the devil; his deadly poison is infused into the life-blood, and has affected the entire nature; but the Gospel stream is all-healing, all-cleansing, all-invigorating, and also an all-sufficient antidote for the most fatal virus from satan's fang.

2. *Like a river, the Gospel is inexhaustible.*

Its supply is abundant, its resources never-failing. Springs go dry, the waters of a well are soon exhausted, and small streams fail; but an army may drink from a river without perceptibly diminishing its waters. Likewise, the Gospel affords a supply sufficient for the human race. It flows through every land, causing the wilderness and the solitary places of the earth to rejoice, the parched ground to become a pool, and the desert to bud and blossom as a rose.

"Its streams the whole creation reach,
So plenteous is the store :
Enough for all, enough for each,
Enough forever more."

3. *Like a river, the Gospel is peaceful.*

A river, in Scripture, is a symbol of peace. "His peace shall be as a river." Seas are ever in motion—"cannot rest, whose waters cast up mire and dirt"; but a river

flows peacefully on. Likewise, the Gospel: it is called
the Gospel of peace. "How beautiful upon the mountains is the feet of him that bringeth good tidings, that
publisheth peace." The Apostle quotes this beautiful
language of the evangelical prophet, and applies it to the
preaching of the Gospel : "And how shall they preach
except they be sent, as it is written, How beautiful are
the feet of them that preach the Gospel of peace, that
bring glad tidings of good things.". Romans x, 15. The
Gospel brings peace with God. God is angry with the
wicked, and the heart of the wicked is enmity against
God. The carnal mind is not in subjection to the will of
God, but rebellious, striving, yea, fighting, against God.
Foolish as is this warfare, ruinous as its final results will
be to the sinner, yet it is continued, and would be continued until the sinner was crushed by the hand of Om-
nipotence, were it not that the Gospel brings peace. It removes the enmity, subdues the carnal mind, puts down
the rebellion, proclaims the Saviour's love, offers mercy,
brings about reconciliation, and makes peace—yea, "the
peace of God which passeth all understanding." The
rebel grounds the weapons of his rebellion, sits at the
feet of Jesus, and sings, "Oh Lord, I will praise thee, for
though thou wast angry with me, thine angry is turned
away, and thou comfortest me."

(1.) *The Gospel brings peace of mind.* It puts down the
war in the members. The sinner is not at peace with
himself. The conscience, the will, the judgment, and the
affections, are constantly at war. The Gospel makes the
conscience tender, breaks down the stubborn will, en-
g htens the judgment, purifies the affections, and thus

establishes peace in the soul—a peace which the world can neither give nor take away. It brought the raving maniac to sit peaceful at the feet of Jesus.

(2.) Finally, *it brings peace among the brethren.* It may not bring them all to see alike in all things: however desirable this may be, it is not at all essential to christian harmony. There is harmony in music, composed of different parts; harmony in a rainbow, of different colors; and harmony in an army, composed of different regiments, with different kinds of arms, and different modes of warfare. Likewise, there may be peace and harmony among christian men, differing from each other in many things. The Gospel makes men respect the opinions of good men who differ with them: it teaches them that God made men to differ. It enforces peaceableness, and proclaims a blessing upon the peacemaker, declaring such to be the children of God. An angry broiler does not adorn the doctrine of our profession, but peaceableness bears excellent testimony to the professor's sincerity.

III. Notice THE PECULIAR CHARACTERISTICS OF THIS RIVER.

"The streams whereof make glad the city of God." It differs from all others in that, it has no tributaries, no contributing branches. It flows from one source only— it rises out of one fountain alone. Other rivers are made up from different sources: springs, lakes and small streams. Our beautiful Cape Fear is made up of many waters; nearly a dozen smaller rivers empty their waters into it. Not so with this river, the streams whereof gladen the inhabitants of God's city: it borrows nothing, save from the one original source. It springs up

from the exhaustible fountain of divine benevolence: it
is poured out of the bowels of God's infinite compassion ;
it flows from the fullness of redeeming love—the love of
God to man. The love of God is the only source of this
Gospel river. John, in Revelation, calls it the river of
life, and says he saw it proceeding out of the throne of
God, and the Lamb. This was not his judicial or great
white throne, from the presence of which the heavens
and earth shall flee away, and from the glorious radiance
of which sinners shall seek in vain for a hiding place;
nor was it that throne from which he displays his sovereign power, in superintending innumerable worlds;
but, his throne of grace; hence the Lamb's connection
with it—"the throne of God and the Lamb." Out of
this throne of divine grace, pity, loving-kindness, and
tender mercy; this life-giving, this health-infusing, soul-
invigorating, heart-cheering river, gushes. "Its streams
make glad the city of God." While the Gospel river,
which rises in the love of God, has no tributaries, yet
there are streams running out from it. While it borrows
not, it lends; nay, more, it gives to a thirsty and perishing world streams of living waters, which overflow the
parched soil, causing the wilderness and the solitary
places to rejoice, and the desert to blossom as a rose.
"Whose streams," &c. In countries where it seldom
rains, the land is sometimes watered by streams running
out from the river. Thus Egypt was watered from the
river Nile, and thus some of our cities are supplied with
water by outlets from rivers. I presume the idea in the
text is borrowed from the manner in which the land of
Egypt was watered, by streams from the river, or, possibly,

from the manner in which some city was supplied by
a stream from a river. There are many streams flowing out from the Gospel river, "which make glad the
city of God." The Gospel is glad tidings. It is good,
wholesome, and soul-cheering news, a gladening message:
tidings which are productive of joy in the highest degree.
Take away the Gospel message from the church, and all is
dull and cheerless. It was the dawn of Gospel day—a ray
of Gospel light, dimly seen through the telescope of
prophecy, that cheered the believing patriarchs while on
their pilgrimage. Faithful Abraham saw it, and rejoiced;
and David, the sweetest singer of Israel's tribes, his harp
to sweetest note did tune, and highest strain did raise—
but even he, of cunning, great beyond degree, had neither
word, nor tune, nor skill, to match the thrill of joy that
pierced his soul, as rising on the wings of faith, he saw
the gladdening stream of Gospel grace.

Idolatry, Mohammedanism, and infidelity are systems
dark and cheerless, because they have no wells of salvation, no living waters of grace, no river of life; sending
out streams of loving kindness and tender mercy, to over-
take the perishing, and relieve their thirsty souls with
draughts from an ever-flowing fountain. But this is the
glory of the Gospel; it gladdens; its streams make glad
the inhabitants of God's city. There are many streams
flowing out from the Gospel river, which make glad the
city of God. We cannot enlarge upon them; the limit
of this hour's service forbids more than the mention of
a few, and a few hints upon the thoughts suggested.

1. *There is a stream of divine illumination.*

Of spiritual enlightenment, of heavenly influence, of

experimental knowledge, of God-blessed assurance of divine acceptance. "Ye shall know the truth and the truth shall make you free." All who accept in their hearts, in faith believing the stream of Gospel truth which is poured into their ears, have the soul cheering, the joy-kindling, the enrapturing assurance, that they are freed from sin, are accepted in the Beloved—that they have passed from death unto life, that they are new creatures, that old things have passed away and all things become new. The Spirit, which Jesus promised to send forth, testifies within them, bearing witness with their spirits that they are born of God. They know in whom they believe, on what their hope rests, and have a foretaste of joys immortal.

> "Rejoicing now in glorious hope,
>   They stand, and from the mountain's top
>   See all the land below:
>   Rivers of milk and honey rise,
>   And all the fruits of paradise,
>   In endless plenty grow."

2. *There is a stream of sanctifying influence.*

The Gospel is a complete system of redemption; it is the power of God unto full salvation. It is the divine arrangement for the salvation of, and restoration to man, of all that was lost by the fall. Jesus prayed—"Sanctify them through thy truth." Then there is the declaration, that God wills our sanctification. If our will accords with his, there is nothing to hinder our sanctification at any time. The apostle tells us that Jesus suffered without the camp to secure our sanctification by his blood. He also reminds us, that if the blood of beasts put away the filth of the flesh, much more shall the blood of Christ cleanse us from all sin. The stream of sanctifying influence is destined to sanctify, and make holy all who are subjected to its power, and to bring them into that state of perfection, in which they shall feel the fulness of divine love, and be wholly freed from sin. This is God's will, and to this end he pours out his Spirit, sends out a stream of sanctifying influence, gives his all-sufficient grace—not by measure, but in all its overflowing abundance. Hence, we sing:

"Oh joyful sound of Gospel grace,
Christ shall in me appear,
I, even I, shall see his face:
I shall be holy here."

If we seek holiness of heart, we shall obtain it, and he that is holy must be happy.

3. *There is a stream of joyful consolation.*

The author of the Gospel is called the God of all consolation. And the consolations which stream forth from the Gospel are numerous, rich and cheering. The world through which the believer journeys is a wilderness, of dark nights and clouds, and gloomy fears—but the Gospel is full of consolation. Listen to the voice of Jesus: "Fear not, little flock, it is your Father's good pleasure to give you the kingdom."

Paul reckons that the sufferings of the present time are not worthy to be compared with the glory which shall be revealed in us. There is one expression which, it seems to me, should quiet all our fears. It is this: "All things work together for good to them that love God." It matters not, then, what trials, what afflictions, what disappointments, what losses, what pain, what suffering, toil, labor, sorrow, persecution or distress we may have to endure; it is all a part of the divine arrangement, on our behalf, and to result in our eternal good—our highest well-being.

> " God moves in a mysterious way,
>   His wonders to perform :
> He plants his footsteps in the sea,
>   And rides upon the storm.
> Deep, in unfathomless mines,
>   Of never-failing skill,
> He treasures up his bright designs,
>   And works his sovereign will;
> Ye fearful saints, fresh courage take—
>   The cloulds you so much dread,
> Are big with mercies and shall break
>   In blessings on your head."

SERMON XIV.

THE PERFECT FELICITY OF THE RESUR-
RECTED SAINTS, A RESULT OF CONFORMITY
TO THE DIVINE LIKENESS.

"As for me, I will behold thy face in righteousness : I shall be
satisfied, when I awake, with thy likeness." Psa. xvii, 15.

There is nothing more evident than the fact, that this
world does not afford an adequate supply of bliss to meet
the cravings of the human mind. The eye is not satisfied with seeing, nor the ear with hearing; neither is the
heart filled with joy. Solomon was wise above all that
were before him: he piled up gold, until it lost its en-
chantment and became a burden. He feasted upon good
things, until his soul loathed the honey-comb. He drank
from earth's fountain of bliss, until it became insipid and
nauseating. He inhaled the fragrance of flowers and
feasted his eyes with their beauties, until their very loveliness was a burden to his soul. He plunged into sensual
indulgences, until nature revolted against itself. And
yet, when he could take in no more of earth's bliss, he
was not satisfied. He wrote upon it all, " Vanity of vanities, all is vanity."

The soul that can be filled with earthly good, must be
miserably small. Good men of all ages have realized

that earth affords not a perfect satisfying portion for the soul.

> " This world can never give
> The bliss for which we sigh."

The Psalmist fully realized this, and living in an atmosphere nearly akin to that purer state, his soul thrilled with rapture at the thought of perfect satisfaction in the glorified state. " I shall be satisfied, when I awake, with thy likeness." In the verses which precede the text, the Psalmist prays for deliverance from his enemies, whom he calls the sword of the Lord. God frequently employs the wicked to punish his people for their sins; hence this language, " Deliver my soul from the wicked, which is thy sword." He characterizes them as men of the world—men whose hearts are set upon the world, whose thoughts are occupied with its vanities, whose time is spent in the pursuit of them, and who, though merely passengers through a world that is swiftly passing away, are content to enjoy its beggarly portion, and seize upon its wealth, honors and pleasures, as the best objects of human aspiration. He had previously referred to his own integrity in verse 3, " Thou hast proved mine heart.' Thou knowest exactly what manner of man I am, for thou hast searched and discovered the secrets of my soul. By temptations, afflictions and vexations, thou hast tested my sincerity. " Thou hast visited me in the night," when no other eye could pierce the darkness—when others slept. In the season when wicked men do their dark deeds, thou hast watched and found no wickedness in me. And having passed the ordeal of divine scrutiny and not found wanting, I am determined that my future life shall be pure. "I am purposed that my mouth shall not transgress." However much I may be persecuted, I will keep a strict watch over all my words and actions. "I will keep my tongue from evil, and my lips from speaking guile." And while the wicked are before me, vexing and tempting me to sin, "I will keep my mouth as with a bridle." After thus expressing his assurance of the perfect work of God in his soul, he, in the language of the text, expresses the hope naturally arising therefrom : "As for me, I will behold thy face in righteousness: I shall be satisfied, when I awake, with thy likeness." I do not envy the wicked their portion, nor men of the world the felicity they may hope to reap therefrom. They may, if they will, cleave to these fleeting vanities ; but as for me, my hopes are bent in a very different direction. My hopes centre in the felicity I expect to enjoy in the glorified state, when in my resurrected body I shall appear in the likeness of my Redeemer. Temporal things are not my portion ; the vanities of earth cannot fill the desire of my soul : I have laid hold upon the hope set before me, of joys which are immortal and eternal ; and to these I shall cleave.

"As for me, I will behold thy face in righteousness." I will labor to maintain that imputed righteousness which will qualify me to see thy face. "Blessed are the pure in heart, for they shall see God." The wicked, if they will, may labor for the meat that perisheth ; but I will labor to maintain that purity and meetness in which I shall behold thy face, and appear in thy likeness.

Our theme is THE PERFECT SATISFACTION OF THE SAINTS IN THE GLORIFIED STATE.

And we may remark, that perfect satisfaction can only be enjoyed as the sequence of perfect conformity to the divine likeness. We shall not be satisfied until all that was lost in the fall is restored, and all will not be restored until we awake with God's likeness on the resurrection morning. Hence, our happiness will be complete then, and then only.

I. We observe THAT GOD'S WORK IN US IS DESIGNED TO RESTORE US TO THE DIVINE LIKENESS, AND TO RAISE US TO THE ENJOYMENT OF ALL THE HAPPINESS OF THE GLORIFIED STATE.

This was man's original state. "And God said, Let us make man in our own image, after our likeness." The divine likeness shone forth in every faculty of man's original nature. Like his Maker, he was holy, and consequently happy. He was God's vicegerent, his visible representative, the visible head of his creation, and monarch of all below the skies. Sin robbed man of his purity, defaced the divine image, stripped him of his glory, tore the crown from his head, sowed the seeds of disease in his nature, and exposed him to death and decay; yea, to eternal death. Now the design of the work of grace in us is to restore all of that, of which sin has robbed us, namely, holiness, happiness, and eternal life.

1. *For this, was the Son of God sent into the world.*

That, " As we have borne the image of the earthy, we shall also bear the image of the heavenly." This was God's eternal purpose. Knowing from all eternity, even before man was created, that he would fall, he arranged in the counsel of his grace for his deliverance and restoration. So wrote the great Apostle of the Gentiles: "For whom he did foreknow, he also did predestinate to be conformed to the image of his Son." Romans viii, 28. It was God's eternal's purpose, appointment, determination, will and pleasure, that all those, whom he knew would truly re- pent and believe, should be conformed to the likeness of his Son, should bear his image and be like Christ, viz., "holy, harmless, and separate from sinners"—that we should have the mind that was in him, and walk as he walked.

2. *To this work, of bringing us to a conformity to the divine likeness, is the Holy Spirit appointed.*

He will not only teach us all things, and guide us into all truth, but will make us every whit whole. The influence of the Holy Spirit, operating upon us, leads us to holiness. Jesus says, " It is the Spirit that quickeneth." We are raised from the death of sin to a life of holiness by the power of the Holy Spirit, which quickens our dead nature, and testifies within us that we are born again. The Apostle Paul speaks of the Holy Spirit as the grand agent in bringing about this change in our nature. "But we all, with open face beholding as in a glass the glory of the Lord, are changed into the same image from glory to glory, even as by the Spirit of the Lord." 2 Cor. iii, 18. Here we are represented as "beholding" the divine "glory," and being "changed into the same image." But the Spirit of the Lord is the efficient agent by which this wonderful change is effected. The Spirit is He who has prepared the glasses, through which we behold the glory of the Lord. The Gospel is one of those glasses, and this

was written by the Spirit's inspiration. The human nature of Christ is another glass, and this the Spirit formed
in the womb of the blessed virgin. The Spirit tears the
vail away from our eyes, opens our understanding, trans-
forms our nature by his renewing and sanctifying power,
and thereby fixes upon us the divine likeness.

II. But we notice THAT PERFECT CONFORMITY TO THE
DIVINE LIKENESS IS NOT ATTAINABLE IN THIS LIFE.

And here we must distinguish between things that
differ. Christian perfection is one thing, but the perfect
conformity of the resurrected saint, in the glorified state,
to the divine likeness, is another, and a very different
thing; yet, if we attain to the former, and live and die in
it, we are sure of the latter. Christian perfection is a
characteristic of the saint on earth; but perfect conformity to the divine likeness is a characteristic of the saint
in glory. The sanctified state is a degree of that conformity, but not that perfect fullness of it that we shall
possess in our resurrected bodies—*when we shall awake
with the divine likeness.*

Perfection under the Mosaic dispensation fell far short
of that under the Christian dispensation, for Jesus tells
us that John the Baptist, who was the greatest of the
prophets, was less than the least in his kingdom. Likewise,
christian perfection falls short of the state of the glorified
saints. Christian perfection is an attainment belonging
to this state. The perfect likeness and consequent happiness contemplated in the text belongs to the future
state.

There is, however, a degree of conformity to the divine
likeness attainable here; and to possess, and live in this

state was the fixed purpose of the Psalmist, as declared in the text. "As for me, I will behold thy face in righteousness." I am resolved to possess and maintain that righteousness, in which I shall behold thy face. This righteousness no man possesses by nature, nor is it acquired by education: men are not trained into it. It is called the righteousness of Christ, and we receive it from him as an unspeakable gift; also the righteousness of faith, and is received through faith—"not of works, less any man should boast." Ii ts experimental: he that possesses it, knows it. He is not left to guess that he is righteous, but he has the God-blessed assurance of it. He knows the time when, and the place where, "his dungeon shook, and his chains fell." He knows when he was relieved of his burden, when the load was removed from his back, and his soul went skipping up Zion's hill. He knows when the night of sin ended, when the darkness gave way, when the morning star arose, and the light of day broke into his soul. The change from darkness to light is so great that all who really pass through the transformation, are sensible of it. All will not have exactly the same kind or same degree of emotion. The emotions may be as great in variety as the number of the redeemed. With some, the change may be sudden and violent, and accompanied with much distress. Some may be so powerfully wrought upon, as to imagine that they had a bodily sensation. Paul had the impression of a voice, and a light shining round him. With some, the experience is less vivid: their winter passes out so mildly and the spring comes in so gently, that they need to consult their spiritual chart, or calendar, to tell just when the change did take place.

While the experiences through which believers pass, in being made righteous, differ, yet in some things there is an agreement. Each one can say, "whereas I was blind, now I see." I know that which no man could teach me, which the unregenerate mind has never grasped, and cannot: "For except a man be born again, he cannot see kingdom of God." He that is made righteous is sensible of the relief from the burden of sin, and can testify that he has peace with God. All who are made righteous also feel their relationship to the Father, for into the hearts of the sons of God he sends the Spirit of his Son, which cries, "Abba Father."

But righteousness is practical as well as experimental, and capable of being demonstrated. There is an outward as well as an inward righteousness; a righteousness in the life, conduct and conversation, as well as in the heart of the believer. That in the heart is the vine or branch; that in the life is its fruit. If the branch is righteous, it will bear the fruit of righteousness, nor can it retain its relation to the vine in a fruitless state. For Jesus says: "Every branch in me that beareth not fruit he taketh away." Our righteousness must conform to the pattern given. It must be Christ's righteousness, working in, running through, and governing all our thoughts, words, and actions. To be like him in the resurrection, we must be like him in the regeneration. The transformation effected in the regeneration is the prelude to the transformation effected by the resurrection. We need the resurrection from the death of sin to a life of righteousness, to have a sure hope of a future resurrection; and the fruit of righteousness is the best and only sure evidence of a regenerate nature.

1. *We must have all the characteristics of Christ's humanity.*

Be like him as a man, follow his steps, walk in his ways—in a word, our life and conduct must be like his. He was distinguished for meekness and humility, and he said: "Take my yoke upon you, and learn of me; for I am meek and lowly in heart." And again: "Tell ye the daughter of Sion, behold, thy King cometh unto thee, meek, and sitting upon an ass, and a colt the foal of an ass." As an example of humility, he washed his disciples' feet. And the Apostle tells us that he humbled himself, that he made himself of no reputation, and took the form of a servant, notwithstanding his equality with the Father. The Apostle, therefore, urges lowliness and humility of mind. He was distinguished for great self-denial. He demands this of us, and lays it down as the basis of acceptable discipleship. Our conformity must include filial obedience—a loving, cheerful obedience; an obedience which is the fruit of a right state of heart. Jesus is represented as saying, to the Father, "I delight to do thy will;" and again, "Not as I will, but as thou wilt." To his parents, who had sought him for three days, and who complained of the trouble and anxiety he had caused them by his absence, he said: "Wist ye not that I must be about my Father's business?" Thus, must we render unto God a hearty and cheerful obedience in all things.

2. We can possess *some of the characteristics of his divine nature.*

We can be just, in such degree as we have light. The

good man walks in the light of the knowledge he possesses.   He deals justly, just in proportion as his mind
is enlightened.   A good man may mean well, and yet do
a great injury to one whom he desires to serve, because
he lacks an enlightened judgment.   In order that a
judge may dispense exact justice in every case that comes
before him, he must know the merits of every case.   Yet
he has done his duty, when, after giving due attention to
the case, he decides it according to his honest convictions.
Still persons might go from the bar of a judge, who was perfectly honest, unjustly condemned, on account of the want
of better knowledge on the part of the judge.   God can
dispense perfect justice, because he has perfect knowledge.   Human justice, though not exactly equitable,
if the intention is pure, and every possible means to
obtain information has been exhausted, is perfect.   This
is christian perfection in judgment.   But if the light
that is in you be darkness, you must stumble; that is, if
your judgment be at fault, you are likely to err, no matter how good your intention.   The intention, however, is
what God regards: if that is pure and holy, we are accepted of him.   To this extent, we can possess the likeness ot divine justice here.

     We can also be holy here, and must, "for without ho-
liness, no man shall see the Lord."   None but the pure in
heart have the promise that they shall see him; and,
therefore, to have a well-grounded hope of this unspeakable privilege, we must purify ourselves, as he is pure.
Our affections must be pure, our thoughts pure, our
words and actions pure.

Finally, *we must have divine love.*

Human love extends to its own, and to them only. "If ye love them which love you, what reward have ye?" The love that God commends, takes in those that hate us. "Love your enemies, bless them that curse you, do good to them that hate you, and pray for them which despitefully use you, and persecute you, that ye may be the children of your Father which is in heaven." This is divine love: he that has it, has this feature of the divine likeness. The great commandments are, "Thou shalt love the Lord thy God with all thy heart, and with all 'thy soul, and with all thy mind, and with all thy strength. This is the first commandment, and the second is like unto it, Thou shalt love thy neighbor as thyself." "Love is the fulfilling of the law, and perfect love casteth out fear." He that loves God with all his heart, will serve him with all his might. He that loves his neighbor as himself, will treat his neighbor as he would wish his neighbor to treat him. He that keeps these two commandments is a perfect christian—is perfect, so far as perfection can be obtained here. What a happy world this will be, when all humanity comes up to this standard of perfection. For this all true christians are praying daily, "Thy kingdom come, thy will be done on earth, as it is in heaven." This prayer will eventually be answered, for at the sounding of the seventh angel, there were heard great voices in heaven saying, "The kingdoms of this world are become the kingdoms of our Lord and his Christ." But even this state of things on earth would not give entire satisfaction. I repeat,

"This world can never give
The bliss for which we sigh."

No matter what our condition here, either temporal or spiritual; no matter what temporal wealth, social standing, or official honors we may enjoy; no matter what attainments of grace or spiritual rapture we may reach, we shall still be affected with the impression that this is not our home.   We shall still feel that,

> "Beyond this vale of tears
> There is a life above;
> Unmeasured by the flight of years,
> And all that life is love."

For this happy state the christian sighs.   He longs to put off mortality, and be swallowed up of life.   To this gratifying state of perfect felicity the text directs our thoughts.

III.   Notice, THE RESURRECTED SAINTS IN THEIR GLORI-FIED BODIES, WILL BE COMPLETELY CONFORMED TO THE DIVINE LIKENESS, AND WILL THEREFORE BE ENTIRELY SAT-ISFIED, OR HAPPY.

"I shall be satisfied, when I awake, with thy likeness." All our desires will then be met, all our expectations more than realized, and every aspiration of the soul entirely satisfied.

> "Of all my heart's desire
> Triumphantly possess'd;
> Lodged in the ministerial choir,
> In my Redeemer's breast."

In what state the saints shall be, from their departure from time till the resurrection day, is not part of our present inquiry.   There are different opinions advanced by the learned, which we have not time now to consider. The text bears us across that period, without permitting

9

us to linger for a moment, and lets us at once behold the light of the resurrection morn. "I shall be satisfied, when I awake, with thy likeness"—when I arise from the dead, with my glorified body; with the image of Christ indelibly fixed upon my entire nature—(for "as I have borne the image of the earthy, I shall also bear the image of the heavenly.")

1. We shall be satisfied, *because our souls and bodies, which were separated at death, will be united again.*

It is written, "All that are in their graves shall hear the voice of the Son of God, and shall come forth;" "the trumpet shall sound, and the dead shall be raised incorruptible," "and we (who are on the earth) shall be changed in the twinkling of an eye"—"mortal shall put on immortality." The glorified body, with which we shall be clothed, will be a source of great and endless satisfaction. The old body was a burden—a body of death. It was afflicted with disease, sickness, infirmity, pain, age, decrepitude, death and decay. But when we awake with our glorified body, these will all have passed away. Not an ache, nor pain; no infirmity, deformity, nor age: these terms are not found in heaven's vocabulary. Youth, health, vigor, and beauty, will be among the characteristics of our glorified body.

2. *We shall be satisfied, because we shall be in the likeness of our Redeemer.*

This is spoken of as one of the unspeakable blessings secured by the surpassing love of God. "We shall be like him, for we shall see him as he is." "If we have been planted together in the likeness of his death, we shall be also in the likeness of his resurrection." Our souls shall be completely conformed to his, and our bodies transformed and made like unto his glorious body. So wrote the Apostle. " * * The Lord Jesus Christ, who shall change our vile body, that it may be fashioned like unto his glorious body," &c.

3. *We shall be satisfied, because we shall be permitted to gaze upon his divine perfections.*

" I will behold thy face." There were certain Greeks (who, having heard of Jesus, in the days of his incarnation, when only occasional rays of his glory shone out,) came to the disciples, saying: " Sirs, we would see Jesus." If a sight of him in the days of humility was so much to be desired, with what rapture will the saints gaze upon him, when they shall see him as he is! When they shall see his glory—the sight for which Moses longed but could not behold. He was permitted only to stand in the cleft of the rock, while God caused his glory to pass by, he being hid, by the Almighty hand, from the overwhelming rays of his glorious face; yet, this mere glimpse of Jehovah's glory, gave to the face of Moses a radiance upon which the Israelites could never look. Ever afterward, he appeared before the congregation only with a veiled face. If, by chance, a ray from his naked face beamed forth, its incomprehensible radiance filled them with awe. But when we awake with the divine likeness, we shall not only behold the unveiled face of Moses, but we shall see Jesus—we shall behold him that sitteth upon the throne! We will not need to be covered by the divine hand, or that he turn his face from us, or give us merely a transient view; but we shall gaze upon him, have an abiding view—see him just as he is. We shall neither be afraid, nor ashamed, to fix our gaze upon him.

4 *We shall be satisfied, because we shall know all we want to know.*

One of the most vexing things of this state, is the want of knowledge. And the more we know, the more fully we realize how little we do know. When we awake with the divine likeness, there will be no more mysteries. Ignorance will not vex us in the gloried state—" we shall know." Our knowledge will be unlimited. We shall sit at the fountain whence streams of knowledge flow, and drink; and to enable our intellectual capacities to receive the never-ceasing stream, which will flow from the living fountains, to which the Lamb shall lead us—they will be continually expanded and enlarged. We shall never feel the want of knowledge, for the moment the desire arises, the supply will meet it. Before this unceasing flow of knowledge, all mysteries will fade away forever, and we shall dwell in the noontide of celestial light.

Beloved brethren, have you a sure hope of enjoying this endless felicity of the glorified saints? I don't ask do you sometimes think about it? I don't ask, would you like to be there?—but can you say with the Psalmist, "I will behold thy face in righteousness: I shall be satisfied, when I awake, with thy likeness?"

SERMON XV.

THE NATURE AND DOOM OF THE HYPOCRITE'S HOPE.

"He shall lean upon his house, but it shall not stand: he shall hold it fast, but it shall not endure." Job viii, 15.

The afflictions which passed upon Job, in rapid succession, and the depths of wretchedness into which he was suddenly plunged, were a puzzle to his neighbors. They could not understand why the most wealthy of all men among them, and possibly the wealthiest man then living, should in so short a period be reduced to poverty, and become the most miserable of all on earth; and their astonishment was heightened by the fact, that he was regarded as the most righteous of all men.

"Job's substance was seven thousand sheep, three thousand camels, five hundred yoke of oxen, and five hundred she asses." Besides this, it is said that he had "a very great household; so that this man was the greatest of all the men of the east." His wealth, together with his seven sons and three daughters, was all swept away, as with a besom of destruction, and the news thereof reached him by four messengers, one following the other as rapidly as they could tell the doleful story.

But this was not all: he he was afflicted with sore boils

from his crown to the sole of his feet, so that he was a
mass of putrefaction, and his breath was corrupt. His
neighbors hearing of his affliction, came to comfort him;
but they were so astonished at the wretchedness in which
they found him, that they sat for seven days, regarding
him in silent amazement. Nor was the silence broken,
until, in the depths of agony, Job opened his mouth, and
in doleful accents expressed the bitterness of his soul.
During the long silence, those who came to comfort him
had been casting about, in their minds, to fix upon the
cause of his affliction; and three of them seem to have
arrived at one conclusion, namely, that Job had been
guilty of some great wickedness, unknown to them, but
known to the all-wise God, and for this God was punish-
ing him. They believed that only by the acknowledgment of his sin, would he be restored to the divine favor;
and hence, they undertook, by arguments, to lead him to
conviction, repentance and confession. No doubt they
set out with the good intention of breaking unto Job
their suspicion by gentle words, and thus to lead him to
repentance; but, the first speaker had not uttered half a
dozen sentences, before he had waxed warm, and was delivering himself in language which must have pierced
Job's very soul: and the second, at his opening, indicated
most clearly his belief that Job was a hypocrite. The
third charged him with falsehood and mockery; and thus
they continued, with argument, ridicule, sarcasm and
irony, to express the thoughts of their hearts. Bildad,
the speaker in the text, attempted to draw an argument
from the prevailing opinion, that worldly prosperity was
an evidence of divine favor, and that afflictions were a

sure token of God's displeasure. It will be remembered that the prosperity of the wicked almost caused David to stumble. When he saw the wicked flourishing as a green bay tree, his feet were well nigh gone.

While Bildad's premises were false, and while he wholly misunderstood Job's case, and therefore misapplied his illustrations; yet he, as it were, stumbled upon a very important truth. It is this: that our happiness—our real well-being, depends upon our being in our right and proper element. All creatures have their own element, or a state in which they perfectly enjoy their existence. Some creatures cannot live at all out of that condition: birds thrive in their native air; but, caged up, where the air is impure and unwholesome, they soon die: water is the element in which the fish lives; remove it therefrom, and it perishes. Now man's true element is to enjoy the love and favor of his God: in this he must dwell, if he would be happy: out of this, no matter what his circumstances, he cannot be happy. The divine favor will constitute our happiness here, and will be the source of our enjoyment hereafter.

> " To dwell in God, to taste his love,
> Is the full heaven enjoyed above:
> The real bliss of christians now,
> Is heavenly love enjoyed below."

This is the truth which, it seems to me, Bildad stumbled upon; for he does not seem to have fully realized the force of his own illustrations. The first is drawn from plants: " Can the rush grow up with mire? or the flag without water?" Verse 11. Can that kind of plants, which are the peculiar product of miry and watery sections, still live and grow, if transplanted on high and dry land? " Whilst it is yet in its greenness, and not cut down, it withereth before any other herb." Verse 12. While the high land herbs all around it flourish, the transplant from the miry and watery soil withers and dies, because it is out of its native element.

"So are the paths of all that forget God." Such is the end to which the paths of all that forget God leads. They will perish: their path leads to destruction. " And the hypocrite's hope shall perish; whose hope shall be cut off, and whose trust shall be a spider's web." All who trust in anything, except in the living God, will miss their expectation, will lose their hope, will meet with disappointment, will come to grief; and will find that in which they trusted, as frail and flimsy as a spider's web. " He shall lean upon his house, but it shall not stand: he shall hold it fast, but it shall not endure."

When the spider has finished, first its outer wall, and then its dwelling, in one corner of the enclosure, it goes over every part of it, and tries its strength. When it is satisfied therewith, it goes into its little house, and standing upon its hind legs, it holds on with its fore legs, and thus leans upon its house, and holds it fast; but woe be unto it, when the housekeeper comes along with her broom: just when it feels most comfortably situated, this spider-web destroyer sweeps the spider, its web and all its hopes away. Such will be the end of the hypocrite, and of all who forget, or fail to put their trust in God. He is the only sure refuge, and out of him there is no safety. He is the rock, all else is sand. He that builds upon this rock shall not be confounded; but he that builds upon any other foundation will, with his house, be swept away by the relentless flood of divine displeasure, that will gather around the wicked, when God pours out his wrath and indignation upon them.

The subject before us embraces two classes of hetrodoxy. The atheist who forgets God or leaves him out of his calculations entirely, and the hypocrite who admits that there is a God, but comes short of the duty which that admission necessarily involves, namely, that they should worship him as God.

The text leads us to contemplate some of the structures which men build for themselves, and upon which they lean; or, in other words, the false premises upon which men base their hopes; and the frail material of which they erect that in which they trust. There are three things of importance in erecting a building: first, a good foundation; secondly, good material; and thirdly, to connect the entire building with the solid foundation. The text especially directs our attention to the materials. The spider's web is very frail material to build a house of. The Apostle cautions us as to the material of which we build, even on a good foundation. After declaring Christ to be the only foundation, he says: " If any man buildeth on the foundation; gold, silver, costly stones, wood, hay, stubble; each man's work shall be made manifest: for the day shall declare it, because it is revealed by fire; and the fire itself shall prove each man's work, what sort it is." (I Cor. iii: 12, 13. Revised Version.) Gold, silver, and a certain kind of stone will stand the fire; but wood, hay and stubble will soon be consumed by the flame.

We remark, that a sense of divine displeasure and of the indispensable necessity of a means of escape from impending wrath, naturally forces itself upon the human heart. Man would drive away this impression if he could, but he cannot. Sometimes daring ones exhibit their pride, and their ambition to be gods, themselves, and to usurp prerogatives which they do not possess; but ere long they are made to feel their littleness. The king of Babylon, who boastingly " spoke, and said: Is not this great Babylon, which I have built by the might of my power, and for the honor of my majesty?" (Daniel iv, 30,) was brought, by power divine, to realize his weakness and insecurity, and the need of something in which to trust, more substantial than any power he possessed.

Now, God has a variety of means by which he awakens in the minds and hearts of men a sense of human helplessness. Sometimes he unfolds his strange providences, as in the case of the king just mentioned, who was driven out from among men, and ate grass as an ox: his body was wet with the dew of heaven; his hair became as eagle's feathers, and his nails like birds' claws; until seven times (seven years) passed over him, and until he knew and acknowledged the power of the Most High. He then lifted up his eyes to heaven and praised and honored Him that liveth forever.

Sometimes, ordinary afflictions are the means of leading men to reflect, and to seek a refuge for the soul. Men, who are thoughtless and indifferent, yea, even hardened and scornful in health, are brought to repentance in sickness, and tremble at the approach of death. Indeed, affliction seems to be a challenge from the Almighty, a call to man to give an account of his stewardship; and many are thus awakened, and brought to repentance.

Sometimes, the motion comes from an internal sense of guilt. At the hour of midnight when no other, but the Eye that never sleeps, sees them, men are troubled, and lie in sensible recognition of the heart's palpitations. Sometimes, the mental excitement is so intense, that the flesh is moistened with perspiration produced by fear. Such is a most critical moment—it is sometimes the last effort of the Holy Spirit to obtain entrance into the heart. If a genuine sigh for relief ascends to heaven, as the result of this final wooing of the Spirit, he draws nearer and knocks; if he finds an open door he enters, drives out the foes and fills the soul with peace, love and joy. But sometimes the Spirit is insulted, is driven away, and never returns! More frequently, however, the struggle is continued until some kind of a compromise is effected—a compromise suggested by the evil one; and one which involves the erection of such a structure as he shall suggest. Knowing the peculiar turn of mind with which he has to deal, he, in every case, suggests what is most likely to be adopted. Whatever he suggests, you may be sure is a refuge of lies.

With the text in view, let us notice some of the spider-web houses on which Satan induces men to lean; and to which they hold fast, to the neglect of the sure refuge. I say some, for they are too numerous to mention, even if we knew them all. And they are all Satan's devices, and all equally delusive. They are all frail and flimsy as the spider's web. You may lean upon them, but they will not stand; you may hold them fast, but they will not endure.

First among the false systems, (if system it may be called) is *Atheism*. But, if we follow the example of the inspired pensman, we shall not attempt to argue with the Atheist. The folly of the man, who can look abroad and behold the vast universe which surrounds him, and the evidence of design upon every hand; who can contemplate the harmony and regularity in the motions of the heavenly bodies, rolling through the vast expanse—conducted, as they evidently are, by an unseen but unerring hand; each in its appointed path, from age to age: who can mark the accomplishment of events, wholly out of the range of the means which appear to be employed; who can contemplate his own body, fearfully and wonderfully made, and yet deny the existence of an All-wise and Almighty Creator, can only be fitly characterized by the language of the Psalmist: "The fool hath said in his heart, There is God." I suspect that the character mentioned by the Psalmist was ashamed to utter such an idea with his lips, and hence is described as saying it "in his heart." The Apostle Paul declares Atheism to be inexcusable folly: "For the invisible things of him from the creation of the world are clearly seen, being understood by the things that are made, even his eternal power and Godhead; so that they are without excuse." Romans i, 20. With these examples before us, of the manner in which the inspired writers treated Atheism, we feel justified in dismissing all who trust in this frail structure, with the solemn words of our text: "He shall lean upon his house, but it shall not stand : he shall hold it fast, but it shall not endure."

Infidelity is another frail tenement to which men cling, which we don't think deserves more than a passing notice. The man who rejects the Bible, is not likely to pay much attention to anything we can say. We should have more faith in Infidelity, however, if its advocates would hold out to the end; but they do not. They do not die Infidels. We have never known nor heard of one who did. The testimonies of dying Infidels are all against the system. Doleful and distressing have been the last words of many Infidels. They have been known to tremble at the approach of death—what then, must have been their horror, when they entered the dark valley and shadow! If their confidence failed them on the banks, how did they fare in the billows of Jordan? A system that only sustains you when you don't need it, is not worth the name.

We have touched upon *fatalism* in another discourse, and need not enlarge upon it here.

But the text leads us especially *to consider the hypocrite's hope*

"The hypocrite's hope shall perish." I doubt whether the Atheist, or Infidel, has much hope. It is more an exhibition of bravado—an effort to appear daring. But there are hypocrites who suppose themselves to be what they are not, and therefore have a hope, which their real state does not warrant. This seems evident from what is said to the church at Laodicea, Rev. iii, 17: "Because thou sayest I am rich," &c., "and knowest not," &c. These were evidently deceived, and did not know their wretchedness. I fear there are thousands just in this condition. They have a name that they live, but are dead. They are among God's people, but not of them. They say, " Lord, Lord," but do not the things which God requires. They have the form, but not the power of god-liness; they have entered the vestibule, but not the temple of grace. Their affections are on the world; and they have much more love for theaters, balls, parties, and other worldly amusements, than they have for the services of the sanctuary. A little rain, or cold, or heat, is sufficient to keep them from church ; and when there, they can't en-dure to be crowded—must have plenty of room; but to the theater they can go in heat, cold, or storm, and crowd into uncomfortable seats without a word of complaint. In church the services are too long and dry, especially if the minister repeats himself; but they can sit for hours in a theater, and enjoy the stale nonsense, which they have heard over and again. If collections are frequent for church expenses, or charitable purposes, there is much complaint in consequence. "Its money, money, all the time money: I don't see what they do with so much money." But they can go to the theater, and pay money every night. Now Jesus says, "Where your treasure is, there will your heart be also." Is it not pretty evident that the hearts of such people are set on the world, and that the world is their portion, their treasure, their all? If their treasure was in heaven, would they not have more interest in heavenly things? Can such persons be genuine christians? If not, they must be hypocrites— "lukewarm." Jesus says, "I would that thou wert cold or hot, * * because thou art lukewarm, I will spew thee out of my mouth." I imagine some of my congregation are saying, "That don't fit me, I am not a professor." Some people think that there are no hypocrites but such as are members of the church. There could be no greater mistake. There are thousands who imagine themselves not far from the kingdom; but if they are not in it, they are as far from being acceptable to God as the most wicked. They are "lukewarm." I said once to a lady friend, "I fear you are lukewarm." She was decidedly amiable, and might have passed for a right good christian; but she had not embraced the Saviour, nor had she united with God's people. To my remark, she answered, "O, I hope I am not in that disgustful state." "Very well, let us see," I replied. "There are three states—cold, hot, and lukewarm. Which is yours? Are you cold? Have you no interest in religion? Do you hate the people of God? Do you believe them all a set of miserable hypocrites? Is that your state?" I asked. With a discouraged look, she answered, "No." I continued, "Have you then the heat of divine love in your soul? While musing, does the fire burn? Is there a flame of heavenly rapture kindled in your heart by the assurance of your acceptance in the Beloved? Can you say, 'I know that my Redeemer liveth,' that 'my name is in heaven—my record is on high?' Is that your state?" I asked. With an effort to maintain her composure, she answered, "No." "What then?" After a few moments' silence, she answered, "I suppose I must be lukewarm." And this would be the answer of very many, if they would acknowledge the truth. This is, as she characterized it, a very "disgustful state." There is no state more so in the sight of God. Men ought to be one thing or the other. If they believe in religion, they ought to embrace it. If they don't believe in it, they ought not to encourage it, by their presence in the sanctuary, nor their gifts at the altar. Every time you contribute to the cause of God, you testify that you are not cold. Religion is either a grand and glorious reality, or a most detestable fraud. If a fraud, it deserves to be exposed, and voted out of society; if a reality, it has claims which we can only withhold at our peril—claims that no honest man can withhold; and he that hopes to escape the hypocrite's doom by refusing to enroll himself with the people of God, will find in the end that his trust is a spider's web, and utterly useless.

But "*time enough*," I suspect, has a large and heavy burden of souls leaning upon it; and, oh, what a fearful sweeping away there will ultimately be, of souls that are leaning upon "time enough !" You admit that you know that you must die, and that a preparation for death is necessary, and that it must be made in time; but still you put it off. Is this wise? Is it in accordance with our practice in other matters? If we were promised a million of dollars in gold, which we could get by simply going to the bank and asking for it, would we say, " Its time enough ?" I think not. Why, then, put off this matter in which the eternal interest of a priceless soul is involved?—a soul that must forever live in raptures or in woe? "Time enough," was the language of a young man who lived in New Berne, N. C., some years ago. He was greatly respected, and worthily so, too; for he was genteel, good-natured, and free from the grosser vices of youth. But like the young man in the Gospel, he lacked the one thing most needed. Hasty consumption seized upon his vitals, and in a few days he was at death s door. I approached him, as his feet touched the waters, and asked him if it was well with his soul? He answered: "You know it is no time to talk upon that subject now." It was all that I could get out of him, and soon after that he dropped into eternity. My brethren, time is flying, and with it we are being hurried on to the house appointed for all living.

> "Our wasting lives grow shorter still,
> As days and months increase,
> And every beating pulse we tell
> Leaves but the number less."

What if our pulse should cease to beat before our work is done? "Time enough!" If you could have seen that young couple sitting in church at Edenton, on a Sunday night, as I saw them some moths ago; if you had heard their merry voices as they returned to their home at a late hour, (for the services were protracted,) you would have thought there was plenty of time for either of them to prepare for death. The husband was, to all appearance, in perfect health when they retired and fell asleep; but sometime before day the wife awoke and found the lifeless form of her husband lying by her side! "You may lean upon that house, but it shall not stand."

We shall mention but one more of these flimsy structures, upon which men lean, and to which they hold fast. It is near of kin to the one last considered. I refer to *death-bed repentance.* I presume that in this christian land, there are more people depending upon death-bed repentance than upon any other delusion. They say they don't mean to be lost; they expect to get to heaven; they mean to attend to their soul's interests, but when? To-day? "No." To-morrow? "No." Next week? "No." Next year? "No." No, they have not fixed upon any time to commence this work, but expect to be ready when death comes. There seems then to be nothing left but death-bed repentance. I have not the greatest faith in death-bed repentance. I will not say that none are saved on their death-bed: but it is not the most satisfactory experience. I have known persons who thought they got religion, on what they thought would be their death-bed: it proved otherwise, and they found afterward that they had no grace. What if they had died with what they afterwards found was not religion? I would not discourage the effort, even in the last moment, for there is too much at stake to think of giving up while there is a single ray of hope. Especially may they be encouraged who, like the dying thief, have not had favorable opportunities before. But after all is said, now is the best time. "Behold, now is the day of salvation."

"Now God invites, how blest the day,
How sweet the gospel's charming sound."

Much is said about quiet deaths. "I think he died all right," says one, "he died very quietly, just as though he had dropped asleep." What if he did drop off quietly, what does it signify? Would it be a strange thing, that a person who had not enough mental and moral energy to raise a sigh to heaven while in health, should be too lazy to raise a groan when dying? The testimony of one life spent in the service of God is worth a thousand quiet deaths.

But you may not have any death-bed. You are, perhaps, anticipating a long spell of sickness; during which time you will have nothing else to do but to get ready to die; you will then repent, give God your heart, and thus prepare to die. But you may not have this lingering illness. You may not be confined to your bed for a long period. You may be suddenly cut off. I could tell of numbers who died suddenly. Some time ago, a friend came to convey me to one of my appointments, and on his way he stopped at a neighbor's gate, talked with him a few moments and started on; he had not driven but a little way when a cry arrested his attention, and looking back, he saw his neighbor's wife trying to raise the lifeless form of her husband, to whom he had just before been talking! Oh, how uncertain is life! We know not what a day may bring forth—not even what an hour may bring forth!

> "And yet how unconcerned we go,
> Upon the brink of death."

But I admit that the chances are that you will die in bed; most people do. But you are not sure that you will be granted repentance at the last hour, or that you will have the grace given you to call on God for mercy. Remember you cannot come unless God draws, also that he says: "My Spirit shall not always strive with man." And again: "Woe also unto them, if I depart from them." We are also reminded that if once the good man of the house rises up and shuts the door, our crying without will be in vain. Remember also the young man who said, that it was no time to talk about the soul's interests at the dying hour. Sometimes the mind loses its balance, and the light of reason goes out, before the lamp of life ceases to burn. My unconverted friends, don't lean upon death-bed repentance. It is one of Satan's delusions; it is a spider-web refuge; it is one of those frail and flimsy structures which will eventually be swept away. As we have already intimated, they may be swept away before we have passed from time. We may realize their worth-lessness when it is too late to lay hold of anything stronger. However this may be, they surely will be swept away in the floods of Jordan.

But blessed be God, there is one sure refuge—*the Gospel.* This is not only God's great means of showing men their danger, but it also points to the only ark of safety. It throws a full flood of light upon the subject of the weakness and helplessness of human nature; it also tells us in whom is our help. He who trusts his soul upon the Gospel promises, will find that they will sustain him. The Gospel establishment will stand when all else fails. The rains may fall, the desolating floods may beat upon it; the thunders of God's wrath may shake the pillars of nature out of their sockets, and his fiery indignation burn the seas; yet amid the crash of falling worlds, the Christian edifice will stand. Yea,

> Those who make the Lord their trust,
>   And faithful to the end endure,
> Shall stand in Jesus' righteousness—
>   Stand as the rock of ages, sure.

Yea, with folded arms, they may stand and sing:

Hail, sovereign love, that first began,
The scheme to rescue fallen man;
Hail, matchless, free eternal grace,
Which gave my soul a hiding place!

Enraptured in dark, Egyptian night,
And fond of darkness more than light,
Madly I ran the sinful race,
Secure without a hiding place.

Vindictive justice stood in view,
To Sinai's fiery mount I flew;
But justice cried, with frowning face,
This mountain is no hiding place!

But, lo! a heavenly voice I heard,
And Mercy to my soul appeared,
She led me on, with pleasing face,
To Jesus Christ, my hiding place.

And now I feel the heavenly flame,
My trust is all in Jesus' name;
I all his sovereign truths embrace,
And find in him my hiding place.

Should storms of seven-fold thunders roll,
And shake the globe from pole to pole;
No thunder-bolt would daunt my face,
For Jesus is my hiding place.

A few more rolling suns at most,
Will land my soul on Canaan's coast;
There, I shall sing the song of grace,
Safe in my glorious hiding place.

SERMON XVI.

THE GLORY REVEALED IN THE CHRISTIAN CHARACTER.

[An Eulogy, by Bishop J. W. Hood, on the life of Robert Harris, late Principal of the State Colored Normal School, delivered at Evans' Chapel, Fayetteville, N. C., November 14, 1880.]

REPORTED STENOGRAPHICALLY BY C. W. CHESNUTT, FOR THE STAR OF ZION.

"For I reckon that the sufferings of this present time are not worthy to be compared with the glory which shall be revealed in us." Romans viii, 18.

If the Apostle Paul, under the many afflictions, persecutions, trials, pains, and labors that he passed through, could use this language; if, after carefully calculating the difficulties attending the labors of the pioneers in God's cause, he could come to the conclusion that those sufferings were "not worthy to be compared with the glory which shall be revealed in us," it seems to me that there is scarcely a mortal being who ought to complain of suffering.

Paul knew what suffering was. He was caused to

suffer from various causes: from false brethren; from being misunderstood by his own brethren—those who were connected with him in the ministry—in the cause of God; yea, even by these was he caused to suffer.

The present state of mankind is one in which there are few exempt from suffering. "Sickness and sorrow, pain and death," are the common lot of humanity. I doubt whether a man has ever lived on this earth that never felt pain.

But, I presume, in the passage before us, the Apostle had special reference to the sufferings peculiar to good men. While all suffer, there are some sufferings which are peculiar to the people of God—sufferings which they have to endure, that others are exempt from; trials through which they have to pass, that others know nothing of. And as the Apostle had been pointing out the characteristics of a perfect man, and the blessings connected with that state, it is fair to conclude that his mind was still occupied with that character. Now, the sufferings of a good man arise from various causes, among which we notice—

1. *From the envy of the wicked.*

I place this first, because it stands first in the history of a good man's sufferings. The envy of the wicked stands recorded as the source of the first attack ever made upon a human being. It was envy that caused Cain to kill his brother Abel. Abel had done nothing to him; he had simply offered sacrifice in accordance with the divine command, and had received the commendation of his God. That was all there was against him—all the provocation he had given his brother, if that can be called a provocation. If to be good—to serve God, fulfill the divine requirement, is sufficient to provoke envy, then Cain had a provocation; and that was the only provocation for the first murder. It was envy that moved the sons of Jacob to destroy Joseph; it was envy that caused Haman to scheme for the destruction of all the Jewish nation, in the kingdom of Ahasuerus; it was envy that caused the princes of the Persians to plot against Daniel's life; and last, but not least, it was envy that caused the Jews to crucify the Son of God.

2. *Then there are sufferings arising from " the ignorance of good men's contemporaries,"—the ignorance, or want of information in those that surround him.*

A really good man desires, and labors for, the good of his fellow men. Many around him content themselves with the false notion that they have done no harm, while he is distressed because he has done so little good. He fully realizes the fact that he did not come here simply to do no harm, but to do good; and he is anxious to fulfil the end of his being, to serve mankind and to glorify God. This desire on his part leads him to consider, to investigate and find out in what way he can best accomplish his desire, to benefit his fellow men. His turn of mind, his habit of study, his deep-toned piety are rewarded in a large expansion of his intellect. His mind expands and goes out to grasp the duties that are before him. He is enabled by his investigations to see what he can do, where he can begin that work, and how best complete it. The way of duty is made clear to him. He lives five, ten, twenty, even forty years ahead of his genera-

tion. William Lloyd Garrison was full forty years ahead
of his generation, and he was a martyr to the principles
he taught.

So it has ever been with men who are good and great.
They are frequently so far ahead that they are out of
sight of the multitude, like Moses when he went up into
the mount, into the presence of God. During this period,
some who were between him and the multitude, took advantage of their position to poison the minds of the multitude against the good man, and make them believe he
was not what he pretended to be. "As to this Moses, we
do not know where he has gone; let us make gods to ourselves." These men were so much nearer the multitude,
both in lack of intelligence and piety, that for the time
being they had the advantage; but it does not last.
After awhile the multitude comes up higher; the light
shines so clearly on the good man's way that if they were
disposed to blame him before, when they catch up with
him, as they do, those who honor Christ acknowledge
themselves in the wrong. The good man is not understood—if better understood the multitude would not unite
against him ; yet because he has no time to go back and
explain, his enemies hang upon his rear and harass him.
Although he has no use for the bridges which his enemies burn behind him, as he never intends to retreat, yet
it grieves him to see that mode of attack.

It is the lot of the good man, however, to be bush-
whacked and attacked in every way except from the front.
How mean the attack on Daniel ! Hear the language of
his enemies: "We shall not find any occasion against

10

this Daniel, except we find it concerning the law of his God." We shall not find anything against him unless we attack his righteousness. What a strong testimony this is to Daniel's rectitude! He was chief of the presidents, the affairs of the empire were in his hands, and yet his enemies testify that his management of these affairs was without fault—his rectitude was absolutely perfect, and therefore they could not attack him upon his character. They could not find any thing amiss with his management of affairs. They could bring no charge against him in this. So they could only attack him upon the point where his conscience would not give way.

This is ofttimes the case. A man's enemies seek to find out his opinions on some point, and knowing he is honest, straightforward and unyielding, they seek on that very point to attack him. They know that the multitude are not in that way of thinking, and therefore finding out his opinions they prepare to attack him upon his righteousness, and to condemn him because he is right.

The enemies of Daniel, however, were angels in comparison with men who lived since their time. They would have scorned to raise a false report about Daniel. They might have gotten together and hatched up some nice story; they might have outsworn Daniel, as they were in the majority—being many against one; and with a large crowd of followers, they might have maintained a falsehood against Daniel. But they would have disdained to do it. Men do not scruple in this day and time to coin lies out of nothing, for the purpose of attacking good men, and by misleading the multitude, make them believe that good men are bad men, and that

black is white, because the multitude are ofttimes not
well informed.

But I must not dwell longer upon these things. And
I stop not to make applications. You must make your
own applications. I have referred to these events, to
these attacks upon good men in former ages, for the purpose of illustrating the Apostle's declaration respecting
his sufferings; to show that there are sufferings peculiar
to good men. The good men of all ages have had to suffer from these sources; from the envy of the wicked, and
from the want of information on the part of those by whom
they have been surrounded. Ofttimes because a man's
real worth is not understood, because he is not known—
he lives among people who do not know him—don't know
the depth of his knowledge, nor the breadth of his intellect, the purity of his heart, the honesty of his purposes:
and for these reasons good men are caused to suffer; their
hearts are pained. It is not pleasant to go through this
world, and have the world against you; but the good
man must expect this; the world is no friend of his.

But I repeat, we must not dwell longer upon these things.
The Apostle declares that they are " not worthy to be
compared with the glory which shall be revealed in us."
They are not worth taking into account—they are of little consequence, because they last such a short time.
" What will all my sufferings amount to, if I can but join
that raptured host above?"   " I can tarry here but a night."
" The sufferings of this time will soon end."   Only a few
days, a few moments. Our life is as a span, a bubble on
the wave, and when brought down to the smallest calculation, it is nothing—it is only momentary. What are

ten, twenty, or fifty years, compared with the endless life
above? Suppose you should have to suffer; suppose
things should go contrary to you here; suppose neighbors, friends and relatives should turn against you in
this world, what does it amount to? God will reward
you. It "is not worthy to be compared to the glory
which shall be revealed in us."

"The glory which shall be revealed in us." *There is a
revelation of glory in the child of God.* Not simply the glory
after awhile; not simply the glory of God in Heaven—
the glory of the sanctified host, the glory of the angelic
army around the throne of God; but the " glory revealed
in us." God's glory is revealed in the good man's life.
And this is the command, "Let your light so shine before men, that they may see your good works, and glorify
your Father which is in heaven."

This glory is revealed in the life of a good man.

His life testifies for God. A good man is a walking
evidence, a walking monument of the divine character—
the character of God is displayed in the good man's life.
Well, how is it displayed? A good man " loves his enemies, blesses them that curse him, does good to them that
despitefully use him, persecute him, and say all manner of evil against him." Have you not thought it very
strange, sometimes, when you have seen a man who had
been abused and lied about, go up to his enemy and give
him a kindly hand and indicate that after all he did not
mind it, but was ready to forgive it, and say to that very
enemy, "Come and go with me to heaven?" He is ready
to ask God's blessing upon him. He won't take down
his flag, he won't pull down his standard; he will dis-

charge his duty if the heavens grow black; but he will discharge it in such a manner as not to hurt any body else if he can help it—in such a manner as to indicate that he does it because he loves to do good—because conscience leads him, because he is guided by the hand of God. He goes on boldly, determinedly, yet lovingly. He indicates his love for mankind, and thus glorifies God.

"God sends his rain upon the just and the unjust." So the good man treats his enemies with the same dealing as his friends. He discharges his duty toward them and theirs in the same way as toward his best friends. There is a glory revealed in such a character. Is not that a glorious character? The character of that man who, notwithstanding all that is said or done against him, threatens not; but led as a lamb to the slaughter, he goes on his way; he does not turn around to murmur and complain, but puts his trust in God, and indicates that he feels it his duty to take care of God's cause and let God take care of his character. It is glorious to see such men; such a course of conduct is glory revealed in us—it is God's work within us. A man cannot do this unless he has God in him; unless he has the Divine hand to lead him. If this were all, it would be enough—to know that we are able to show forth the glory of God in our lives, would be enough to induce us to bear patiently all the sufferings of this life.

But there is also a revelation of God's glory in the good man's perseverance.

It is said that "the righteous shall hold on his way; he shall persevere; he shall not stop." He knows he must fight—he must meet the hosts of night. He counts the cost, makes up his mind, puts on his armor, goes out for the fight, and is not satisfied if he does not get into a fight. When soldiers are well drilled they burn for a fight; their swords are well rubbed up, their ammunition is in good order, and everything is ready for the fight. "Hast thou given the horse strength? Hast thou clothed his neck with thunder? The glory of his nostrils is terrible. He scenteth the battle afar off." And the good man, like Job's war horse, wants to fight. He goeth out to the battle; he holds on his way, perseveres; and he cares not how many enemies he has, so long as they are in his front. They harass him some, but if they will stay in front of him, he is always ready; he does not fear an open enemy; he expects them, he is ready to meet them. God's glory is revealed in him, in the manner in which he stands the contest. He throws himself in the battle; he says, "I must fight, if I would reign;" and if he feels any weakness, he cries, "Increase my courage, Lord." He glorifies God in overcoming the world; he shows in his life and character that God has power to bring his saints out "more than conquerors." The man of God will go on his way; you cannot stop him.

But I must pass on. *The glory of God is revealed in the death of a good man.*

He dies in triumph! He more than conquers death. Having lived a righteous life, meeting his last enemy, he is not afraid. He says: "Come, welcome, death; the end of fear—I am prepared—I am standing joyful on the margin of Jordan. The golden bowl will soon be broken, the silver cord loosed; the doors shut in the streets; the

sound of the grinding is low." In that hour, the death
of the child of God is a revelation of glory. Have you
ever stood by the bedside of a dying Christian? There
may be no rapture—sometimes there is; but there is a
peace, a calm, which even death cannot distrub. In the
hour of dissolution, when death is untying the heart
strings, breaking the pitcher at the fountain, and the
wheel at the cistern, I hear the departing spirit ask:
" What, what is this that steals upon my frame? Is it
death ?

> If this be death, I soon shall be,
> From every pain and sorrow free;
> I shall the King of glory see:
> All is well!
>
> Weep not, my friends, weep not for me,
> My sins are all pardoned—I am free;
> There's not a cloud, that doth arise,
> To hide my Jesus from my eyes,
> I soon shall mount the upper skies:
> All is well!"

And, while standing upon the banks of the mystic Jordan, awaiting the coming of heaven's chariot, the dying
saint beholds the heavenly host moving up the shining
avenues of the golden city; heaven's armies on dress pa-
rade upon the sea of glass, and the harpers near the
throne, and, filled with rapture he exclaims:

> " Tune, tune your harps, ye saints in glory,
> I soon shall join your pleasing story;
> The angels are from glory come,
> They are 'round my head, they are in my room,
> They 've come to bear my spirit home:
> All is well! "

And as the pearly gates of the celestial city open to receive the triumphant saints, he salutes the heavenly hosts:

" Hail! all hail! ye blood-washed throng;
I've come to join your rapturous song,
Now all is peace and joy divine,
Heaven and glory now are mine,
O, hallelujah to the Lamb:
All is well!

Now permit me for a moment *to refer to the experience of our departed brother.*

During his illness some months ago, he had, as he afterterwards informed me, a most joyful and glorious experience; a happiness so great, a joy so complete, a fullness of glory which is the result of holiness of heart. As he expressed it—"I had got to Beulahland; that happy place where the Christian rests after his labors. He had connections here, friends here, that were pulling him back; but his mind was going after God." If he had departed in that state at that time, he would, he said, have been perfectly happy. He was sanctified then, but he stayed here eight or nine months longer. He was one sanctified soul who remained upon earth after sanctification. And that is better than all argument—the testimony of a living witness, one who feels that perfect rapture. What complete resignation he showed to the will of God! and that I claim as the key-stone in the arch of sanctification. This state of resignation which comes from a complete yielding of everything, body and soul to the will of God, brings with it a peace which we generally call sanctification; and you must get there before you go.

Blessed be God! brother Harris had got there. I have his testimony—the testimony of a dying man—that he had gotten there; a testimony from the gates of death. "Lord," he said, "I am willing to go now up to heaven, or to stay here, as thou seest fit."

Then there is a revelation of the glory of God in a good man at the judgment.

I had almost said that this would be the most complete revelation. There is a revelation of glory at the judgment in the fact that the good man shall be entirely vindicated. It is said that "a lie will go a thousand miles while truth is getting its boots on." But at the judgment, truth will catch up. And that is one great purpose of the judgment—that all wrongs may be made right, and that a good man may be vindicated before all who ever heard of him. Slander can outrun the truth; and, therefore, if there were no judgment at which all nations should be called together, the truth would never be made known to all—the falsehood would never be exposed. But we shall all be at the judgment; all who did, and all who did not hear of us, will know the truth, and the good man's character will then shine. We shall then see the heart, the motive, the intent, as God sees it. "Then we shall be like Him; we shall see Him as he is;" "we shall know even as we are known." As the Apostle says, "We shall no longer know in part," but absolutely. We may not know all that God knows—we may not be able to grasp the infinite—but everything that our minds shall come in contact with, everything that is necessary to make us happy, we shall know. There will be no mysteries then. Our knowledge will be ever increasing. I do not know when we shall get to it all, but when we come to it, we shall know it. And in seeing the real character of every man that is born of God, we shall see the real glory of the christian character.

Finally, *there is a revelation of glory in the christian character through all eternity.*

We shall be constantly entering into new revelations of divine glory. "These sufferings are not worthy to be compared with the glory which shall be revealed in us." God's glory shall be revealed in us throughout all eternity! We shall outshine the sun! We shall have palms of victory, crowns of glory! We shall there never hunger, there never thirst! We shall have no sickness there; we shall bathe our souls in the river of eternal pleasure; and through endless ages we shall sing "the song of Moses and the Lamb."

Oh, may God lead us to seek this glory: to seek to exhibit what belongs to us in our lives. Then like our beloved brother, who is departed, we shall be able in the dying hour, to fold our arms in peace and die the death of the righteous.

Let me say to the Conference, we have often met Bro. Harris in our assemblies; we have loved to have him with us; we have enjoyed his talents; we have received instruction from his counsels He was an honor to the connection, and to the General Conference of which he was a member; an honor to Christianity.

Adieu, my brother. We shall soon meet where parting shall be no more.

As I said of him the other day, of all men whom I have met, there was never one whom I would have been more willing to call " Master." When in his presence I felt the shadow of a great man resting upon me; I-felt little. I have never been able to sound his depth, to measure the breadth of his mind, and I do not know the man who has.

We do not know the extent of our loss, in the State, in the community, in the church. But, O blessed be God! our loss is his eternal gain; and He that knoweth all things, and doeth all things well, knows what is best for us. No doubt he had some good purpose in taking him away from us. Let us imitate his virtues, and seek to conform to the will of that Saviour he loved and cherished. So that when our days are numbered here below, we may meet him on the shining shore.

To his weeping relatives I would say, weep no more; dry up your tears. He is gone where

"Sickness, sorrow, pain and death,
Are felt and feared no more."

He will have no more distresses, no more dark nights, no more burning fevers. But in the presence of God, he shall shine forevermore. May God help us to live right, to die right, and we shall then, like him, be saved to all eternity!

SERMON XVII.

A DESIRABLE CONSUMMATION.

"Made ready before it was brought thither." 1 Kings vi, 7.

It will be seen that the text is not a complete sentence. It is taken out of its connection, in such a way, that its full import is not apparent. This is done for the purpose of presenting, forcibly, the points we wish to illustrate. The text suggests the idea of a preparation, for an end in view—"made ready." It also indicates the time and place in which this preparation must be made, if made at all, " before it was brought thither." The whole verse reads, "And the house, when it was in building, was built of stone made ready before it was brought thither: so that there was neither hammer, nor axe, nor any tool of iron heard in the house, while it was in building." The house referred to was the temple built by Solomon at Jerusalem, which was erected according to the divine plan as a place of divine worship and service; wherein God might dwell among his people in visible appearance. This was the most interesting and beautiful structure ever erected by mortal hands, and was a type of that building not built by man, but eternal in the heavens. We shall not attempt anything like a minute description of the temple, but will speak only of a few of its features. It was three-

score cubits long, thirty in height and twenty in breadth.
The common cubit was about eighteen inches—about
the distance from the elbow to the extremity of the middle finger, or the fourth part of a well proportioned man's
structure. Its length was, therefore, about ninety feet,
its height forty-five and its breadth thirty. There were
towers extending up to the height of a hundred and
eighty feet. Its length was from east to west, and its
breadth between north and south ; and represented what
was anciently supposed to be the shape of the world, viz:
an oblong square. There was a porch extending across
one end, ten cubits broad and thirty high. Besides the
supporting columns of this porch, there were two massive
pillars set up as monuments, or ornaments, or both.
There has been a question in controversy respecting the
height of these columns, as in Chronicles, they are said
to have been thirty-five cubits high, in Kings eighteen.
It is possible, however, that they were cast in one piece,
and then cut in two, and that in Chronicles, the length
of the whole piece is given. The statement in Kings is
best supported by other facts. It is accepted by the great
Jewish historian, Josephus, and to say nothing of chapiters and globes, a column of thirty-five cubits could not
be set up under a porch only thirty cubits high.

There was some reason, I have no doubt, for the massive proportions of these columns. Of an ordinary well-
proportioned column, the height is supposed to be about
nine times its diameter. The diameter of these was four
cubits, indicating a column of thirty-six cubits. Their
names seem also to indicate extraordinary proportions.
The name of the one on the left hand was Boaz, which

denotes strength, the name of the other Jachin, signifying, "It shall be established;" hence the worshippers,
coming up to the temple, beholding these massive pillars
and calling to mind the signification of their names,
would exclaim : "In strength is this house established."
And to us, there is in them a typical signification of the
strength which God will put forth to establish his church
and to defend his people, against all the assaults of the
powers of darkness. Some suppose that the object of
Solomon, in setting up these columns, was to represent
the two imaginary pillars that the ancients supposed
were placed at the equinoxes to support the heavens:
this would account for their massive proportions. But
if tradition should be admitted into consideration, we
should prefer to conclude that they were erected to commemorate the two pillars, said to have been set up by
Enoch before the flood. Enoch enjoys a most honorable
distinction among the antideluvians. Jude informs
us that he was a prophet, and that he foretold the destruction of the world by fire, and a judgment, to be followed by an eternal state, either of happiness or misery.
Tradition informs us that Enoch, vexed by the wickedness of his time, assembled those in whom he had confidence, (including Adam, Seth, Jared and Methuselah)
and implored their assistance in stemming the tide of
wickedness, which was overflowing the world.

It is said, that at this time he communicated to them
the terrible prophecy of the destruction of the world by
either fire or water, and that to preserve the sacred mysteries, committed to his charge, he built two great columns on a high mountain. Not knowing whether the

destruction would be by water or fire, he built one of a
kind of granite, which is said to resist the fire, and the
other of brass, which he supposed would resist the force
of a flood. We are told that the granite column was
overturned, swept away, and washed into a shapeless
mass by the force of the flood; but the other, by the
providence of God, stood firm. If this tradition is true,
the mystery of these columns is solved. They were two
in number, to commemorate the original two, and composed of brass, to commemorate the one which withstood
the force of the flood. They were cast hollow, and were
the depository of the archives. The chapiters were
adorned with wreaths of net work, lilly work and pome-
granite, symbolizing the unity of the three master minds
engaged in the work (Solomon, King of Israel; Hiram,
King of Tyre; and Hiram, the architect and beautifier
of the temple); and also the peace, plenty and prosperity
which the people enjoyed under their direction and care.
Upon one of the balls, which surmounted the columns,
was traced maps of the earth's surface; upon the other,
a view of the heavenly bodies.

The temple was built of stone so completely squared,
that it was difficult to find the joints, and so white, says
one writer, that it resembled a large snow-bank. Its
gold-covered top, when viewed in the sunlight, presented
a brilliancy which dazzled the eyes of beholders. Grand
and complete as this building was, it is said to have been
erected without the sound of any iron tool being heard
on it while it was being constructed. Iron was considered
polluting. In Deuteronomy xxvii, 5, we read that God
commanded Moses to build an altar of stone, but not to

lift an iron tool upon it. Also, in Exodus xx, 25, we have the following: "And if thou wilt make me an altar of stone, thou shalt not make it of hewn stone: for if thou lift thy tool upon it, thou hast polluted it." For this, with other reasons, no iron tool was used in the erection of the temple. But how could such a splendid structure be erected without the sound of some iron tool being heard? The Hebrews are said to have a tradition that the stones were not formed and polished by human industry, but by a worm called *samir*, which God prepared for that purpose; and that the stones come together of their own accord, and were erected by angels. We have also read a Mohammedan tradition, that Solomon, being annoyed by the noise made by the workmen in preparing the materials, offered an imprisoned genii his liberty if he would inform him how the hardest materials could be worked without noise. The genii admitted that he possessed no such knowledge, but said it might be learned from the raven. Take (said he) the eggs from a raven's nest and cover them with a crystal bowl, and thou shalt see how the mother bird will cut it through. Solomon followed the instruction, and soon a raven came and flew about the bowl, but finding that she could not get at her eggs, she flew away, but soon returned with a stone in her beak, called samur, with which the bowl, being touched, fell into two halves. Solomon procured a number of these stones and divided them among the workmen, who were thus enabled to continue their work without the slightest noise or confusion. From these fabulous traditions, it is evident that it was generally known that the temple was erected without noise or con-

fusion—which fact is attempted to be accounted for
by the putting forth of these traditions. But respecting
this and everything else in the history of God's ancient
people, the Scriptures are the most satisfactory—most
certain, full and complete source of information. In regard to the matter under consideration, the text supplies
a most reasonable solution: "The house was built of
stone made ready before it was brought thither." The
preparation of the stone only, is mentioned; but the expression is hyperbolic, in which a part is mentioned for
the whole. The preparation of all the material is intended to be included. There were three places in which
the materials were prepared. The stones were prepared
in the quarry, the wood in the forest, and the metals in
the clay ground, on the banks of the river, between Suc-
coth and Zeredatha.

The statement of the text is given for our instruction,
to remind us that in order to our being admitted as a
living stone for that spiritual building, a preparation
must be made before we cross the narrow stream of death.

We have remarked that this Jerusalem structure was a
type of the temple of the saints on high—composed of glorified believers. To prepare us for a place in the temple
not made with hands, is the purpose of the arrangements
of grace in the plan of redemption.

1. *There is an external preparation.*

We sometimes call it a professional preparation. It is
our duty to make a public profession of faith in Christ.
We should neither be ashamed nor afraid to stand up for
Jesus, to tell the world that we are no longer in love
with it; that it has no charms sufficient to hold us longer.

This we can do, and this God requires of us He never
does what man can do; hence he did not take away the
stone from the grave of Lazarus. He wanted to teach
them that they had a work which it was their duty to
do. They could not bring Lazarus back from the dead:
he did that himself; but they could take the stone away,
and that he required them to do. The joining of the
church, like the taking-away of the stone, is our part.
We cannot ungrave ourselves, and come forth from our
death of sin to a life of righteousness: that is God's work.
We must break away from our sinful habits, and strip
ourselves of all dependence in anything we have or can
have, growing out of ourselves. No matter what we have,
whether a favorable lineage, wealth, honors, titles, or anything else of a worldly nature, it will not give us admission to the enjoyment of the saints in light. We shall
be stripped of all these in the ante-chamber of death, and
if we enter heaven, it will be without them; and the
work of stripping from our affection the love of the
things of this world, is a most important part of the work
of preparation for heaven. "Love not the world," says
he that spake as man never spake, "for if any man love
the world, the love of the Father is not in him." So long
as we love, and trust in, the things of this world, we
shall not be prepared for that which is to come. We
must wear this world as a loose garment, and be ready to
drop it off at any time. We must be ready and willing,
if necessary, to part with all things here to obtain an
eternal inheritance. This is most frequently taught, and
yet what dull students we are: how slow we learn that
the life is more than meat, and the body more than rai-

ment; that we must put off the filthy rags of unrighteousness, and be clothed with the garment prepared for
us—the wedding garment, the garment of salvation,
which constitues our vital union with Christ, and gives
us a title to, and a meetness for all the blessings of the
marriage supper of the Lamb.   The outward sign of this
vital union with Christ, is a public declaration of our
having accepted the offered grace by uniting with the
church—the people of God.   To refuse to make this public profession is rebellion: it is sin—it is robbery.   It robs
God of the affectionate homage and honor due him.   It
robs the soul of the peace this secures, and robs the church
of the influence that we should exert in its behalf.

2. *There is an internal preparation.*

A preparation of the heart.   The heart, by nature, is
deceitful and desperately wicked.   The guile thereof must
be removed, the stony nature must be taken out—its hardness must be melted, and its coldness consumed by the
flame of divine love.   The rough and unpolished state
of the stone in the quarry, the timber in the forest, and
the metal in the quartz, is a fit emblem of human nature
in its fallen and depraved state.   There is much rubbish
of sin to be removed from our nature, much earth to be
shoveled off from our affections, and much dross to be
burnt up, before we shall appear as stones squared, polished and numbered for the building, or as sparkling
gems, or as gold tried by fire.   This transformation from
our natural deadness to the enjoyment of spiritual life, is
a most important part of the preparation for a place in
the heavenly structure.

3. *There is a practical preparation.*

There is work to be performed—not meritorious work—not work which produces righteousness, but work which is the fruit of righteousness, by which our righteousness is evinced. " By their fruits ye shall know them," said the great Teacher. The secrets of the heart may be read in the conduct—in the life an individual lives. Men imagine that they pass through the world unknown, but it is a mistake : those who are observing, read the character of their neighbors in their manner of life. Indeed, there are many who wear their marks so prominently, that none need be deceived. However well the cautious ones may conceal their defects, there is one Eye from which none can hide ; and because it is the eye of the Inspector General, under which we must pass, it is of the utmost importance to us that our works are such as will bear inspection : only such as spring from love to God and humanity will be accepted.

We remarked that there were three places in which the material for the Jerusalem temple was prepared. There are also three places in which the material for the New Jerusalem temple is being prepared, viz: the family, the social circle, and the church. We must not forget that children have souls as well as bodies, which must be fed and clothed. While we are trying to outdo our neighbors in providing fine dress for our children, we must not neglect to endeavor to secure for them the garment of salvation which is freely offered. Then there is the social circle, in which much work is to be done, or great loss will be sustained. Brotherly love and relief are used as motors in society ; but their demands are not fully met by administering to the wants growing out of bodily afflictions. There are distressed, afflicted, and perishing souls, which must be relieved, and clothed now, or being found naked at the judgment, will be ashamed. Whatever is done by us to advance the happiness of others, is a help to prepare ourselves for the temple above; for, in watering others, our own souls shall be watered also.

4. *There is the church, and its circles, which constitutes the chief place of preparation.*

All its energies are put forth to the end that there may be no lack of material for completion of the building. The material from the quarry and the forest was all prepared before it went down to the sea. Likewise, the material for the heavenly structure must be prepared on this side of the waters of death.

5. *Let us notice briefly the end in view.*

This is a place in the building. And about this, we need not concern ourselves, if we are prepared. Every stone prepared will find its place in the building. In Psalms we read that, "the stone which the builders refused became the head of the corner." This suggests the idea that a stone must have been carried up for inspection, which, owing to the ignorance of the inspectors, was refused, but afterwards had to be accepted, as it proved to be the key-stone to a principal arch in the building, without which it could not have been finished. The Master overseer of the heavenly building will make no such mistake: he knows the place for every piece, whether corner or cap-stone. Just here I may remark, that this passage has been sometimes taken as a foundation of discourses delivered to benevolent societies, which have been greatly praised as promoters of human happiness. Whether they are or not, depends largely upon their subordination to evangelical religion. If they claim soul-saving efficiency, encroach upon religious duties, or claim the time or talents which belong to the church, they are guilty of userpation, and are a curse to mankind. From such I would say, " Arise and depart; for this is not your rest." Only that which tends to fit us for heaven, is really useful to us. God grant that our preparation may be perfected in due season, and then we shall be admitted, as lively and living stones in His spiritual temple.

SERMON XVIII.

LOSS OF FIRST LOVE.

"Nevertheless, I have a few things against thee, because thou hast left thy first love. Remember, therefore, from whence thou art fallen; and repent, and do the first work: or else I will come unto you quickly, and will remove thy candlestick out of his place,-except thou repent." Rev. ii, 4, 5.

Our text is a part of the message which God gave unto his servant to write in a book, and send unto the seven churches in Asia.

John, the beloved. disciple of Jesus, having survived all his companions, became the special object of the persecuting enemies of the christian church and worship. Other attempts having failed to silence him, he was finally cast upon the isle of Patmos by the Emperor Domitian (it is generally believed). While thus in exile on account of his testimony to the truth, it pleased the Lord to give him a prophetic view of the conflicts and triumph of his kingdom on earth. The things which he beheld in this vision, he was commanded to write in a book and send unto the churches, over which he is supposed to have been the presiding Bishop.

God sometimes permits men to remove his servants from a particular field of usefulness, but not to hinder them from doing good. Indeed, it has often happened, that the very means employed by men to hinder, God has overruled to accomplish his purpose. If a man wants to be usefully employed, God will find means to employ him, let men do what they may to prevent it. John Bunyan was cast into Bedford jail, to keep him from preaching and comforting true believers, but while there, he wrote a book that has gone forth preaching in all the earth.

Likewise, while John, the disciple, was in exile, God employed him in writing a work, which will carry comfort to the persecuted followers of Jesus, through all ages, till time shall be no more. Before entering upon his prophetic vision, John was instructed to write a special message to each of the seven churches named. The epistles, each begin with some attribute of the Redeemer. Thus, "These things sayeth He, that holdeth the seven stars in his right hand"—"These things sayeth the Amen, the Faithful and true witness." Then follows the declaration, "I know thy works." After this there is a statement of the condition of the church designated, a commendation of that which was good, and a condemnation of that which was bad. In two of the churches, Smyrna and Philadelphia, there was nothing to condemn: in one, Laodicea, there was nothing to commend. The other four was a mixture of good and bad. To three of them there is an exhortation to repentance.

Ephesus, to which the language of our text is addressed, was not in quite so bad a condition as Laodicea or Sardis, yet we have no account of its improvement, by reason of the exhortation sent, and its total extinction affords a striking evidence of the infliction of the punishment threatened in the absence of repentance. For many ages there was not a single christian in the city, indeed the place itself was for ages without an inhabitant. To this church, John was told to write thus, " I know thy works, and thy labor, and thy patience, and how thou canst not bear them which are evil, and thou hast tried them which say they are apostles, and are not, and hast found them liars, and hast borne and hast patience, and for my name's sake hast labored and hast not fainted. Nevertheless I have somewhat against thee," etc.

Notwithstanding there was much in this church to commend, there were also a few things amiss, and we have reason to believe that the evil finally predominated, to the exclusion of every thing that was good. Such is the prevailing and growing nature of sin that, unless it is rooted out by repentance, faith and obedience, it will eventually root out every good desire, and leave its victims in a state of entire destitution.

I wish upon this occasion to apply the text to the condition of this church.

A little over a month ago, while steaming down the Tar river, on board the steamer Greenville, I was studying this passage, not with a view to preaching from it at any time, but simply for my own edification. I was suddenly impressed, however, with the idea that I was called upon to bear the message contained in the text to this church. This church, or its condition, had not been in my thoughts during that day, or for days, until that moment, but the impression was so vivid, that I felt it my duty, if called upon to preach here during the meeting of the Bishops, to discourse from this subject. I confess that a very dif-

11

ferent subject would have been my choice, had I been left to select without any special inspiration. Nevertheless, I think it best to follow the dictates of the Holy Spirit. A God-called ministry have no business with the conse-quences: they have only to follow the directtions of the Spirit and word of God, in the use of such means as God gives them ability to command. The more I thought upon this subject, the more I felt the burden of the mes-sage resting upon me. Nor did I feel relief until I began to write down the cogitations of my heart.

There is certainly some resemblance between the situa-tion and history of this church and the church at Ephe-sus. That was the first church named among those to whom a message was sent—most likely the first one formed, and the chief of those over which the Apostle presided. Ephesus was a flourishing maritime city, possibly the most flourishing of its time. Likewise, this church is situated in the first of American cities, and was the first African Methodist Episcopal church formed upon earth. It stands forth as the great pioneer in the contest, in which the race has had to engage against caste—preju-dice. Before the foundation of any other of the early African M. E. churches was laid, her walls were towering up toward the heavens, and her sons and daughters were frequenting her courts. When Richard Allen, the foun-der of the Bethel connection, was, according to their own history, a local preacher in the M. E. Church, Zion's lay preachers were upon her walls raising the horn of salva-tion, and declaring their determination to enjoy the blessings of religious liberty.

But the context refers to *the characteristics of the church at Ephesus.*

"I know thy works, labor and patience." This was also once a working church. Some of you can remember her labors of love in years gone. Both the ministry and the laymen were untiring in their efforts for the salvation of souls. Young men united in bands to attack the powers of darkness in their strong holds, and by their persuasions and prayers brought sinners out from their haunts of iniquity, and gave them no rest until they found rest in Jesus. Night after night, week after week, and month after month, they were found at the sanctuary. The word "tire" was not known to them. And the sisters—the daughters of Conference and daughters of Zion connected with this church, made sacrifice and performed labor, the far-reaching results of which will only be fully known, when they are read in the light of eternity. Many a poor minister, dispirited and ready to give up a poor field, received such substantial encouragement from the charitable sisters of this church, that they were caused to return with joy to their labor, and thus church after church was planted, and the borders of Zion were extended East, North, West, and finally South.

Ephesus was commended for her patience, under the reproaches and persecutions. Certainly, no church ever bore her persecutions with more patience than Zion has. I have thought at times that her patience had ceased to be a virtue. The slanders of her enemies have passed into proverbs, and are believed because not contradicted. Every misrepresentation that malice could set afloat, has been kept in circulation for nearly a century, and she has suffered them to take their rounds unchecked by even a denial.

The church at Ephesus was commended for its aversion to evil-doers: "And how thou canst not bear them that are evil." Likewise this church has been fearless in its opposition to evil-doers. Our fathers opposed every kind of evil, so far as they had light on the subject of evil. Some of our ministers refused to administer the sacrament to persons who came to the table with rings on their fingers, or in their ears, or with flowers in their bonnets. You may call this "old fogyism," but it was their idea of what religion required. Plainness of dress was a part of their religion, and, to their notion, there was no religion without it; hence, they insisted upon it. As they opposed vanity, so they opposed whatever else seemed to them evil.

The church at Ephesus was commended for its acuteness and faithfulness in detecting imposters. "And thou hast tried them which say they are apostles and are not, and hast found them liars." Likewise has this church been rigid in its examination of those who claimed to be called to the ministry. She has admitted none but such as gave evidence of a divine call.

Such is the favorable—the bright side of the picture we have to present. I would that there was no other-side to it; but alas! there is, and the text leads us to contemplate it: "Nevertheless I have somewhat against thee, because thou hast left thy first love." Notwithstanding the general commendation of the church at Ephesus, there were some things that were not approved. And I fear that if judgment was laid to the line, and righteousness to the plummet, the same complaint would truly be brought against old Zion. Come now! you have been with me thus far, you must go with me to the end. Face the truth : if it is unpleasant, the fault is not in God or his word, but in us. If we are not wholly acceptable with God, the lack is not in him, but in us, and the sooner wo know it, the better. I told you in the beginning that I was not following the line of my choice, but of duty.

Notice the COMPLAINT.

"Thou hast left thy first love." Literally, thou hast lost, remitted or let down thy first love—thy early affection. It has become less glowing and ardent than at first: love to Christ and to the souls of men has declined. The doctrines of religion probably are still maintained and error still opposed, but that glowing zeal which moved thee to make any reasonable sacrifice in the interest of the Redeemer's kingdom, thou hast lost. There is still an attendance upon divine worship, but it is cold and formal. There is little of that holy, burning Christian love which fills the heart with joy at the thought of entering the sanctuary—a joy which was once so overflowing that it broke forth from the lips, in the language of the Psalmist, "I was glad when they said unto me, let us go up into the house of the Lord—our feet shall stand within thy gates, O Jerusalem."

It is not an uncommon thing, either with individual christians or with churches, to lose their first love. You have often seen young converts start out so full of zeal and good works, as to throw old christians in the shade; and the same may be said of churches. They are formed under the influence of a great revival, or a godly zeal, which takes possession of a portion of the members of an old organization, and causes them to break away from their cold and formal associates, and form a new organization for the promotion of holiness. Such were the circumstances under which the Methodist Church was formed. Sometimes larger religious liberty is desired. This desire gave birth to the A. M. E. Zion Church. These young organizations, like young converts, usually show great activity; but after a time, they lose the fire of their zeal, and become as formal and dead as the older bodies from which they sprang. This is seen in the Wesleyan church in England ; it is seen in the Methodist Episcopal Church; it is seen in our own church. This declination of love is the result of various causes. With individuals, it is often the result of neglect of God's house, and the various means of grace—such as reading the Scriptures, fasting, meditation, prayer, and other holy exercises. The enemy is so deceptive and crafty, and leads men away so gradually, that his influence is not discovered until one finds himself cold, and almost without hope. Awakening to a sense of his condition, he exclaims:

"Ah where am I now!
When was it, how
That I fell from my heaven of grace?
I am brought into thrall,
I am stripped of my all,
I am banished from Jesus' face.
Hardly yet do I know
How I let my Lord go,
So insensibly led from his love."

Worldly association, and the indulgence of the inclination to worldly pleasures, have a chilling effect, and tend to the declension of love.

Some are led away by temporal prosperity. Abundant blessings from our Heavenly Father ought to fill our hearts with gratitude, and lead us to greater devotion and thankfulness; but alas! the opposite is too often seen.

Sometimes people get too respectable to have much love to God, or for the souls of men. As churches are composed of individual members, whatever tends to the declension of love in the members, affects the entire body. There is such a thing as a church being ate up with respectability—too respectable to be a working church. Wrapped up in old moth-eaten garments of self-righteousness, they imagine themselves well dressed, in old-fashioned finery—than which nothing looks worse. There is such a thing as a church wearing its old clothes, till they are entirely out of fashion and threadbare; or, in other words, living the past—what it has been—old-time respectability. Sometimes the members of a church get so respectable, that they don't want anybody in church but themselves. They are especially opposed to new comers. They can pay the minister themselves, if they can have one to order, and what is the church for, but for their comfort, and credit, and glory?

Sometimes a set of old officers cling to the offices long after their usefulness as such has ceased, and think it would be sacrilege to diffuse any fresh blood into the body; and the result is, the church goes to seed. It loses all healthful growth and vigor; and from its scattered seed,

there springs up around it a number of young and vig-
orous plants, whose branches shoot out and cover all the
ground, leaving the old respectable stock in the shade.
Is this picture too striking? If so, I would have you
view it until it disgusts you beyond endurance—until
you resolve to shake off that spell of lethargy that has
dwarfed your efforts, and rise up in God's might and en-
graft into the old stock a sufficiency of youthful energy to
reproduce the healthful growth which distinguished the
early days of Zion.

II. This brings us to consider the EXHORTATION.

The duty or exercise required as an antidote for the
evil complained of is—

1. *Remembrance.* "Remember, therefore, from whence
thou art fallen." Call to mind the eminence Old Zion
once occupied, when her gates were crowded with happy,
enthusiastic worshippers, coming up to the sanctuary to
worship the God of Jacob. Think of the influence Zion
once wielded in this city. She was the great centre of
attraction: the other little bodies exhibited only a reflected
light, borrowed from the refulgence of her poured-out
splendor. She was the queen of christian beauty, sending out her rays to enlighten the dark places of the earth.
When her sister churches were struggling for existence,
she was floating on the bosom of prosperity. We are
urged to recollect—to remember, to bring up into our
minds a remembrance of our former state; to think of the
warmth of love, the ardor and zeal that once characterized this church. Such a recollection of our former state,
when religion has declined in our hearts, or in the church,
will most likely produce a good effect. Nothing is better

suited to produce a good effect upon a backslidden christian, or a backslidden church, than to get them to thinking about the former happy days, until their thoughts
burst forth in song—till they sing:

"What peaceful hours I once enjoyed!
How sweet their memory still!
But they have left an aching void,
The world can never fill."

As our thoughts rest upon the blessedness we knew
when the love of God was blown to a flame in our hearts,
by the soul-refreshing view of Jesus and his word; holy
desires spring up, and holy resolutions are formed,—and
by the aid of divine grace, we are encouraged to call back
the insulted Spirit.

"Return, O! holy dove, return
Sweet messenger of rest:
I hate the sin that made thee mourn,
And drove thee from my breast."

We will then feel a desire to have Jesus reign in the
soul, and to this end—ask help from on high.

"The dearest idol I have known,
What e'er that idol be,
Help me to tare it from thy throne,
And worship only thee.

So shall my walks be close with God,
Calm and serene my frame;
So purer light shall mark the road
That leads me to the Lamb."

A remembrance of former happy days will remind the
backslidden of what they might have enjoyed, had they
continued as they began—how much good they might

have accomplished, and how great attainments they might have reached. Think of what vast results this church might have accomplished, if she had continued to weild the influence she once wielded: she might have been sitting here in the garden of prosperity, with a large number of full grown and flourishing daughters in this and neighboring cities. We have sent you from the South hundreds of promising lambs, but you have suffered them to be gathered into other folds.

2. We are exhorted *to repentance.* " Repent and do thy first works." Let there be in you a change of mind, purpose and action. All of this is included in the word " repent"—a godly sorrow for sin, disobedience and slothfulness—a fixed purpose, a firm and active resolution to forsake sin, and engage in the practice of every virtuous and benevolent work. Sometimes there is a desire in the heart of backsliders to return to the practice and enjoyment of religion, but they don't know how. And there may be those who long for the prosperity of Zion, but they don't know where to begin. The text directs us: " Do thy first works." God has done his works once and for all. The work now is ours: you will not be happy now until you work. It is not so much the loss of faith that causes people to backslide as it is the neglect of duties. It is work that has been neglected, and work that is required. The unregenerate are justified by faith, but believers can only feel the evidence of divine reconciliation, by actively and continually engaging in works of righteousness, which are the fruit of the Spirit. If you have backslidden, and feel cold and lifeless, and desire to feel the joy of former days, go to work for the Lord, for the salvation of souls, for the up-

building of the church; and you will soon feel the flame
of love re-kindled in the bosom. Don't sit in silent meditation, waiting for some supernatural influence—some
special visitation from above, to call you back and restore
you to the joys of better days, but get up and go to work.
The counsel of the Savior to those who have left their first
love; is, "To do their first works,"—to engage themselves
at once in doing what they did in the days of their early
piety, the days when the light of heaven shone upon their
path, when they went about doing good—when no kind
of weather, and no kind of amusement kept them from
the prayer-meeting, or class-meeting. "The day of thy
espousal." Do you wish to see the borders of Zion enlarged? Go to work as our fathers did in the early days
of the church, and as you did when in the enjoyment of
your first love. Bring in the stragglers, call back the
wanderers, raise up the fallen and gather the lost sheep,
and let Zion's gates be crowded with a throng of happy
worshippers. We cannot regain all that has been lost by neglect, but there is much ground that can yet be occupied, and
cheered by the hope of future possibilities: let us live, and
work for God and Zion. Let us emulate the holy determination of the evangelical prophet. "For Zion's sake
will I not hold my peace, for Jerusalem's sake will I not
rest until the light thereof goes forth as the brightness,
and has glory as a lamp that burneth."

III. Notice the FEARFUL CONSEQUENCES OF NEGLECTING
THIS ADMONITION.

"Or else I will come unto thee quickly, and will remove
thy candlestick out of his place, except thou repent." The
church at Ephesus was the spiritual light-holder for that

city—the means of dispensing light; which, if removed, darkness would prevail. This was the punishment that God threatened to inflict, if they repented not: He would put out the light and leave them in darkness. The obvious meaning is, that the church in that place should cease to exist—the light go out, to be lit no more. We have already remarked how fully this judgment was inflicted. Mr. Gibbon, though not a believer in revelation, bears testimony that will show with what exactness the prediction in regard to this church has been accomplished. Speaking of the conquests of the Turks, he says: "In the loss of Ephesus, the Christians deplored the fall of the first angel, the extinction of the first candlestick; the desolation is complete; and the temple of Diana, or the church of mercy, will equally elude the search of the curious traveller." Thus it appears that the heathen temple of Diana, at Ephesus, and also the Christian church there, have both passed away, and nothing remains but unsightly ruins. What God did in Ephesus in the fulfillment of his word, he has frequently done, both to individuals and to churches. He has removed the light, and left them in darkness. During the last ten years I have frequently seen church buildings in which a sermon has not been preached for years. Others have been turned into barns and dwellings, and not a member to be found who will own the name—"Christian." God forbid that his light should ever go out in this church or city, or that any backslider should be left in eternal darkness. But fruits meet for repentance is the only preventative.

Perhaps some will feel discouraged, as so much time has been lost. You have no need to be. Let each do his part now Whining over the past will avail nothing. We have nothing to do with the past, except to be admonished and instructed by its experience. To the future we must look. Thank God there is a future—a bright and glorious future—a future for the Church on earth—a future for old Zion, I fully believe. A future in which the youth, whose eyes are now sparkling with delight, will take the helm, and man the old ship Zion, and steam her across the pitching and tossing waters of prosperity, and bring her into port laden with a full Christian cargo.

Then there is another future, an eternal future, for the promise is, "To him that overcometh will I give to eat of the tree of life, which is in the midst of the paradise of God." The fruit of this tree is eternal life.

> " O what are all my sufferings here,
>   If Lord thou count me meet
> With that enraptured host to appear,
>   And worship at thy feet.
> Give joy, give grief, give ease or pain,
>   Take life or friends away;
> But let me find them all again,
>   In that eternal day."

SERMON XIX.

THE HELPLESSNÉSS OF HUMAN NATURE.

"No man can come to me, except the Father which hath sent me draw him." John vi, 44.

Jesus, having heard of the death of John the Baptist, left Nazareth, passed over the sea of Galilee, and retired, with his disciples, to a desert belonging to Bethsaida. To this place the multitude followed him, received his instructions, and many were healed of their diseases. His miracles, and the force of his doctrines, held the attention of the people so long, that the disciples thought they needed rest and refreshment, and they suggested that for this purpose he should dismiss and send them away. The Lord Jesus, however, had compassion on the people, and said to Philip, (who was a native of that country), "Where shall we buy bread that these may eat? And this he said to prove him : for he himself knew what he would do. Philip answered him, Two hundred pennyworth of bread is not sufficient for them, that every one of them may take a little." Andrew remarked that there was a lad present with five barley loaves and two fishes, but that these would go but a little way among so many. Jesus commanded the multitude to be seated upon the grass : he gave thanks, broke the bread, gave it to his disciples, and they gave it to the multitude. After all were satisfied, they took up twelve baskets full of the fragments that remained. This miracle convinced many of them that Jesus was the Messiah promised them, and they were desirous to crown him and proclaim him king; which, when he perceived, he retired to a mountain alone. After his mysterious departure, his disciples took ship, and returned to Capernaum; but as Jesus went not with them, the multitude remained. The next day, however, when other ships passed by, they also crossed the lake. To their astonishment, when they reached Capernaum, they found Jesus there. As he did not embark with his disciples, nor go in any of the ships which followed, they could not imagine how he had reached that shore. It had not occurred to them that he, who could multiply a few loaves and fishes into a meal sufficient to feed thousands, could also walk upon the bosom of the deep. Hence, they asked: "Rabbi, when camest thou hither?" He refused to gratify their curiosity by giving them an account of his passage over the water, but proceeded to criticise their motive in following him, and to teach them the lesson they should have learned from the miracle he had wrought the day previous. "Verily, verily, I say unto you, Ye seek me, not because ye saw the miracle, but because ye did eat of the loaves, and were filled. Labor not for the meat which perisheth, but for that meat which endureth unto everlasting life, which the Son of man shall give unto you: for him hath God the Father sealed." They had not been duly impressed with the purpose for which the miracle had been wrought; he, therefore, took the occasion to teach them, that they

should not make it their chief object to obtain nourish-
ment for the body, or temporal blessings, which perish
with the using of them, and at most can only give momentary satisfaction, but that their chief object should be
to obtain that spiritual food which gives eternal life, and
secures to us those blessings which are lasting, and that
felicity which is eternal. "Then said they unto him,
What shall we do to work the work of God? Jesus answered and said, This is the work of God, that ye believe
on him whom he hath sent." All the work required of
a truly penitent enquirer after righteousness, is faith in
Christ. It is this work—the exercise of faith—that God
is well pleased with ; nor do we begin the work, which
he requires, until we believe on his Son. The perverseness of the hearts of most of his hearers, however, caused
them to reject this way of salvation : not all, for some
believed on him, and of them he declared that all those
whom his Father gave him should come to him, and that
he would not cast them out. But the Father, according
to his own plan could only give him such as believed on
him, for they alone are acknowledged as his. All who
remain in unbelief are children of the wicked one. Some
of his hearers, notwithstanding they had seen his latest
miracle, yet desired a sign as evidence of his Messiahship.
They intimated that, in comparison with the miracle by
which Moses had fed their fathers for forty years in the
wilderness, the one he had performed was but a small
thing. "Our fathers did eat manna in the wilderness, as
it is written, He gave them bread out of heaven to eat."
But he answered, "I say unto you, Moses gave you not
that bread from heaven ; but my Father giveth you the
true bread from heaven." That was not the gift of Moses

but of God ; it came not out of heaven, but out of the air. The Psalmist spake of manna simply as a type of the true bread, which God has now given out of heaven, and which giveth life to the world. When Jesus declared himself this bread out of heaven, which God had given to the world, some of the Jews were displased, and said : "Is this not Jesus, the son of Joseph?" To this Jesus answered, "Murmur not among yourselves." Don't murmur at my sayings, as though they were incredible, or hard to be believed : it is not the want of truth in them, but your prejudice against me, and the perverseness of your will, which cause you to reject them. For such is the degeneracy of your nature, such the hardness of your hearts, such the stubbornness of your will, and such your depraved and helpless condition, that nothing but the power of grace divine can prevent your eternal ruin. "No man can come to me, except the Father which hath sent me draw him." The text is one of those passages which emphatically declare the universal degeneracy and helplessness of human nature, and the absolute impossibility of restoration, without divine aid. Mankind is so weak and helpless, so under the reigning power of sin, that he cannot come to Christ until drawn by cords divine. He cannot savingly believe until God helps his unbelief. He cannot open his eyes to behold the light of the glory of God, in the face of Jesus Christ, unless God gives him strength to do so. Hence the language of the poet : .

"How lost was my condition,
Till Jesus made me whole;
There is but one physician,
Can cure the sin-sick soul."

A figure, however, representing a more helpless state than that of sickness, is frequently employed to represent the soul's condition, namely, death. It is dead—dead in sin. Hence the Apostle exclaims, "Arise from the dead." And the change is spoken of as passing from death unto life, and also as a resurrection from the dead. If these figures do not express a state of utter helplessness, none could. The sinner is spiritually dead—destitute of spiritual life, of the image of God, which is the essence of vital union with him; of his favor, which is life, and his loving kindness, which is better than life. The sinner is judicially dead—dead by sin through the law. "Sin," says the Apostle, "finding occasion through the commandment, beguiled me, and through it slew me." (Revised version) The sinner is doomed to natural death, and exposed to the danger of eternal death.

I. But the text reminds us of THE SPIRITUAL AND MORAL DISTANCE WHICH SIN HAS WROUGHT BETWEEN MAN AND HIS MAKER.

Sin has separated man from the Author of his being, caused man to take his departure from his God, to go away from him—not out of his sight; for if I borrow the wings with which the rays of morning light fly across creation with incomprehensible speed; and with them fly —and dwell in the uttermost parts of the earth, his all-seeing eye shall follow me: not beyond his power; for if I take up my abode in hell, that is his prison, and his hand shall hold me there: but away from his holiness, away from his reconciled love; away from that vital union with him, which constitutes our spiritual life and joy unspeakable,—

"Away on the mountain wild and bare,
     Away from the tender Shepherd's care."

Now the object of Christ's visit to this world was to
bring man back to God. "He came to seek, and to save
the soul which was lost."

    . "We all like sheep had gone astray,
         We had left the fold of God:
      Each wandering in a different way,
         But all the downward road."

We had all departed from God, and the distance was
continually growing greater. Christ left heaven to bring
us back to God. By the sacrifice of himself, in the humility, poverty, shame, and the agony of his incarnation and
death; and by His resurrection; He has made an atonement, which meets all the demands of divine justice.
"He was bruised for our iniquity, the chastisement of
our peace was upon him, and by his stripes we are healed."

But in order to our being brought back to God, we must
come to Jesus. We can approach God only through him.
He is the way, and there is no other. He is the door;
and there is no other entrance: by him, if any man enters, he shall be saved. He is the true way; all else is
deceptive—is false. He is the life; without him is death.
He invites us to come to him: "Come unto me all ye that
labor and are heavy laden." He urges us to come—ex-
hibiting his wounds—his pierced hands, his feet, his side,
his temples torn by a crown of thorns, and his back fur-
rowed by a wire whip. He dwells upon the easiness of
the terms: "Without money and without price." He
proclaims the richness and costliness of the provisions—
"My oxen and my fatlings are killed, all things are ready,

come!" And when every effort has been exhausted in vain, he complains: "Ye will not come to me, that ye may have life." (Rev. Version.) It is our interest to come to Christ: our well-being in this present life hinges upon our coming to him; nor can there be any present peace, security, or real happiness here without him. That we may be truly happy here,

> " Christ must be the sea of love,
> Where all our pleasures roll;
> The circle where our passions move,
> The center of our soul."

Then, our future well-being depends upon our coming to Christ: all the immortal concerns of eternity are involved —heaven, with all its glories; and hell, with all its terrors, urge us. It is our duty to come to Christ; to refuse, is rebellion—is sin, yea, sin unto death—temporal, spiritual and eternal. Hence, finally, we must come to Christ, or be forever lost and undone—"For there is none other name under heaven given among men, whereby we must be saved."

II. This brings us to notice that WHILE WE ARE INVITED TO COME TO CHRIST—IT IS OUR DUTY AND INTEREST TO COME TO HIM, AND WE MUST COME OR PERISH ETERNALLY.

Yet, such is the helplessness of human nature, that no man can come to Christ except the Father draw him. Such is the language of the text, and it was uttered by the Son of God. "Then," says the sinner, "if I am not divinely drawn, I am lost." Precisely so. If God should pass you by, you are forever lost. "Then my case is both helpless and hopeless, unless the Lord be pleased to draw me?" It is verily so. "Then I have nothing to do, but

to wait God's time?" This is a false suggestion of the
devil, in which, as usual, he mixes a little truth with his
falsehood. It is true that we must wait God's time, but
it is not true, that we have nothing else to do. If you
were expecting a very dear friend by a particular train—
one you loved more than all others—you might have to
wait the arrival of that train, but you would hardly be
doing nothing, while waiting. If nothing else, you would
be wishing the train might come on time; notwithstanding, this wish might be fruitless. But we have the assurance that a sincere desire for the Saviour's love is
never breathed in vain. Yours would be an anxious
waiting; it would not be regarded as a marvellous thing
for you to go to the railroad station and wait there.
I repeat, it would be an anxious waiting—something
like that expressed by the Psalmist, when he says: "My
soul waiteth for the Lord more than they that watch for
the morning: I say, more than they that watch for the
morning." He repeated it to exhibit the force he wished
to throw into it. You can imagine how a shipwrecked
mariner, alone upon the bosom of the deep, would watch
for the morning—for light, by which his signal of distress could be seen. The Psalmist declares that his waiting for the Lord had in it an energy of soul, an agony, a
thirsting, yea, a longing for the Lord, more intense than
the agony of any distressed, benighted mortal, who
watches for the morning. It was said of Simeon that he
waited for the consolation of Israel, but he was found
waiting in the temple. He had drawn as near to the
Lord as he could get. This is a waiting in which there
is no folding of the arms, no indifference, but an energy

of longing, which sets every fiber of the soul in motion.
Yes, you must wait God's time; but that is now. He
proclaims it, "Behold now is the day of salvation."
Hence, you need wait no longer, but come! Come now,
while he is drawing you; for, blessed be God, he passes
none by: he leaves no soul to perish in its sins—not until
love's utmost efforts, in its behalf, have been exhausted in
vain. While power is given to the Son to save all who
come to God through him, yet the Father is not an idle
spectator of the glorious work. He is not only watching
the process through which sinners are passing in the
washing of regeneration, but is also engaged continually
in drawing souls to Christ, that they may be saved. Do
you say you don't understand the divine drawings? You
must remember that the instrumentalities by which objects are drawn, are as various as are the objects to be
drawn. An apple is drawn from the limb of a tree to the
ground by the power of gravitation: that is, when the
hold, by which it was held to the twig, has relaxed, then
the power of gravitation, takes hold of it, and draws it to
the ground. Till then, the power of gravitation is not
strong enough to bring it down. Likewise, when our
affections relax their hold upon the things of this world,
we are easily drawn to God by the cords of divine love.
This earth, with all its sattellites is drawn around the sun
by the joint action of the centre-seeking and centre-flee-
ing forces. The one keeps the earth from flying off into
unlimited space, the other keeps it from tumbling into
the sun. A train of cars is drawn by the power of steam,
and a wagon is drawn by horse-power—brought to bear
upon traces attached to it. .Thus you see that matter is

drawn by forces suited to its nature. But there is something in man that is not matter, and in that something is the spring of all his moral actions. We call it the soul. As the body has a heart, or fountain out of which life's blood flows, so has the soul a heart, centre, or mainspring of all its action. This mainspring of the soul, I am inclined to believe, is the will. I have heard men speak of doing things against their will, than which there could be no greater mistake. •We act only when the will acts: that which is done against our will, is not our act, but the power of forces which we either cannot or will not control. To make the matter plain: Suppose I lay my hand upon this Bible, a desperado rises up before me and shouts out, "Take that hand up!" I answer, "No, I won't." " Take that hand up, or I will blow your brains out!" he exclaims. Now, if my will does not yield to the force of the danger before me, my hand will still remain unmoved. If I don't say it, in so many words, my act says, " Crack away! I won't move my hand." But if I am not willing to risk having my brains blown out, or am more willing to take up my hand than to take that chance, my will runs down into that hand and it comes up. It comes up by the consent of my will too. That the force operating upon the will was strong, I grant; it had to be stronger than the will, in order to make it yield. Likewise the will must yield to the divine influence; hence, the cords by which men are drawn, are such as can be brought to bear upon the will. Jehovah says, I draw them by bands of men. There are peculiar cords by which human nature is drawn, and which operate upon the will, which I have declared to be responsible for every moral act. And I may here remark, that God lays great stress upon the will. It is, " whosoever will.' To the man who had laid thirty-eight years at the pool, Jesus said, " Wilt thou be made whole?" The consent of that man's will was all that was required. And that is all that is required of many here, this day. There are at least three strong cords, which operate upon the will and draw men to Christ—the cords of fear, the cords of interest, and the cords of love. The fear of hell, the hope of heaven, and the love of God, are the three grand motives prominently set forth in the Book Divine, and they are designed to draw men to Christ. Man is an intellectual being: he has understanding; he can think, he can reason, he can take subjects into his judgment, (the mind's balances,) and weigh them. He can reflect, consider, decide, and act. He has conscience capable of emotions, and affections which can feel the touch of love, and are moved in response to its influence. There came once a man to church, filled with his notions of his own importance: it was during a revival season. I said to him, " Would you like to go forward to the altar for prayer ?" He gave me a look, which seemed to say, " I don't want your prayers!" Now, I might have talked with that man for a month, while he was in that state of mind, without moving him. To have gotten that man to the altar, I would have had to apply physical force, and then only his body would have been there. But the services continued, the Spirit of God touched that man's conscience, tears stole down his cheeks, his head was bowed, and finally he arose and went to the altar, and found peace. That man's con-

science was touched, and through his conscience his will
was reached, and caused to yield to the divine influence;
and it would have taken strong chains to have held him
back from that altar, to which he could only have been
dragged, a little while before. Some months ago, there
came a man to church, who was an unbeliever. He listened to a sermon in the morning, in which human helplessness was set forth. In the afternoon the minister
presented an argument, in which the way of salvation,
through faith in Christ, was made plain. Before the
services closed for the day, that man, who had come in
the morning a thoughtless unbeliever, found that peace
which he had never before thought of seeking for. His
understanding grasped the truth, which he thought had
never before been so plainly set forth, and reason said,
" Why not accept the Saviour now?" That man's will
yielded to the force of reason, and he was thus drawn to
Christ, and saved. Let us suppose a lady, who is a millionaire, is approached with the request that she take the
place of a servant and become a child's nurse. What is
the result? You have kindled the wrath of that lady,
until she could burn you up with her anger, if such a
thing were possible. What! she descend to the position
of a servant! She scorns the thought. But let that lady
be a loving mother, and let her child be at the point of
death, and where will you find her? Clothed in scarlet
robes, decked with jewels of gold, and entertaining the
gay and thoughtless mortals who delight only in exhibitions of sublunary grandeur? No! Where then? You
will find her near that sick child, watching and waiting,
and serving—a servant of the child. That lady has come
12

down from her high notions—her scorn of labor, toil, and service. What brought her down? She was drawn down by the cords of affection for that child. Her will was reached through her affections, and yielded to the force of love. God says, "I draw them with cords of love;" and again, "With everlasting kindness have I drawn thee." You were all drawn to church this day, as you have often been, but I see not the cords by which you were drawn : and yet some of you were drawn so hard, that it would have caused you pain to have stayed away. You would have been unhappy at home, on account of your great desire to be here. Some were not drawn so hard, but they are here. A little rain would have held some back, because they were not drawn by the kind of cords which draw people through all kinds of weather. You were drawn here by a variety of forces. Some were drawn by the cords of affection for the house and worship of God. Like the Psalmist, you were glad when they said unto you, "Let us go up unto the house of the Lord." You said with heart-felt love, with glowing rapture, "Our feet shall stand within thy gates, O Jerusalem." Some were drawn by the cords of duty: though you felt not that burning desire which at times has drawn you, yet there was a sense of duty impelling you. There may be a sorrowing soul, who has come seeking comfort, or a sin-sick soul may have come to inquire for the Great Physician. Of such, the Matchless Speaker has said, "Blessed are they that mourn, for they shall be comforted " Perhaps some have been drawn by the cords of curiosity; possibly, some by the cords of vanity—something new to exhibit. " The bands of men," or cords by which they are led about, are truly various, and there are very many ways by which the Father draws souls to Christ. The danger, therefore, is not that we shall not be drawn, but that we may suffer the divine influence to be employed in vain. For, I repeat, it is a blessed truth, that God passes none by. He leaves none to perish, until all the cords by which he draws men to his Son have been employed in vain. Do you say, "I have never felt the divine drawings?" Possibly they were so gentle and tender, and you so thoughtless and indifferent, that you failed to notice the heavenly influence. If you had been like the Psalmist, waiting for him more anxiously than they that wait for the morning, you would have felt the divine operation. Many are brought to Christ through a painful process, because they will not yield to the milder means. With some, severe providential interpositions have to be employed, before they will yield—such as the furnace of afflication, bereavements, and other domestic troubles. Are you inclined to hang back until the strongest and most severe cords are employed to draw you? Is it not more reasonable to yield to the milder influences? Is it not unfeeling to put the Father to so much trouble to bring us to Christ? No man can truly say, he has never felt the divine drawings. Have you ever felt guilty, or a moment's remorse of conscience? Have you ever felt sorry for sin, or wished yourself better? Such feelings only come through the divine influence; they are his drawings: if yielded to, they will bring us sweetly and joyfully to Jesus. I once knew a man who said he lived to the age of thirty years without having one good impression, or the least remorse of conscience. I never expect

to meet another, who can truthfully say the same. Is
there one here who can? If so, let him now stand up——
I conclude there is none. Then you have all been drawn—
perhaps time and again. Don't you remember a time in
which you were aroused at midnight—a night so dark
that it seemed as though every star had been blotted out,
and the stillness was so profound that it appeared as
though all creation was at silence for a while? And
don't you remember that, notwithstanding the stillness,
you felt a horror as though 'you were in some dreadful
presence? That was God drawing you by filling your
conscience with tormenting fear? Have you at times, like
Agrippa, felt that you were almost persuaded to be a
christian? God was then drawing you by the cords of
reason. Were you almost ready to accept the Saviour,
while urged to do so by your dying mother? He was
then drawing you by the cords of tenderness which you
felt toward that sainted parent. If you have yielded to
these influences, you are happy in the Saviour's love; if
not, you have resisted the strivings of the Spirit: and God
says, "My Spirit shall not always strive with man."

The time will come, and you know not how soon, when
God will cease to draw you, and then you will be forever
undone. O yield now, while you are under the divine
influence.

> " Almost persuaded" now to believe ;
> " Almost persuaded" Christ to receive ;
>   Seems now some soul to say,
>   "Go, Spirit, go Thy way,
> Some more convenient day
>   On Thee I'll call."

" Almost persuaded," Come, come to-day;
" Almost persuaded," turn not away;
    Jesus invites you here,
    Angels are lingering near,
Prayers rise from hearts so dear:
      O wanderer, come!

" Almost persuaded," harvest is past!
" Almost persuaded," doom comes at last!
    " Almost" cannot avail;
    " Almost" is but to fail!
Sad, sad the bitter wail—
      " Almost—but lost!"

SERMON XX.

THE CHRISTIAN CHARACTERISTICS.

"And in the midst of the throne, and round about the throne, were four living creatures full of eyes before and behind. And the first creature was like a lion, and the second creature like a calf, and the third creature had a face as of a man, and the fourth creature was like a flying eagle." Revelation iv, 6, 7. (Revised Version.)

In the three chapters of this book which precede the one in which our text is found, we have a description of the state of the Christian Church as it existed in John's time, as revealed to him by the Son of God. This description is called the things that then were. After giving suitable direction and encouragement to the churches and their pastors, his attention was directed to a second vision, in which things were revealed which should transpire after that time—that is, things that should successively come to pass from the time of the vision until the mystery of God, respecting mankind on earth, should be accomplished. In this vision God is represented as seated upon his heavenly throne in the midst of his saints. His glorious majesty and infinite perfection are set forth in the most lively, beautiful, and expressive images that finite mind could possibly imagine. The picture includes a view of the church triumphant before the throne engaged in unceasing adoration and praise.

As no language of mine can equal that in which the beloved disciple paints this sublimely glorious and heavenly scenery, I transcribe his language: "After this I looked, and, behold, a door was opened in heaven: and the first voice which I heard was as it were a trumpet talking with me; which said, Come up hither, and I will show thee things which must be hereafter. And immediately I was in the Spirit: and, behold, a throne was set in heaven, and one sat on the throne. And he that sat was to look upon like a jasper and a sardine stone: and there was a rainbow round about the throne, in sight like unto an emerald. And round about the throne were four and twenty seats: and upon the seats I saw four and twenty elders sitting, clothed in white raiment; and they had on their heads crowns of gold. And out of the throne proceeded lightnings and thunderings and voices: and there were seven lamps of fire burning before the throne, which are the seven Spirits of God. And before the throne there was a sea of glass like unto crystal: and in the midst of the throne, and round about the throne, were four beasts full of eyes before and behind. And the first beast was like a lion, and the second beast like a calf, and the third beast had a face as a man, and the fourth beast was like a flying eagle. And the four beasts had each of them six wings about him; and they were full of eyes within: and they rest not day and night, saying, Holy, holy, holy, Lord God Almighty, which was, and is, and is to come. And when the beasts give glory and honor and thanks to him that sat on the throne, who liveth

for ever and ever, the four and twenty elders fall down
before him that sat on the throne, and worship him that
liveth for ever and ever, and cast their crowns before the
throne, saying, Thou art worthy, O Lord, to receive glory
and honor and power: for thou hast created all things,
and for thy pleasure they are and were created."

In this vision John beheld a door opened in heaven:
so it appeared to him; and he had the gratifying promise
of a further insight into the divine mystery. There are
several of these openings mentioned in this book, by each
of which John gained a new and more extended prospect. Here a door was opened, afterward the temple of
God in heaven (chaps. xi, 19; xv, 5), and still later heaven
itself was opened (chap. xix, 11). John was bidden to
ascend, which it appears he did immediately, not in body
but in spirit. "He beheld a throne sat in heaven." We
are not to understand this description as literal, but figurative. His mind received the impression of a picture
of Jehovah seated on a throne of majesty, arrayed in
robes of glory, as a king, governor, and judge. The appearance of three precious stones, connected with the rainbow, the lustre of which attracted the attention of the
evangelist, seem indicative of his purity, or righteousness, justice, mercy, and truth: and show, that in him
mercy and truth are met together; righteousness and
peace have kissed each other. The jasper is white, signifying his purity and righteousness. The sardine stone
is red, and denotes his justice, in executing vengeance
upon his enemies. The emerald is green, and betokens
mercy to the penitent. The rainbow signifies his truth
in keeping his covenant: he is true to all his engage-

ments. Around the throne, in a circular form, were four and twenty seats, upon which sat four and twenty elders. These, I think, represent the Old Testament church. Their robes seem to correspond with the patriarchal and Jewish costume, especially that of the Jewish priests: their harps and golden vials seem to indicate their connection with the tabernacle and temple worship. Their golden crowns indicated that they were made kings and priests unto God. Understanding the elders to represent the Old Testament church' I think we must regard the four beasts as a representation of the Christian Church.

Dr. Doddridge remarks, that it was a very unhappy mistake in our English translators to translate this word, beasts: it should have been translated "living creatures," as it is in the Revised Version. One had wings, and another the face of a man, neither of which belong to beasts. I, therefore, adopt the term "living creatures;" and shall consider them as representing the Christian Church. These were nearest the throne. Their number indicates universality, and corresponds with the Christian Church, which is to extend to all nations. The new song which they sang—"Thou hast redeemed us out of every kindred, and tongue, and people; and nation," would not well apply to the Jewish church, for it was composed of one nation only; much less to angels, who were not redeemed. The elders sang of creation, with which the ancient church was best acquainted, the living creatures sang of redeeming love.

I. Let us consider THE CHARACTERISTICS OF THE CHRISTIAN CHURCH, AS SET FORTH IN THE DESCRIPTION OF THESE LIVING CREATURES.

Some think that by the living creatures, the characteristics of the Christian Church at different periods is intended to be set forth; that in the first age, the Church was distinguished for undaunted courage; that in the second age, when the people of God were slain like sheep for the slaughter, the Church was distinguished for unwearied patience; that further on in its history, intelligence was its peculiar characteristic; and, finally, when all the enemies are overcome, and every obstacle removed, she will go forth upon wings as an eagle, extending her conquests to earth's remotest bounds. I think, however, that the picture is intended to represent the complete christian character: that the creatures named include a combination of characteristics, which should adorn every disciple of Christ.

1. The idea of *undaunted courage is set forth.*

" The first living creature was like a lion." How frequently this lion-like courage has been exemplified in the life and character of the people of God: undaunted they have gone forth, as it were, with their lives in their hands—few in number, but facing thousands. Forty days after the crucifixion of the Founder of the Christian religion, Peter stood up, in the city of His death, and boldly charged His death to the enmity of the Jews; and declared that God had raised Him from the dead. Kings, princes, and potentates forbade the disciples to speak in the name of Jesus; but they answered, " We should obey God rather than men," and continued to speak in his name. While in all civil matters, they both taught and practiced obedience to the ruling powers, yet in matters of religion, they regarded not the edicts of sovereigns,

Paul stood before Felix, Festus and Agrippa, and fearlessly professed his faith in the despised Nazarene. The disciples faced danger and death in the cause of their Master, and counted not their lives dear if spent in defence of the truth. Paul at Athens, the seat of science, charged the learned Grecians as being in the darkness of ignorance and superstition, and urged them to repent and embrace the light which is revealed in the Gospel. To king Agrippa, associated with his beautiful sister Bernice, he put truth so pointed that he drew from the king's lips the acknowledgment that he was almost persuaded to be a Christian.

To-day we see men and women of God, going forth as missionaries in foreign lands, bearing the lamp of truth into the dark regions of heathenism, regardless of danger—not with carnal weapons, but with weapons that are mighty, through God, in pulling down the strongholds of the devil: not by secret stratagem, but with open boldness.

2. The picture reminds us that *Christianity includes patience—unwearied patience.*

"The second creature was like a calf," (or ox.) Horses are sometimes balky, and mules grow stubborn; but not so with the ox: I have seen him when the load was heavy get down on his knees, and hang to it, until his eyes seemed ready to start from their sockets. There is also a quiet submissiveness in the well trained ox, that is not seen in other beasts of burden. Now patience is a most commendable virtue. We are thus admonished by the Apostle James: "Let patience have her perfect work, that ye may be entire, lacking nothing." He also refers us to the prophets, as an example of suffering and patience; and to Job, who endured to the end, and thereby secured the gracious favor of God. James v, 10, 11. Also, the Apostle Paul exhorts us to be imitators of those who, through faith and patience, inherited the promises· Speaking of the suffering and endurance of the Old Testament saints, he says, "they were stoned, they were sawn asunder, were tempted, were slain with the sword; they wandered about in sheepskins and goatskins, being destitute, afflicted, tormented; of whom the world was not worthy: they wandered in deserts, and in mountains, and in dens and caves of the earth." Hebrews xi, 37. Yet through all of this they possessed their souls in patience, and obtained a good report—were faithful to the end. These things being said of them, reminds us that patience especially becomes us as christians. How fully this virtue was displayed by the early christians is plainly seen in the history of the martyrs. Patient resignation to the will of God, under every dispensation of his providence, is, in our judgment, the capstone of christian perfection.

> "Who suffer with our Master here,
> They shall before his face appear,
> And by his side sit down ;
> To patient faith the praise is sure,
> And all that to the end endure
> The cross shall wear the crown."

The Captain of our salvation was made perfect by suffering; and we, to be conformed to him, must patiently endure our sufferings.

3. The figure in the text reminds us that *Christianity bears the marks of intelligence.*

The third living creature had the face of a man. The religion of Jesus is not a system of dark sayings, nor a mass of ambiguities, as were the responses of the heathen oracles: it is not superstition, nor fanaticism, nor cunningly-devised fables. It is truth capable of being demonstrated, and worthy of the deepest meditation, and the profoundest thought of the highest order of intelligence. We are told that the angels desired to look into it: yea, breaking off from the contemplation of every other object in God's dominion, they exhaust the utmost effort of their celestial powers in studying the mystery of redemption. It is the true wisdom, which cometh down from heaven—from God, the fountain or source of all knowledge. They who embrace it are not mad, as Festus supposed Paul to be. He, who had been so mad that he dwelt among the tombs in a nude state, cutting his flesh with stones and could not be held with chains, was brought by its power to sit at the feet of Jesus, clothed, and in his right mind. "Then shall we know," says the prophet, "if we follow on to know the Lord." There is no limit to the knowledge secured through the religion of Jesus: we shall reach the source whence knowledge flows in streams divine. The idea of intelligence is not only expressed by the face of a man, as a characteristic of one of the living creatures, but "they were full of eyes." It would be impossible to present the idea of intelligence more forcibly than by the representations in this vision. They were full of eyes round about and within. They had not only eyes without, but within also—to see them-selves. Those who only have eyes without, cannot see themselves. They can see everybody else, can detect the smallest defect in the character of others; but not in their own—can see a moat in their brother's eye, but not the beam in their own eye. The genuine christian has large self-knowledge: he discerns his own faults; can see wherein he is wrong; discovers evil in his own nature; studies and knows himself: finds the plague in his own heart, and rests not until it is removed. Light and knowledge, and their natural product—joy and peace, increaseth, wherever the religion of Jesus prevails. Everyerything beastly in humanity vanishes, as Christianity goes forth bearing on its face the beams of angelic intelligence.

4. But the representation also includes the idea of *unceasing activity.*

"The fourth creature was like a flying eagle." It is also said of the creatures, that they "rest not day and night, saying, Holy, holy, holy, Lord God Almighty, which was, and is, and is to come." They also had each six wings. It must be a dull mind that does not perceive the idea of activity in this three-fold figurative representation. Activity is the general order of created things. The subordinate planets cease not to perform their stupendous revolutions, and the burning orbs, which are suns and centers of planetary systems far from us, have each their path in unlimited space, over which they never cease to travel. Even Satan's crew are always busy. For it is written, "They have no rest that worship the beast." Mark the difference. The hosts of heaven rest not, but those who worship the beast have no rest. The heavenly hosts employ themselves in the delightful service of holy adoration. The hosts of hell are kept busy: they cannot rest; their agony forbids rest; tossed upon the bosom of a burning lake, they shift and turn, like one upon a bed of thorns, seeking ease or rest, but find it not. Even here on earth they have no rest; their master, the devil, keeps them busy. Some he employs in useless vanities—such as going to the circus, card-playing, dancing, and other vain amusements; others he employs on coarser, baser, and more daringly wicked work—such as slander, adultery, robbery, drunkenness and murder. They are not only kept busy, but they are kept in pain.

> " In pain they travel all their days
> To reach eternal woe."

If the wicked cannot rest on earth, or in the world of woe, and saints in heaven will not rest, or cease their holy exercise; surely saints on earth, or those groaning to be such, ought not to let their hands hang down, until they have done all in their power to bring themselves, and all others within their circle, into that meetness and perfectness of heart and life, which will insure the divine acceptance.

We are urged to activity by the flight of time. "My days," says Job, "are swifter than a weaver's shuttle." David says, "Thou hast my days as an hand breadth"—only four inches of time, but he reduces it still—"Mine age is as nothing before thee." But we are admonished, by the vast concerns that hang upon these fleeting moments. The immortal poet shall tell it:

"Lo! on a narrow neck of land,
Twixt two unbounded seas I stand,
Secure, insensible,
A point of time, a moment's space,
Removes me to that heavenly place,
Or shuts me up in hell."

Short as time is, our souls, if saved at all, must be saved while time lasts. Our eternal interests, if secured at all, must be secured while time lasts. We conclude with the following lines of poetry, which speak volumes:

"No room for mirth or trifling here,
For worldly hope, or worldly fear,
    If life so soon is gone;
If now the Judge is at the door,
And all mankind must stand before
    The inexorable throne!

O God, mine inmost soul convert,
And deeply on my thoughtful heart
    Eternal things impress :
Give me to feel their solemn weight,
And tremble on the brink of fate,
    And wake to righteousness.

Before me place in dread array,
The pomp of that tremendous day,
    When thou with clouds shall come
To judge the nations at thy bar ;
And tell me, Lord, shall I be there,
    To meet a joy doom?

No matter which my thoughts employ,
A moment's misery or joy,
    But, O! when both shall end,

Where shall I find my destined place?
Shall I my everlasting days
  With fiends or angels spend?

Nothing is worth a thought beneath,
But how I may escape that death
  That never, never dies!
How make mine own election sure,
And when I fail on earth, secure
  A mansion in the skies.

Jesus, vouchsafe a pitying;
Be thou my guide, be thou my way
  To glorious happiness.
Ah! write the pardon on my heart,
And whenso'er I hence depart,
  Let me depart in peace."

SERMON XXI.

DAVID'S ROOT AND OFFSPRING, OR VENUS IN THE APOCALYPSE.

"I am the root and offspring of David, the bright, the morning star." Revelation xxii, 16. (Revised Version.)

The human vocabulary has been exhausted in vain attempts to find language, sufficiently expressive, to set forth the characteristics of the world's Redeemer. Words are too sparse, and language inadequate, to express the beauty, the glory, the wisdom, the power and the grace of this immutable and incomprehensible Being who appears as our Daysman. The inspired penmen have employed the most beautiful and expressive figures that heaven and earth afford, to aid our limited comprehension; and yet, they have failed, as all finite effort must fail, to grasp the Infinite. He is the " Branch," the " Dayspring," the " Plant of Renown "; a " Rock," a " Refuge," a " High Tower," a " Shield," a " Hiding Place," a "Shelter from the Storm," a " Covert "; the " Shadow of a Great Rock in a Weary Land," the " Way, the Truth and the Life," the " Rose of Sharon," the " Lilly of the Valley," the " Fairest among Thousands," and the " Altogether Lovely." In the text he is the " Root and Offspring of David, the Bright, the Morning Star."

The figures in the text are used by Jesus himself. He had employed an angel to show many things unto his servant John, but he came forth himself to close up the prophecy. He introduces himself as the Alpha and Omega, but this language is not sufficiently broad and expressive: he, therefore, adds the figures in the text. "I Jesus have sent my angel to testify unto you these things in the churches. I am the root and offspring of David, the bright, the morning star."

The first figure is expressive of the two-fold character of Jesus as God and man—"the root and offspring." If he possessed but one nature, and that the divine, he might be the root, but not the offspring of David. If he had but one nature, and that the human, he might be the offspring, but not the root of David. In his divine nature, he is the root, the source, the first, the underlying principle; hidden from view, but upholding and sustaining all things. As a root, he sends forth the bough and branches of the visible creation—unseen, but as surely sustaining all things as the unseen root sustains the tree. He is elsewhere spoken of as God's fellow and companion; his possession in the beginning of his way, before his works of old—before the mountains were brought forth, before time was born, or light conceived. We feel back through countless ages, but cannot touch the beginning of his way: we throw our thoughts back through the mental telescope, back, back, back! and attempt in vain to survey the eternal regions, in which he hides himself with curtains too thick for mortal thoughts to pierce. He is the Everlasting Father and Eternal Son, the great First Cause of all things,

Himself uncaused and eternal. He is also the offspring of David—sprang from David. This eternal, self-exist-ing Being condescended to appear in human form, as the descendant of a mortal. He, who in the beginning was with God, and was God, became flesh and dwelt among us in mortal form—was really and truly man, with all human infirmities, sin excepted. As a man, he was hungry, thirsty, and weary—as a man, he ate and slept. He had the human passions of love, desire, fear, sorrow and joy. He was really and truly man—had a human body, and a human soul and spirit; had a will of his own, separate from, but in all things yielding to that of his Father. He said to his Father, "Not as I will, but as thou wilt." That he might die for us, he took upon himself our nature in all its weakness and infirmity, ex-cept sin. Like Adam, "sufficient to have stood, yet free to fall." Hence he is called "the second Adam."·

The other figure in the text, "the bright, the morning star," is a symbol of his subordinate character—the char-acter he assumed, in the form of a servant, to become our Daysman. In his divine nature, he is the Eternal Son. As such, the planet referred to would not fitly represent him: the sun would be a better figure. The star re-ferred to is the planet Venus, which, like our own planet, the earth, is a dark body, which shines only by reflection. If Venus is inhabited, (as is most likely,) to its inhabi-tants the earth appears as Venus does to us, except much brighter. In the first place, the earth is larger; and sec-ondly, it having an orbit outside of Venus, the inhabi-tants of that planet view its whole illuminated surface, when at its nearest point; at which time it must reflect a light most beautiful to behold. We only see the whole illuminated surface of Venus when it is farthest from us: when it is on the other side of the sun, a hundred and fifty-six million miles away. When at its nearest point to us, we only see its rim, like the new moon. Being between us and the sun, most of its illuminated surface is turned from us.

This star, or planet, is a fit emblem of the human nature of Jesus. The beams which occasionally shone out from him were the reflection of the rays of his Father's glory. The true character of Venus is only seen when in transit across the sun's disc. Its illuminated side is then wholly turned from us, and it is seen in its true character as a dark body. Likewise, the human nature of Jesus was most clearly seen when he hung upon the cross, when the rays of the divine glory were wholly withdrawn from our view, and his lifeless body hung between the heavens and the earth. His suffering and death were convincing evidences of his humanity, while his miracles testified of his divinity, especially the last great miracle by which he broke the bars of death, bore away its gates, spoiled principalities and powers, drew out death's sting, snatched victory from the grave, and came forth as the spoiler of hell and conqueror of death, and exulting in his possession of universal dominion. These reflected rays of the divine glory, however, were frequently displayed, in a greater or less degree, by the person of Jesus, through the whole period of his incarnation. It was the rays of the divine glory, reflected by him, that brightened the morning of his advent—amid which light angels broke the silence, and to the astonished ears of.

Bethlehem-shepherds proclaimed his birth in songs of praise :

> "Shepherds, rejoice, lift up your eyes
> And send your fears away;
> News from the regions of the skies,
> Salvation's born to-day."

" For unto you is born, in the city of David, a Saviour, which is Christ the Lord."

I cannot think that the manger and the swaddling clothes in which they were to find the child wrapped, were alone the sign to which the angel alluded ; but also the light—the divine glory, which he bid them not to fear—this, no doubt, illuminated their path, and guided them to the place where the young child was. It was the rays of divine glory reflected by him that caught the attention of the far-off eastern wise men, and guided them to Jerusalem, to which they came, saying, " Where is he that is born king of the Jews, for we have seen his star in the east, and have come to worship him." We are not to understand that they saw this star to the east of them ; but that they were in the east when they first saw it, westward from them. Looking toward the west, they discovered a light which appeared to them as a star, which they had never noticed before. They called it his star, and no doubt it was a brightness emanating from him : possibly the same that appeared to the shepherds. It was a sure guide, designating the very spot where he dwelt. Just before they reached Jerusalem, its rays were withdrawn, that they might inquire, and thus announce his birth to the reigning king. So soon as the divine purpose was accomplished, and they had started to Bethlehem, they again beheld the light, which differing from other stars, to which you never seem to get nearer, it stood over the place where the young child was, and guided them to the very spot, which, when they reached, they found not a star, but the infant Jesus, amid the splendor of divine glory. The lustre of this brightness distinguished him so clearly, that, had there been a thousand children present, they would have known this one to be the Messiah, the Christ—the anointed of God. The divine rays were reflected by him, when at twelve years old, he sat in the temple among the doctors, asking and answering questions with such wisdom and grace that all who heard him were astonished.

In the miracles of Jesus also, as before mentioned, his divinity shone forth. Before the splendor of his divine power, darkness fled, and a flood of light rushed into the eyes of those who were born blind. Infirmities retreated at the approach of his rays; diseases sought in vain for a hiding place from his all healing power, and icy death itself melted away before the lustre of his brightness.

A display of divine wisdom was exhibited in the answers of Jesus to those who attempted to catch him in his words. Behold the Scribes and Pharisees, with a woman, an adulteress; they have brought her for him to judge, that they may accuse him; but they find themselves condemned, and the woman left without an accuser. They thought to place him, either in the attitude of contradicting Moses, which would have moved the enmity of all who revered the memory of that great prophet,

historian and law-giver—or of assuming the functions of
a magistrate, which would have brought the Romans
down upon him—or of refusing to take cognizance of the
case, which would have been inconsistent with his kingly-
claims. They thought they had him completely cornered, and therefore pressed him for a decision. They
declared the case to be a clear one, the woman was taken
in the very act, and could make no defence. There was
nothing left but to decide as to what disposition should
be made of her. "Now Moses in the law commanded
that such should be stoned, what sayeth thou?" When
he stooped down and wrote upon the ground as though
he heard them not, they pressed him for an answer with
an energy which seemed to be inspired by a feeling of
assured triumph; but when he arose, he easily swept
away the webs they had woven around him. He neither
contradicted Moses, nor assumed the authority of a magistrate, nor denied his authority in the matter; but he
demanded that the innocent should begin the execution
which they said the law required. "He that is without
sin among you, let him first cast a stone at her." At
this their guilty heads went down, and they retired, confounded by his wisdom and penetrating power; and the
woman was left, without an accuser; alone with Jesus,
to hear, in accents of matchless tenderness, the encour-
aging words, "Go in peace and sin no more." In company with the Herodians, the Pharisees made a second
great effort to catch him in his words: they came with
a question about the tribute money, and thought they
had him securely cornered. "Is it lawful to give tribute
to Cæsar or not?" This, it seems, they thought was not

sufficiently direct, as he might have simply referred them to the law, hence, they quickly added, " Shall we give, or shall we not give? " Mark xii, 14, 15. If he had said that they should give tribute, they would have said that he was a pretty king, teaching his subjects to pay tribute to another! The throne of David, which it was promised that Messiah should restore, would not be restored, in its former grandeur, so long as they were tributary to a foreign power, and besides this, the people looked upon the tribute as a burden under which they groaned; and they held those in contempt who justified it. We ourselves know in what contempt our own revenue officers are held by many. On the other hand, if he had said they should not pay tribute, they would have accused him before the Roman court. It will be remembered, that this accusation was brought against him before Pilate, but was not sustained. If they could have proven this, they would have had a case against him. Thus it will be seen that they felt sure of bringing him into discredit with either the Romans or the multitude. But his wisdom compelled them to decide the question themselves, by acknowledging that the tribute money belonged to Cæsar; and it necessarily followed that Cæsar must have his own :—" Render unto Cæsar the things that are Cæsar's, and unto God the things that are God's." In other words, if by your wickedness you have fallen under Cæsar's subjection, if you are reminded of that subjection by every financial transaction, if you have no currency but Cæsar's, both the laws of God and man require that you should support the power that protects you and provides the means of intercourse with your

13

neighbors. But remember that, notwithstanding this, there are also duties which you owe to God, the performing of which alone will relieve you of the burdens under which you groan.

The Scribes, Pharisees and Herodians having been silenced by his wisdom, the Sadducees came next, with a question by which they thought to render the doctrine of a future state ridiculous. The Sadducees disputed the doctrine of the resurrection, and a future state, and held that there was neither angel nor spirit. Coming to Jesus, they recited the law of Moses, which required a man to marry the widow of his deceased brother, in case the brother died childless : they named a case, in which under this law seven brothers had married one woman, all of whom had died, leaving no children, and last of all the woman died also. They asked : " In the resurrection, when they shall rise, whose wife shall she be of them, for they all had her to wife ?" They, no doubt, thought they had pictured a delightful heaven, where seven men would be quarreling over one woman ! But he answered, " Do ye not therefore err, because ye do not know the Scriptures, neither the power of God ?" They had not known that in the world to come they don't need to marry. Here sickness wastes, and death depopulates, and marriage is necessary to maintain the human species. There death is unknown : sickness, sorrow and pain have no place ; for the heavenly atmosphere is untainted with disease, and marriage is unnecessary to maintain the population of the better country. Neither did they know the power of God. He who at the beginning made two natures out of one, can as easily transform them again, and give them an angelic nature, who neither marry, nor are given in marriage, " For in the resurrection they neither marry, nor are given in marriage, but are as the angels of God in heaven." Matt. xxii, 30. He then turned upon the Sadducees, and said: " But as touching the resurrection of the dead, have ye not read that which was spoken unto you by God, saying, I am the God of Abraham, and the God of Isaac, and the God of Jacob? God is not the God of the dead, but of the living." Then Abraham, Isaac and Jacob are living, and as they live, we shall live also. After this we are told, they asked him no more questions, and thus acknowledged themselves confounded by his wisdom.

But he is the Bright and Morning Star. Venus is pre-eminently the bright morning star; appearing as such for months at a time, rising a little before the sun. Mercury is so near to the sun that it is seldom seen. Mars, Jupiter and Saturn, having orbits outside of the earth, arise at all hours of the night, and at times shine all night long; their rising and setting, therefore, do not mark any particular period of the night. But Venus, having an orbit inside of ours, in making its journey around the sun, it never rises over about three hours above our horizon, and therefore never rises more than three hours ahead of the sun: its average being only one hour and a half ahead of the sun ; hence, when it rises, we know that day is coming—that its dawn will soon appear. It is truly the certain harbinger of day. Other lights may mislead, deceive and disappoint us, but it, never! When it arises, we know that the sunlight will soon follow. It is the forerunner, the usher, the introducer of day. Now

Jesus may be called the Morning Star, because he introduced the first ray of hope into this sin-cursed world.
Man had lost the divine image and favor, the last ray of
hope had faded from his soul, and there was nothing but
a fearful looking for the blackness of eternal darkness—
a darkness so dense that no star was seen, nor was there
hope of a morning to follow. In the midst of this darkness the Morning Star of hope arose out of the promise:
" The seed of the woman shall bruise the serpent's head."
This promise gave hope to a lost world: it was the harbinger of the day dawn; it ushered in the morning of redemption; it introduced the day of salvation, and proclaimed the approach of the dayspring from on high. In
its light the patriarchs walked: its rays illuminated their
path, and cheered them on their journey to the Celestial
City. As the Morning Star, Jesus ushered in the day of
freedom from the rigor of the legal economy. What a
burdensome system that was; what an almost endless
round of ceremonies, of new-moon feasts, and many kinds
of offerings, of fasts, affliction of soul, and long and te-
dious journeys to the place of worship. These were types
of the one offering for sin, of the intense agony of him
who should be bruised for our iniquity, upon whom our
chastisement should fall, and by whose stripes we should
be healed. His coming in the flesh lifted the burden of
these rites and ceremonies from our shoulders, and proclaimed the day of Gospel liberty—a day in which we
have no need to make a pilgrimage to some high mountain, or to Jerusalem to worship, but wherever two or
three are assembled, in his name, truly believing, there

we may expect his presence, yea, wherever a holy aspiration ascends from a sincere heart, the answer of peace is assured ;

> " Not heaven's wide range of hallow'd space
> Jehovah's presence can confine;
> Nor angels' claim restrain his grace,
> Whose glories through creation shine.
>
> It beam'd on Eden's guilty days,
> And traced redemption's wondrous plan:
> From Calvary, in brightest rays,
> It glowed to guide benighted man.
>
> Its sacred shrine it fixes there,
> Where two or three are met to raise
> Their holy hands in humble prayer,
> Or tune their hearts to grateful praise."

In this glorious day, we have no need to wait at the pool for the troubling of the water, but a physician awaits the approach of the impotent folk.

> " Free from the law, oh happy condition,
> The star hath appeared and there is remission,
> No burdensome rite henceforth on us laid,
> For Jesus the price of redemption hath paid."

As the Bright and Morning Star, he ushers into the soul, the light of joy and peace. What darkness envelopes and fills the soul of the sinner! He is represented by the Great Teacher, as sitting in darkness, in the valley and shadow of death—in gross darkness. And we who have been called out of darkness into God's marvelous light, can testify how dark that night of sin was, and

with what rapture we beheld the rising of the Morning
Star. As its glorious rays brightened the morning of our
espousal, we sang:

> " In darkest shades, when he appeared,
>   My dawning was begun:
>   He is my soul's bright morning star,
>   And he my rising sun,"

I can think of nothing more appropriate, with which
to close this discourse, than the closing words of Jesus,
to the beloved disciple—the prophetic valedictory: "And
he saith unto me, Seal not up the words of the prophecy
of this book; for the time is at hand. He that is righteous, let him be righteous still : and he that is filthy, let
him be made filthy still; and he that is holy, let him
be made holy still. Behold, I come quickly; and my
reward is with me, to render to each man according as
his work is. I am Alpha and Omega, the first and the
last, the beginning and the end. Blessed are they that
wash their robes, that they may have a right to come to
the tree of life, and may enter in by the gates into the
city. Without are the dogs, and sorcerers, and fornica-
tors, and murderers, and idolaters, and every one that
loveth and maketh a lie. I Jesus have sent mine angel
to testify unto you these things for the churches. I am
the root and offspring of David, the bright and morning
star. The Spirit and the bride say, Come. And he that
heareth, let him say, Come. And he that is athirst, let
him come: he that will, let him take of the water of life
freely. I testify unto every man that heareth the words
of the prophecy of this book, If any man shall add unto

them, God shall add unto him the plagues which are written in this book: and if any man shall take away from
the words of the book of this prophecy, God shall take
away his part from the tree of life, and out of the holy
city, which are written in this book.   He which testifieth
these things saith, Yea; I come quickly.   Amen: come,
Lord Jesus.   The grace of our Lord Jesus Christ be with
all the saints.   Amen."

THE END.

BISHOP S. T. JONES. BISHOP J. J. MOORE.

BISHOP J. P. THOMPSON. BISHOP THOS. H. LOMAX.

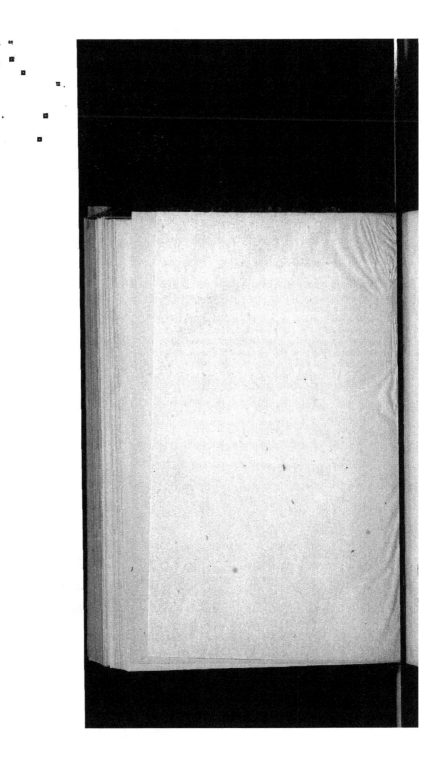

BISHOP S. T. JONES.

BISHOP J. J. MOORE.

BISHOP J. P. THOMPSON.

BISHOP THOS. H. LOMAX.

APPENDIX.

SERMON I.

THE UNPARDONABLE SIN.

BY BISHOP J. J. MOORE, D. D.

"Verily, I say unto you, All sins shall be forgiven unto the sons
of men, and blasphemies wherewith soever they shall blaspheme:
but he that shall blaspheme against the Holy Ghost, hath never
forgiveness." Mark iii, 28, 29.

Upon this subject men and women's minds have been
much exercised. The great difficulty that has attended
a proper solution of this grave subject, has arisen from
the confounding of passages of Scripture referring to other
classes of sins, with this sin, to which the text refers, and
from not properly understanding the nature of the sin
as named in the text.

There are three classes of sins in which men may put
themselves beyond God's pardoning mercy in this life,
beside the sin referred to in the text.

I. There is the SIN UNTO DEATH; as referred to in 1 John
v, 16, "If any man see his brother sin a sin, which is not
unto death, he shall ask, and he shall give him life for
them that sin not unto death. There is a sin unto death:
I do not say he shall pray for it." This same class of
sins is alluded to in Numbers v, 27, 30, 31: "And if a

soul sin through ignorance, * * the priest shall make an atonement for the soul when he sinneth by ignorance, before the Lord, and it (his sin) shall be forgiven him. But the soul that doeth ought presumptuously, * * that soul shall be cut off from among his people." In the passage in 1 John v, 16, the Apostle has no reference to the sin of blasphemy against the Holy Ghost, as alluded to by the Saviour in the text. Although it is, or was a sin that put the perpetrator beyond a chance of being forgiven, yet it was not the sin of blasphemy that Christ sealed with eternal damnation. This sin unto death, which many confound with the sin of blasphemy against the Holy Ghost, has an exemplification in the case of the prophet or man of God sent by the Lord to reprimand Jeroboam, the King of Israel, for his practicing idolatry at Bethel. See 1st Kings xiii, 17—24. This man of God sent to Bethel was instructed by the Lord, when he had delivered his message, not to tarry at Bethel, nor eat bread, nor drink water in the place, and not to return by the same way he came. There was an old lying prophet at Bethel, who heard of the man of God that had delivered the message to Jeroboam : his sons were present at the altars of worship or sacrifices at Bethel ; they saw all that had transpired, and told their father (the lying prophet), all that had happened. The old lying prophet went to bring the man of God back to eat with him. The man of God disobeyed the divine injunctions given him by the Lord, not to eat bread nor drink water in that place, but he both eat bread and drank water. Thus disobeying the Lord, God prepared a lion, and as

the disobedient prophet started from the old lying prophet's house to go on his way home, the lion met him and
slew him in the highway.

This sin of disobedience was immediately punished
with death; therefore it was a sin unto death, or a single
sin that the Lord punished with death. In the case of
Ananias and Sapphira, (Acts v, 1,) we have two other
instances where a single sin was punished with immediate death—their sin of lying unto the Holy Ghost. They
told a wilful lie to God's apostles about their earthly possessions. These Apostles were acting under the power of
inspiration—were acting in Christ's stead, under the di-
rections of the Holy Spirit, therefore in lying unto the
Apostles, Ananias and Sapphira lied unto God, and the
Lord punished them with death, and gave them no space
for repentance. In the case of the man of God in 1 Kings
xiii, 17—24, he was acting under the immediate influence
of the Holy Spirit, yet disobeyed God, made the sin at
once damnable, and visited immediate retribution upon
the offender, not allowing mercy unto him. In the case
of Ananias and Sapphira their lie was told, notwithstanding they were under the influence of the Holy Ghost,
therefore it was a damnable sin, and beyond mercy;
hence, none but such as were circumstanced as they were
could sin the sin unto death. It required a person to be
favored with the highest evidence of the influence of the
Holy Spirit to sin the single sin unto death.

2. There is another condition in sin, in which men may
place themselves beyond God's pardoning mercy in this
life; which condition is sometimes confounded with the
case of the sin of blasphemy against the Holy Ghost, or

the sin referred to in our text, pronounced by Christ as unpardonable. This sinful condition, to which we here allude, or act of sin, is that of APOSTASY. This sin is treated by the Apostle in Hebrews vi, 4—8: "For it is impossible for those who were once enlightened, and have tasted of the heavenly gift, and were made partakers of the *Holy Ghost*, and have tasted of the *good word of God*, and the *powers* of the world to come, if they shall fall away, to renew them again unto repentance." See Luke xi, 24, on this subject. As this condition of sin, spoken of by Paul in the Scripture just read, excites anxiety among many common backsliders, I would here say that there was a great difference between those apostates alluded to by Paul, and common blacksliders of God's church in this day. Common backsliders now do not occupy the position those Jewish converts did; hence apostasy, or common backsliding now, is not attended with the impossibility of repentance as then. The Christians may now, as was the case of the Jewish converts, be " *enlightened*," and they may have tasted of the " *heavenly gift*," and of the " *good word of God*," and of the " *powers of the world to come*," as did the Jews when converted, but we are not made partakers of the Holy Ghost in the sense they were. Hence, we can't apostatize as they did, being differently circumstanced religiously. Apostasy with the Jew was the falling away of Christian converts, who had been favored with the miraculous demonstrations of God's power under two dispensations of his grace—a people who had been chosen to peculiar divine favors. Those whom the Apostle warns against the sin of apostasy, were favored with the testimony of those who were the living

witnesses of Christ's incarnation: they had seen and
handled the Messiah before and after his death and resurrection. They had witnessed the Church's miracle-
working endowments. They had been invested with all
the saving power with which the Christian Church is invested, even to the resurrection power. Upon them was
bestowed heaven's highest gift, the special gift of the Holy
Ghost, by the laying on of hands, which Christians now
do not enjoy. Is it any wonder, if they wilfully fell
away from this condition, that they could be renewed
unto repentance again? This was a very different state
from that of common backsliding, which is not a state of
sin on which the door of mercy is closed: the backslider,
therefore, may find pardon, if he will return to his offended Saviour: he is not in a condition to commit the
unpardonable sin, which Jesus seals with damnation in
the text. "Turn, O backsliding children, saith the Lord.
Return, ye backsliding children, and I will heal your
backslidings." Jeremiah lii, 14, 22.

3. We come next to consider what is called the UN-
PARDONABLE SIN, or the SIN OF BLASPHEMY AGAINST THE
HOLY GHOST—the sin which the Saviour declares in the
text would never be pardoned. This is the sin that
those that are solicitous about it, want explained. In
considering this grave question, we must not simply take
into account the mere act of blaspheming against the
Holy Ghost, which was in itself, according to the common meaning of the term, speaking irreverently of the
Holy Spirit, or the Deity, or Holy One. So far as the
simple act is concerned, persons might blaspheme against
the Holy Ghost, or Holy Spirit, and yet be within reach

of pardoning mercy. It was the *nature of the act of blasphemy*, that caused Christ to seal it with eternal retribution. By the nature of the act, we mean two things: first, the feeling, or disposition of heart, that prompts to do the act; and secondly, the circumstances with which the act stood connected.

First, we notice the feeling or disposition that incited them to that act of blasphemy.

(1.) The feeling of *malevolence or extreme hatred:* as the Scripture states, "They hated me without a cause."

(2.) They were prompted by a spirit of *arrogance or pride*. They were too proud to admit the divine work of the Saviour.

(3.) It was prompted by a *deliberate, determinate obstinacy*, to resist every evidence of Christ's being the Son of God.

First, it was prompted by falsifying their convictions, declaring what, in their minds, they did not really believe and feel in their hearts—that the Saviour cast out those evil spirits by the prince of devils: their knowledge and conscience told them better.

Secondly, let us notice some of the peculiar circumstances connected with their religious experience, that added to the enormity of the act.

(1.) They had been favored with the highest developments of God's miracle-working power in their behalf. They had seen and confessed the works of the Holy Spirit —confessed His power in other instances, which they now blaspheme.

(2.) They here blasphemously deny the highest attestation of the divinity of Christ.

(3.) No people ever have had God's special and supernatural interposition in their behalf, as had the Jews, yet they presumed to pour out blasphemy in God's face, because it was uttered in the face of Jesus Christ. Those are the aggravations of that awful sin of blasphemy against the Holy Ghost, that Jesus sealed with eternal damnation. This sin none but a Jew was circumstanced to commit; therefore, men and women need not be solicitous about committing it now.

But there is a condition, or state of sin, into which men may place themselves in this life, and put themselves beyond God's pardoning mercy. That is the state of REPROBACY. Men and women may reach this state in sin, and still remain on earth for a time. This condition is alluded to in various passages of Scriptures. Prov. i, 22—30: "How long, ye simple ones, will ye love simplicity? and the scorners delight in their scorning, and fools hate knowledge? Turn you at my reproof: behold, I will pour out my Spirit unto you, I will make known my words unto you. Because I have called, and ye refused; I have stretched out my hand, and no man regarded; but have set at naught all my counsel, and would none of my reproof. I also will laugh at your calamity; I will mock when your fear cometh; when your fear cometh as desolation, and your destruction cometh as a whirlwind; when distress and anguish cometh upon you. Then shall they call upon me, but I will not answer; they shall seek me early, but they shall not find me: for that they hated knowledge, and did not choose the fear of the Lord." Again we have this condition of sin referred to in 2 Thess. ii, 11, 12: "And for this cause

God shall send them strong delusion, that they should believe a lie: that they all might be damned who believed not the truth, but had pleasure in unrighteousness." Again in Rom. i, 28: " And even as they did not like to retain God in their knowledge, God gave them over to a reprobate mind." Again in 2 Cor. xiii, 5: " Know ye not your ownselves, how that Jesus Christ is in you, except ye be reprobates?" Luke xiii, 34, 35: "O Jerusalem, Jerusalem, which killeth the prophets, * * behold your house is left unto you desolate." ·

This is a condition that sinners in these days can fall into. It is a state of sin that not only individuals have reached, but the antideluvian world of mankind reached this condition. It is a state of sin that nations have reached ; and there could be with them nothing but the certain fearful looking for of the fiery indignation of God. This is a state into which every sinner living can reach by often rejecting God's proffered mercy. Heb. x, 22. That men may not procrastinate their acceptance of mercy, and get beyond the reach of pardoning mercy, a warning is given them in Proverbs xxix, 1: " He that being often reproved hardeneth his neck, shall suddenly be destroyed, and that without remedy." This is a loud warning voice to sinners to shun the sin of *reprobacy,* which is the sin that fills up their cup of iniquity, which seals their fate, putting them beyond God's pardoning mercy, as were those that blasphemed against the Holy Ghost.

SERMON II.

THE FIRST PAIR BANISHED,

BY BISHOP J. P. THOMPSON.

"He drove out the man." Genesis iii, 24.

Never was there a sight so solemn, or a scene so mournful, as that displayed in the banishment of man from the garden of the Lord. The sentence had been heard, but still they were unapprized that banishment awaited them. They had learned that they were doomed to toil and to die, but they doubtless consoled themselves with the reflection that they might spend their Sabbaths amid the bowers of Eden and repose at night within the sacred enclosure, or rest at noon beneath its ample shades: but alas! they discovered that they were soon to be hurried away to parts unknown. The preparations which were being made by Deity himself for clothing them with coats of skin, betrayed a purpose to send them forth to less salubrious climes to a rigor in which the fig-leaf covering of Eden would not protect them. "Unto Adam and to his wife did the Lord God make coats of skin and clothed them." How changed their condition! Thus rudely clad, they stood as silent spectators of this mysterious work of Deity, whose wrath seemed strangely mingled with compassion. They queried the meaning; what need of clothing beyond the fig-leaf, where chilling winds had never blown, and frost had never nipped the virgin flowers that-bloomed on the plains or skirted the rivers of Eden? They doubtless guessed as to the designs of God, and longed to know the worst. A hush most deeply solemn was in the garden—a stillness pervaded the earth and the sky. No sound was heard save only a moan of distress, mingled with a sound of confusion in the breeze, which came over from the world of animals among the neighboring hills that seemed portentous of evils before unknown. On the far-off sky the first dark clouds were seen. The first storm gathered thick and fast—the lightnings, it may be, played on its bosom. New-born thunders shook the heavens, but in the garden all was calm. On golden pinions angels gathered among the trees while God in silence prepared to drive them forth into the world of tempests without the gates of Paradise, which was then to them forever lost. The man looked on the woman—her glory had departed; with anxious solicitude she returned the gaze upon the man, and he was a fallen monarch! How appalling the scene! They fain would have talked of the thrilling scenes which were enacting around them; but they were culprits and dare not speak. Indeed, no time had been allowed them for consultation, from the time they had first partaken of the forbidden fruit until the time of their condemnation. Step by step they had been hurried from their hiding place in the garden to their trial, their sentence and their banishment.

New scenes were about to be revealed; new trials

awaited them, and new developments of wrath were soon
to be disclosed, and still no time was afforded for consultation. Amid the trees a Trinity were seen in council
as to the manner of disposing of the culprits, whose lives
had been spared by the interposition of the promised
seed. "And the Lord God said, Behold the man is become as one of us, to know good and evil : and now, lest
he put forth his hand, and take also of the tree of life,
and eat, and live forever ; therefore the Lord God sent
him forth from the garden of Eden, to till the ground
from which he was taken. So he drove out the man."
Until then, perhaps, they had never ventured beyond the
gates of Paradise, but now the Deity, with angels and
cherubim who thronged the sacred place, prepared to
conduct them to the world beyond. With despairing
look they gazed upon the much loved spot, then turned
away in all the agonies of despair, and slowly and with
faltering step retired to the world of their future toil.
The sun, perhaps, was just retiring from the western sky,
when the guilty pair passed out of their native Paradise,
to return no more. How solemn their reflection as they
cast a lingering look upon their forfeited inheritance,
How lonely the spell that came over them, when they
saw the glittering trains of the Almighty disappearing
in the distance, while they, in solitude, were left upon
the untented field, with no other covering than the deep
blue sky ! A time for reflection had arrived, the culprits
were alone in a state of banishment from their native
home. No angel voice was heard ; no whispers of mercy
were in the breeze ! They felt that they were banished
in a strange land with none to help and none to pity,

Never did solitude appear less charming, and yet no way
of escape was seen. They fain would have ventured back,
but God had driven them forth, and they knew they could
not return, and to make the attempt would be to incur
his greater displeasure.   The night approached; the
beasts of the field were reposing in slumber; all nature
was hushed in silence; no sound was heard save now and
then perchance the growl of the tiger as he passed, the
howl of the wolf among the neighboring hills, or the
lonely hoot or startling shriek of the owl of the wilderness. The world around them was desolate. Thistles and
thorns were the product of the soil, and rank and abundant did they grow. No bowers of peace were there.
No bow of promise was on the cloud. No gentle mur-
murings of the brooks of Paradise were heard.   The stars
were brightly twinkling in the distant sky; but to them
they had no charms, as they only disclosed the barren
waste of the sin-cursed world, with which they were
surrounded. Gloomy beyond description were their reflections, as they mutely sat upon the ground.   They
remembered the pleasures of Paradise from which they
had been driven—their nightly rambles amid its bowers
—their fearless star-light musings and unbroken slum-
bers within its walls. But with respect to these, they
were then as those who dreamed. They could scarcely
realize, while retrospecting their former glory, riches, and
power, that they were then reduced to poverty, toil, and
peril, in a state of lonely exile from that glorious kingdom
over which the Almighty had so recently given them
dominion. They fain would have fancied it all a dream;
but alas! the anguish of spirit they felt, the goadings of

conscience they endured, and the damp and chill which distressed them, demonstrated clearly that all was lost. With sleepless vigilance they watched the foes with which they were surrounded, and longed for the approach of day. Angels, it seems to us, might well have wept, when silently gazing on the banished pair, as they nerved themselves to resist the first pangs of their depraved moral nature, and the first sorrow of their fallen state. With sleep they struggled as with a foe, for they did not dare to slumber, as the moan of death to them, seemed sounding in every coming breeze, in the far-off heavens. The glittering spheres were wheeling, and glowing, then as now; but that with them was not the moment for meditating upon nature's beauties. Their thoughts were turned upon themselves—reflections upon their own melancholy future held pre-eminence, and a burden of grief, almost intolerable, overwhelmed them. Bitter were their recollections of the past, and bitter the tears that were shed for the ruin they had wrought upon themselves and the unborn millions of the race for all ages then to come, O! what a night was that first spent beyond the gates of Paradise! Crushed hopes and tormenting fears were blended with bodily pain, from fatigue and exposure to the damps of earth and the piercing chills of the night-winds of heaven. Among all the stars that twinkled in the dusky depths of the sky, there was to them no star of hope—no gleam of joy. They watched the seemingly slugglish movements of the spheres and longed for day, that they might see the worst of the untried theatre assigned them, and seek some means of safety and support.

The day dawn came! With what tears of joy they saw

the coming morn! as the sun's first beams gilded the eastern sky—as the king of day arose, and nature stood forth revealed to the eye of man. But oh! how changed! The earth was cursed; weeds and briers sprang forth from the ground where once the lilly grew, and the guilty pair were compelled to eat the herbs of the field for their morning repast. They thought of the fruits of the garden, and resolved to return and risk the vengeance of God rather than perish in the wilderness world with which they were surrounded. Slowly and with anxious solicitude they retraced their steps. In the distance they beheld the garden of the Lord, and lo! it was in full bloom as in days gone by. To it the curse had not extended. Its trees, as at first, were bending with fruits; its fountains were gushing and flowing amid its bowers; in the east of the garden was the Tree of Life, and thither they bent their way, with joyful expectation of partaking of its fruit that they might live forever. But suddenly they paused, as though some danger threatened! A sentinel was there! Grim and terrible he appeared; a flaming sword was in his hand and fiery indignation in his eye. They retreated from this awful presence, and the last ray of hope was gone.

This awful banishment is recorded for our instruction and improvement. This was the punishment inflicted for the first act of human disobedience. In it, God gives us the first picture of the exceeding sinfulness of sin—a picture painted by the hand of Infinite Purity, and displaying in fearful colors the evils of disobedience. If by this one sin, the original Paradise was forever lost, we have much cause for care, lest there should be in us a spirit of disobedience, producing presumption, which may rob us of the promised inheritance—the Eden on, high, where the Tree of Life, laden with immortal fruits, flourishes on either side of the river.

May God grant unto each of you grace to listen to the warning voice, to give earnest heed to the importance of obedience, as designed to be taught by the historical fact we have briefly delineated ; that you may finally be admitted to the everlasting enjoyment of that Paradise which the second Adam has prepared for all who are partakers of His nature.

Grace, mercy, and peace, be with you, and keep you in the love of God the Father. Amen.

SERMON III.

THE LOVE OF GOD—ITS OBJECTS, GIFT AND DESIGN.

BY BISHOP THOMAS H. LOMAX.

"For God so loved the world, that he gave his only begotten Son, that whosoever believeth in him should not perish, but have everlasting life." John iii, 16.

Can this extraordinary announcement be received as actual truth? Dare we credit it, or lift up our guilty hearts to comprehend its terms? It is so exceedingly strange and thrilling, that it seems to stunn us, and only on recovering from our amazement, are we able to grasp this blessed declaration. There is so much of God in it, that we recognize his awful presence, and fear, as we are entering "into the cloud." "God so loved the world." If I may use the expression, God created the world, or God preserves the world, or God governs the world. The language I employ is, to my mind, the symbol of infinite wisdom, power, and benignity. But when I repeat this statement, "God so loved the world," the apparently simple clause reveals at once a depth of meaning at which the mind is almost startled into incredulity: and yet these precious words afford the true explanation of many mysteries in God's providence. Why, for example, may the saint exclaim, I have been redeemed, I have been brought into the conscious possession of divine peace and joy—and the dark shadows that lay on my mind have all fled away; or, Why does the throne of the universe now stand out as a throne of grace, to which there is for me daily access, continuous welcome, and rich response? or, Why are there in heaven the spirits of our human kindred, whose bodies are lying yet in the darksome pollution and thralldom of the grave? Are not such changes, privileges and blessings to be traced upward and backward to the grand and ultimate fact, that *God loved the world?*

Now, the introductory shows that this text presents itself as the reason for the previous statement. The reference in it is to a remarkable incident in the history of ancient Israel. They had in one of their periodical fits of national insanity, so provoked their divine Protector, that he sent among them fiery serpents, and many of them were bitten and died. But, to modify the chastisement, and make its terror of salutary effect, Moses was commanded to frame a brazen figure of one of the poisonous reptiles, and place it upon the summit of the flag-staff, so that any wounded Hebrew might be able to see it from the extremity of the camp, and every one, no matter how sorely he felt the poison in his fevered veins, if he could only turn his languid vision to the sacred emblem, he was instantly healed.

It is then asserted that salvation is a process of equal simplicity, facility and certainty. Jesus Christ must be lifted up, and he that looks may live and be saved from death. This is a pledge of safety and glory to the be-

liever. "He that believeth shall be saved." The scheme
of salvation is here presented to us in its origin, its
means and its designs; or we may contemplate the love
of God, first in its object—the world; secondly, in the
provision he has made for its deliverance—the gift of
his Son; and thirdly, in the instrumentality by which
this provided salvation is brought into individual possession—the exercise of faith.

1. *The object of God's love.*

Again we recur to the startling thought, if God so
loved this guilty world, what an unplumbed depth of
grace must be in his heart! For the object of his love is
not the world in its fairest condition, such as it was when
his eyes resting on it with beaming complacency, he pronounced it "very good," but that same world ruined by
sin, and condemned for its apostasy. There would have
been no wonder had the divine Lawgiver assumed the
stern functions of the Judge and doomed our guilty earth
to the death which it deserved. Might it not have been
enveloped in flames, which, gleaming far into other
orbits, would have taught other creatures that "our God
is a consuming fire"? But, though he had armed his
law with a terrible penalty, and allowed the incipient
elements of the menace to fall upon the sinner; though
the holiness of his nature and the interests of his government seemed to demand that punishment shall instantly and immediately follow transgression, yet, without any change in our claims or character, he loved us.
And that love is not a mere relenting which might lead
to a respite, or a simple regret which might end in a
sigh, but, thrice blessed be his name, it is a positive af-

fection. It is as true as his existence, as real as our sin. Now there is no merit in loving what is lovely, for by a necessity of our emotional nature, our affection throws itself out upon any object that presents an aspect of loveliness. Such an instinct within us is only the reflection of a similar law in the character and actions of God. He cannot but love what bears his image, and therefore the bright and happy essences who surround his throne are forever sunning themselves in his ineffable smile. But, ah! man has washed out and lost his moral loveliness: originally like God, he is now as unlike him as he can be, and there is nothing about him but his misery to attract the Divine attachment. Paradise loathed and expelled him, and the globe into which he was exiled out of Eden, has been cursed for his sake—" the whole creation groaneth and travaileth in pain together"; the bleak rock on which no seed can vegetate; the eternal snows where no animal breathe; the blasted oak of the forest. stretching its leafless arms to the wintry sky; the beach spread over with the wreck and corpses of the hurricane; the desolations of volcanic fires and the rocking and chasms of the earthquake; the bed on which tosses the invalid, to whom wearisome days and nights are appointed; the hand which the laboring man uplifts to wipe the perspiration from his brow; and those monuments of victory that tell of thousands lying beneath them uncoffined and unknelled—these are tongues by which nature proclaims in melancholy emphasis that she has wandered from her God. And this sin of man is not his misfortune, but his fault. Sometimes those around us are overborne in providence; wave after wave breaks upon them, and, as they stagger and fall, they are more to be pitied than to be blamed. Alas! on the contrary, man is not only a ruined, but a self-ruined creature: he has lowered himself to what he is—the victim of his own pride and disobedience.

I presume not to solve the mystery of the origin of evil. I cannot tell why, with God's possession of infinite power and purity and love, sin was ever permitted to find its way into our world; but this I know, that amidst all subtile speculations on this dark theme—amidst all daring and devious attempts to climb these heights of eternal Providence—this one truth is very apparent: "God made man upright, but they have sought out many inventions;" there is, therefore, no palliation for our crime. Our Master is not an "austere" one reaping where he had not sown, and gathering where he had not strewn. The law under which man was placed was holy, and just, and good; and he was furnished with power of perfect obedience. The test by which he was tried was an easy one, and he was, but for one restraint, lord of the world: besides, it was simply a respect for the divine will which could lead him to obedience. There was no commingling motives such as that which spring out of natural relationship and originates moral obligations; but man broke this simple covenant, and wantonly disobeyed the clear injunction not to eat of the tree. And yet that world, which has in this way made itself so guilty and helpless through its perversity and disloyalty, is not thrown off by God—is not flung into oblivion by him, and covered with his frown—is not merely tolerated, or, like a condemned criminal, indulged with a few provi

dential and minor kindnesses; but is really loved by him.
The marvel is this, there is nothing he hates so much as
sin, and yet no one he has loved so much as a sinner. In
spite of our alienation and hostility; in spite of our low
and loathsome repugnance; in the midst of so much that
he hates and condemns and nauseates, God has loved,
yes, has "so loved the world!" What infinite grace in
this amazing love of God! Let me sing,

> "Thou shalt walk in robes of glory;
> Thou shalt wear a golden crown;
> Thou shalt sing redemption's story
> With the saints around the throne,
> Thou shalt see that better country
> Where a tear-drop never falls,
> Where a foe may never enter,
> And a friend ne'er said farewell.
> Where upon the radiant faces
> That will shine on thee alway,
> Thou wilt never see the traces
> Of estrangement and decay."

2. *If God loved, and so loved this little world, surely his love
was wholly disinterested in its nature.*

Should some large and important province of an empire rise in rebellion, the sovereign will use every means
to induce it to return to its allegiance ere he proceed to
arms against it; but should an insignificant region be involved in insurrection, summary vengeance will be taken
at once on its folly. Now, our rebellious world was only
a small portion of God's universe. What a melancholy
thought did we look up to the sky and see in every orb
a wreck and in every star a prison of ruined spirits!
The great unfallen universe is a vast territory on which

its Creator can still look with complacency. If, therefore, worlds unnumbered roll around his throne, brighter in their glories of light and mass of structure and motion than ours; if the absence of our earth from creation would be as little felt as the removal of a single particle of sand from the mound which girds the ocean; and if another divine fiat could at once fill its place with a new orb, and with another population whose obedience should be coeval with existence and co-extensive with their faculties —will it yet be affirmed that it was from any selfish motive, or with any selfish purpose, that God has prolonged our existence, when life and all its enjoyment has been forfeited? or that we are of so much importance to himself, his happiness, or the harmony of his empire, that, rather er than allow us to perish, he gave up his only begotten Son to death, even the death of the cross? "When I consider the heavens, the work of thy fingers; the moon and stars, which thou hast ordained; what is man that thou art mindful of him? and the son of man, that thou visitest him?" Higher beings are even the servants of humanity.

> Of highest God, that loves His creatures so,
>   And all his works with mercy doth embrace—
> That blessed angels he sends to and fro, ·
>   To serve to wicked man—to serve his wicked foe.

The same truth has been pictured out to us by the great teacher. The shepherd had a hundred sheep, and only one had gone astray. But his fond anxieties go out after it; and leaving the ninety and nine in comparative neglect, he flees into the wilderness and seeks everywhere, till he comes upon the object of his solicitude—the one poor wanderer; and when he finds it, there is more joy in his bosom over the recovery of the solitary straggler, than over the entire flock that had not deserted the fold. Oh, there is more of the heart of God exhibited in our salvation than in all his benignity to the universe, in which this orb is truly a "little one;" and yet it has called out emotions which other and mightier spheres have failed to elicit. Now, such is its moral magnitude, that in its connection with Christ, it stands out in unrivalled glory from other worlds, and over its redeemed inhabitants is the chant raised, this my son "was dead and is alive again; and was lost, and is found." Therefore, we may exclaim "The Lord is my shepherd, I shall not want." "Not unto us, O Lord, not unto us, but unto Thy name give glory, for thy mercy, and for thy truth's sake."

3. *If God loved this world, this world of fallen men—and not of fallen angels—his love must be sovereign in its essence, for man was not the only sinner in his dominions.*

Beings of higher original nature, and having their position in heaven itself, were mysteriously involved in the guilt and doom of apostasy, and expelled from their bright domain. And yet, though they dwelt in heaven, they are not summoned back to it; no pardon is offered to them; no means of purity are provided for them; no mediator has taken on himself the nature of angels, in order to make atonement for them: they are left to the endurance of death—death for ever—ever sinning, ever suffering, while pardon and restoration have been proclaimed to the human family—our weak and erring race!

So nearly allied to the ground they tread, so proud in their debility and so impious in their thraldom, would it not have been a more natural operation, so to speak, to have saved these lofty exiles, and called them again to the heaven in which they once lived, and for which they were created, than to select this distant and miserable world, and by an abnormal and mighty process to purify and refine its wretched earthy outcasts for a realm of existence to which they are strangers, and to which they reason, inducing infinite wisdom to make this choice? We may neither search nor maintain this preference of fallen man to fallen spirits, as the recipient of divine love can only be resolved into a mysterious exercise of uncontrolled sovereignty. The loved of earth and hell both might have been punished with eternal penalty, and neither the one nor the other could have complained of the equity of its doom, and both might have been forgiven and redeemed, and the one and the other would have equally felt its salvation due to the blessed Jehovah's tender pity. Nay, though hell had been taken and earth had been left,—though the earliest transgressor only had been saved, and brought again to the awful presence before which they once mixed, and the hallelujahs which they once sang, while this world was left to pine and grow hopeless and helpless. But Christ's universal and everlasting kingdom hath been gloriously set up.

> Jesus shall reign where'er the sun
> Doth his successive journeys run;
> His kingdom spread from shore to shore,
> Till moon shall wax and wane no more.

4. *The gift of God's love.*

Now, we estimate the value of a gift by various *criteria.*
First, the resources of the giver must be taken into consideration. If a man be loaded with the blessings of
fortune himself, and occasionally part with some of his
superfluity, such a fraction, if estimated by its proportion to what remains behind it, is really far less in value
than another gift that does not possess it semblance of
magnitude. Our Lord reckoned by this scale, when he
declared that the poor widow, who cast her last mite into
the treasury, gave truly more than the wealthy worshippers with the ringing shekels and talents of their abundance, for "she gave her all." Nor can the motive of the
giver be left out of the calculation; one may heap favor
upon the head of a fallen foe to wound his pride and
produce within him a rankling sense of his inferiority.
But such a donation suffers a sad discount when compared with other and in themselves smaller benefactions
bestowed in cordial warmth and generosity of spirit. The
manner, too, in which a gift is conferred, must enter into
the estimate; if it be withheld till it be rung out of the
donor by repeated and humiliating importunity, or if it
be offered in a surly spirit, and its amount enlarged upon
with undue exaggeration, or if it be meted out slowly and
with a prolonged comment upon the trouble and self-
denial it has cost the benefactor—it sinks at once in importance, especially if placed in contrast with a lesser
boon given. The reader may note that God gave his
only begotten Son. Look, then, with enlightened vener-
ation at the resources of the Giver—are they not infinite

and endless? The riches of the universe are at his dis-
posal. But oh, when he gave his Son, did he not give his
all? What other gift remained superior to him—equal
to him—or next to him? There was no second Christ
to confer, the divine treasury containing many gifts.

5. *The design of God's love.*

But the same fervor of the divine love is seen, too, in
the end contemplated, and in the peculiar instrumentality
by which that end is achieved. He gave his only begotten Son for this purpose, that "whosover believeth in
him should not perish, but have everlasting life." The
language plainly implies that the race were all in a lost
condition. The Son of God is given to keep them from
perishing—from sinking into irretrievable ruin. It was
a perdition great and terrible which sin had produced.
What a frightful spectacle! a soul in ruin—away from
God, and hostile to him; his image gone; his glory in the
dust; a darkened mind; a distracted or sensualized heart;
a spirit in thraldom; appetite predominates; the divine
law forgotten; conscience bribed, hushed, or quelled; and
the end of man being not unrealized, of all enjoyment.
Life, how eagerly cherished by all; the sick man tugs for
it; the bad man dreads its termination, and the good
man prays for its continuance. The whole struggle of
world is for life—for means to enliven and prolong it. It
is full of contrivances to shut out the idea of death. Now,
if there be such anxiety for the life that now is—a life that
is brief and chequered by clouds and trials—a life that is
rarely stretched to three score and ten years, and it is
ended amidst spasms and tears—Oh, what intense aspi-

rations and prayers and wrestlings should there not be
after a life that is not measured by centuries or by mil-
lenniums—a life far above change and sorrow—a life serene as the bosom of its Giver, and endless as God's own
eternity !

> "Let every tongue thy goodness speak,
> Thou sov'reign Lord of all ;
> Thy strength'ning hands uphold the weak,
> And raise the poor that fall."

6. *The result of God's love to the world.*

In the stead of the church he died, to deliver her from
death, the sentence which so righteously lay upon her.
The death of the Son of God is a true and mighty sacrifice. That death might be viewed in a variety of as-
pects; for while it was an instance of undaunted bravery
and a confirmation of his sincere attachment to men, it
was also an example to all his followers, inspiring them
with that patience which they must evince during their
lives, and with that calmness and fortitude which must
not forsake them, even in the hour of trial and desolation. But it was more than a tragedy or a martyrdom.
To suppose the Saviour to be the victim of human persecution is true; but to suppose him nothing more is but
to give an ordinary termination to his extraordinary existence. To bring into one fold all who will conform to
His divine laws is one of the designs of the blessed Jesus;
also it is his design to bring into the church of God all
who are in the fellowship of the church—the communion
that its members enjoy, one with another. The end of
this fellowship is the maintenance of sound doctrine and

of the ordinances of christian worship.   We will preach
Him to all and cry in death, " Behold the Lamb."

> " How sweet the name of Jesus sounds
>   In a believer's ear;
> It soothes his sorrows, heals his wounds,
>   And drives away his fear.
> It makes the wounded spirit whole,
>   And calms the troubled breast;
> 'Tis manna to the hungry soul,
>   And to the weary, rest."

SERMON IV.

A FAREWELL DELIVERED BEFORE THE KEN-TUCKY CONFERENCE.

BY BISHOP S. T. JONES, D. D.

After adoption, amid great enthusiasm, of a memorial to the General Conference for the return of the Bishop to this District, and a short recess, the Conference re-assem-bled to hear the farewell, which was as follows:

"Endeavoring to keep the unity of the spirit in the bond of peace."—Ephesians iv, 3.

No apostolic admonition possesses deeper, broader, and more significant meaning, or is capable of a more general and beneficial application than that contained in the text. Sin has not only exhibited its hostility against God in its stubborn and defiant attitude of disobedience and oppo-sition to his just requirements, but it has also developed a spirit of bitter antagonism and savage encounter be-tween man and his fellows.

The first important event recorded in the history of the race after the fall is a sad commentary upon the truthfulness of this declaration. Cain, with premeditated

purpose and murderous intent, invites his unoffending
and unsuspecting brother into the field, and, in open day,
coolly and without any just provocation, smites him to
the death and leaves him weltering in his blood.

Thus early in the history of the human family were
our parents summoned . to look sadly on the legitimate
results of their own rash act, and the unmistakable development of the malice and hate, the envy and murder
which it had produced. The cause and excuse for this
beginning of fratricides was, that God had respect to the
offering of Abel and had none for that of Cain. The exercise,
therefore, of a preference on the part of the Almighty
toward one of his own loyal subjects, led to the commission of the first foul murder; and how many have since
been murdered in character, reputation, good name, and
even deprived of life itself—simply on account of preference?

Such is the envious character of the human heart that
if you will traduce your neighbor, acquaintance, or associate, you excite for him pity; but commend him—speak
of his merits, his ability, his rightful claims to consideration—and you have aroused for him in the bosom of
your hearers, feelings of jealousy and bitter hate.   David
would have had but little to fear at the hands of Saul
or any of his sympathizers, if, after he had slain Goliath
of Gath, it had been said of him by the popular crowd,
that there was but little valor about his exploit; that it
had been performed in an awkward and bungling manner; and that after all, the credit and glory of the
achievement were mainly due to Saul and his brave army,
and not to the mere accident of this youthful rustic, fresh

from the sheepfold. But, the startling and significant cry which rang out on the evening air, and whose inspiring eloquence and enchanting cadence, as it issued from the lips of the fair damsels of the land, quickened the pulsations of every patriotic Israelite was—"Saul hath slain his thousands, but David his tens of thousands!"

Not, even, with credit announced with equal sweetness from the lips of the same fair maidens—that Saul and his confederates had slain their "thousands"—could they brook the announcement, truthful as they knew it was, that David had slain his "tens of thousands."

"All this availeth me nothing," said the jealous, wicked, envious Haman, "so long as I see Mordecai the Jew sitting at the king's gate." His banqueting, wining and dining with the king and queen, to the exclusion of all the other members of the royal court, the honor of the second place in the kingdom, the rich emoluments of office and all the glittering glories of the house of Haman were soured—blighted to ashes—by this slight, but well-merited mark cf respect awarded to that horrible Jew.

And thus does jealous envy and secret hate, armed with murderous weapons, stalk abroad through all the land to-day scheming, plotting and planning, with a view to circumvention and destruction.

It has not remained in the field where it perpetrated its first dark design; it has not been content to plot its foul mischief and murder in kings' palaces, but, restless of the ordinary walks of life, it has lifted its slimy, serpentine folds into the very inner courts of the visible church, and even essays, and that with alarming success, to desecrate and pollute the sacred oracle. It were by no means difficult to prove that the desolating wars which have drenched so large a portion of the earth in blood, have been the almost invariable fruits of envy, jealousy and hate, that ascendency to the thrones of earth have been more numerous through treachery and murder than by lawful claims or lawful means. The legitimate elements of sin are pride, selfishness, arrogance; these lead to discord, dissension, division, and bitter strife; then come uncharitableness, unmercifulness, wicked conspiracies, sinful plottings, envy, jealousy, hate, and murder—often bloodless, but, nevertheless, murder; for he who hates his brother, under any circumstances, is charged in the Scriptures with murder, though he does not actually shed blood. Hate cherished in the heart—fostered and brooded over—carried to its desired end—means murder as its objective point—its cherished aim. It misrepresents, defames character, destroys reputation; and, in the language of Shakespeare, takes that from another which we cannot give; and is, in the eye of God, equally infamous with the taking of life. It needs no warrant from Scripture to prove that many of those who are converted, justified children of God by many infallible signs, are far from being perfectly freed from indications of the lingerings of these offshoots of sin—the remains of the carnal mind.

Even among the devout and holy men engaged in establishing the Christian Church, we find, at least, one example of the spirit of bitter contention, which distracts the church, and finally leads to division, envy and unholy strife. Paul and Barnabas, by far the more earnest and successful of the apostles, and, doubtless, equally pre-eminent in piety, differ so widely and so fiercely about a matter in which complete harmony might reasonably have been expected, that these good men separated in consequence of the sharp contention that arose between them, long and beneficially as they had traveled and labored together; and, so far as we are informed, they never associated in their labors subsequently. Thus early in the history of the church, and among its most distinguished advocates, do we find the seeds of discord sown, and, taking root, to spring up, as evil seed is sure to, in envy, strife and division. We could hope, for the sake of that homogenial spirit, that harmony of operation, which is the ornament and beauty of christian character, as well as for the power, influence and success of the Christian Church, that this divergence of holy men of God from that path of peace and love which appeared so prominent, so uniform and so captivating in the early experience of the church, were left isolated and alone in its subsequent history and progress; that this huge malformation, marring so greatly the otherwise symmetrical and beautiful form of the Body and Spouse of the Lord, was the single instance of its kind to which infidelity could refer, or anti-christianism take exception against the claim of the church as the repository and dispenser of divine knowledge; but the truth is sadly otherwise.

The implied claim and boast of superiority in judgment; in aptness to teach; in clearer or more correct comprehension of the word of God; in clearness of perception on doctrinal points; in appropriate and fitting ceremonials; in precise Scriptural modes, and in various other less important matters, have, at one time and another, originated the most rancorous dissensions, resulting in the most unfortunate divisions. And many a Paul and Barnabas, whose christian intercourse had been most pleasant, whose fellowship in Jesus had been sweet, and whose labors together in the vineyard of the Lord had been crowned with most brilliant success, have separated, never again on earth to be as lovingly united in a common cause as before. Add to these the jealous envy even in the same society which comes frequently of the seeming preference which the Almighty exercises by endowing one or more of his servants with more ability, more influence and power, and, by consequence, more success than others, and which, not unfrequently, manifests itself in open or covert demonstrations, kindred to those by which Cain sought and finally succeeded in detroying his brother, and you have an inventory of the vast magazine of means with which Satan carries on such formidable warfare against the unity, peace and success of the church.

From these and other considerations, the importance and necessity of christian endeavor in the direction of the careful and prayerful maintenance of the spirit of unity will readily appear.

First—Let us notice briefly the principle urged, "*unity*."

The term signifies—oneness, concord, agreement; in such manner as to insure harmony, friendliness, peace, Differences of views, opinions, doctrines and creeds are likely to exist for an indefinite period; possibly, and most probably, to the end of time. Denominational diversities arising from honest and sincere differences of interpretation of the word of God, seem, therefore, unavoidable; and any serious attempt at uniformity in these respects, much as they may appear desirable, is likely to be unsuccessful and futile.

Uniformity in maternal care, and early training in education, in literature, in lines of thought, and in all the conditions, accidents, and circumstances which enter into the formation and development of mental and moral character, must, in the nature of things, precede any hopeful attempt at uniformity in this respect; and, as nothing in the near future encourages a hope of a uniformity so strange, it would seem useless for us to waste our energies in efforts to accomplish that which seems not only of doubtful accomplishment, but of equally doubtful advantage or benefit.

Christian unity, as urged in the text, is not, consequently, dependent upon either the abrogation of denominational distinctions—not in themselves invidious—or uniformity in any of those circumstances and conditions in human development which render mankind so diverse in their thoughts and actions; but it accommodates itself to all these circumstances and shades of difference, and so blends and harmonizes them as to render each subservient and helpful to the other, and alike beneficial to all.

Secondly—We observe that the nature of the unity, for the maintainance of which we are urged by the Apostle to put forth an earnest endeavor, is "*unity of spirit*"—union, agreement, harmony of spirit; that condition of mind wherein the sentiments, desires and affections are so happily influenced, directed and controlled by a feeling of friendliness and good will, that the one all-pervading, all-controlling and predominating spirit, which disposes us to deal prudently, friendly, kindly and even magnanimously with each other at all times, and under whatever real or imaginary provocation, shall hold its ascendency over every other feeling that would seek to antagonize it, with its banner joyfully thrown to the breeze, floating in triumph over all human selfishness, emblazoned with the Christian motto, "good will to men."

The fostering and exercise of this spirit would prove a panacea for the effectual cure of nearly all the maladies which enervate the church, and shear it so fearfully of its influence and power for good.

However widely we may differ in our opinions, our creeds, our views of church polity, our modes of administration; however diversified our gifts, graces and callings in life; whatever may be our denominational divergencies, we may, and ought to be, firmly and harmoniously united in a spirit of fraternal love. As in nature harmony is made up of diversities or seeming contrarieties; as in music, it depends upon alternate chords and discords, so also in the Christian Church, infinite wisdom and goodness, by a seeming predetermination, has diversified the elements of usefulness in harmony with the order of things throughout the universe, and in loving accommodation to similar diversities in the human family, to the end that all may avail themselves of the means of salvation, and every one may be left without excuse. There is, consequently, nothing in the dissimilarity existing among men, either as individuals or associations, that is necessarily incompatible with Christian unity. It may be difficult for men, influenced and blinded by self-ishness, or dilated to lofty dimensions by pride and vanity, or bending at the shrine of the common prejudices of the times, to comprehend either the possibility or the fitness of a strict observance of the divine injunction. In view of the fact that the Church is composed of what seems to them a crude, heterogeneous mass, made up of all nation-alities, all complexions, all grades and conditions, they regard it as being a most unsavory and incongruent com-mand. And there are those who occupy high positions in the visible Church who share, with the Apostle Peter, the same lofty feeling of superiority, and evince the same loathing repugnance, when summoned like him to a practical recognition of the full brotherhood and uncon-ditional equality of the children of God; who, while the-orizing with captivating eloquence, force and beauty, upon the doctrine and indispensable necessity of Christian unity, practically evince such selfish and repulsive man-ners; such an unholy and unlovable course of conduct; such harsh and uncharitable criticisms, and such a mani-fest disregard for the tender sensibilities of the brethren, as constitute a standing repudiation of the doctrine they teach. In vain to them is the vessel filled with a hetero-geneous mass of living creatures let down from heaven; in vain to them comes the voice from the throne of the universe: "Rise, Peter, kill and eat." They still insist that whatever to their refined and fastidious tastes seems "common and unclean" must necessarily be so regardless alike of the judgment and commands of heaven. Con-vinced of the logical sequence of the startling conclusion at which Peter arrived, they are nevertheless wanting in the magnanimity with which he confessed his conviction of the fact by the bold announcement, "God is no respecter of persons," and in the earnestness and impartiality with which he subsequently maintained his position, notwithstanding its unpopularity among his countrymen. To this class of professors the command in the text may seem neither practicable nor desirable; but to the unselfish and thoughtful it is not only practicable, but, aside from its God-required observance, there is a beauty and fitness connected with it that commends it to the favor and hearty acceptance of all who are capable of comprehending and appreciating the harmony of natural things and their application to those harmonizing influences among men, and especially among Christians, which accord with their best interests. The materials entering into the composition of a house are widely dissimilar; yet, the insignificant and seemingly inferior portions of it are as essentially parts of the building as are the more conspicuous and apparently useful—each and all contributing its share to the stability, the beauty and utility of the dwelling. Thus, by the appropriate and beautiful figure of the human body, the Apostle strikingly illustrates the unity and harmony of the Church under the symbolical representation of the mystical body of Christ; assuring us here as elsewhere that whatever diversities exist in the Church of God, exist in conformity with the divine arrangement, and for the interest and edification of the entire body—no part is wanting, none superfluous. Just as each member of the human body is a part of the whole, so each member of the Christian Church constitutes a part of that Church.

The real or apparent inferiority of some parts as compared with others does not destroy their identity nor supersede their usefulness; each performs its function, however inconsiderable, and each makes its contribution to the symmetry, harmony and beauty of the whole.

So intimately are they connected, so harmoniously are they blended in the human system, that the loss, or even the serious interruption of any one member, will be sensibly felt by the entire body. So, likewise in the Christian Church, we are all members of the same body, and whatever affects one affects all.

True, we belong to different nationalities; we are born in different localities; we belong to different denominations, and worship under different forms. We differ in color, in tastes, in conditions and circumstances in life. We differ quite as widely in intellectual endowments; but, having received the same heavenly recognition, the indwelling testimony of the Divine Spirit, we sustain perfect equality before God, and any invidious distinction made as between the children of God is insulting to him, and in its highest degree anti-christian.

There are, indeed, diversities of gifts and operations; some possess, in a remarkable degree, the spirit of wisdom; others, the word of knowledge; others, the working of miracles; others, diverse tongues; some prophesy, some teach and some are evangelists; some exert a wider influence than others, and are more successful. But all belong to the same body, are members one of another, are governed by the same head, are seeking the same

15

object—the glory of God—and therefore should seek and maintain unity of spirit. It may be very desirable to be the eyes, ears, or hands of this body, and we may seem even to quarrel with our Maker, because we do not occupy what seems to us the more important positions, and we may become envious of our brethren, and, like Cain, seek to injure them on account of this seeming preference exercised on the part of the Almighty. But this course will never alter these conditions; and, so far from deriving any permanent advantage from the adoption of a course of such extreme folly and wickedness, it is destined to bring signal disaster upon the heads of its perpetrators. The sad history of Cain, of Saul and of Haman, who were conspicuous in this reprehensible practice in the early history of the race, abundantly illustrate the truth of this averment. And who but recalls some one or more whose premature downfall and ruin was the legitimate consequence of jealous envy? He who digs a pit for his brother is sure, sooner or later, to fall therein himself, with equal or more saddening results than he intended. Many a Haman has, by divine permission, been made to suffer the penalty of his envious guilt upon the same gallows which he had erected for some innocent and unsuspecting Mordecai!

Proper consideration will readily convince us that most, if not all, the causes which constitute the grounds of envy and jealousy, resulting in discord and uncharitableness toward our brethren, are matters over which neither they nor ourselves have any control, but are the result of divine arrangement; and so far from causing disquietude or alienation, they were designed to be beneficial to all. And in the exercise of a liberal, generous spirit of christian charity, they would prove to be a bond of perfectness—a golden chain possessing—indeed multiform, multifarious and multinominal links—but nevertheless, a chain, uniting in spirit every believer in Christ into one bond of peace, harmony and love—so strong that no power on earth could sever it. And with the great link firmly held in the omnipotent grasp of the Head of the Church, no power in hell could seriously disturb its harmony and security.

Let us not, therefore, cherish, much less exercise, any feeling of jealousy or envy in reference to any one; since, as the context assures us, "God hath set the members every one of them in the body as it hath pleased Him."

Neither let us despise any one; since each one is part of the whole. Let not the eye envy the ear, because of its ability to try sounds to the exclusion of the other members. Let not the hand despise the foot, because it occupies the lowest position; for the ear cannot see, the hand cannot hear, neither can the feet manipulate. Each serves a desirable purpose peculiar to itself, designed of God, and conducive to the comfort of all.

Equally absurd and senselessly wicked are those invidious distinctions, so inimical to this unity of spirit, founded on race, complexion, beauty, deformity, or wealth; since these are either accidental or they are in accordance with divine arrangement; and the variety here as elsewhere should be made productive of harmony and love rather than of discord and strife, and especially when Christ is formed in the heart.

Third—Having spoken of the importance of Christian

unity, its spiritual nature and its entire practicability, let us briefly inquire *into the method of maintaining it.* " Endeavor" is the word used in the text, which signifies to try, to labor intensely. Nothing important is accomplished without an effort. Let us, therefore, in view of its beneficial results, both to ourselves and those with whom we have intercourse, as well as the cause of God, which will be so greatly promoted thereby, put forth an earnest, faithful and prayerful endeavor, to maintain the unity of spirit at all times and at whatever cost, by the cultivation of a spirit of meekness, or that disposition which checks the tendency to provocation in ourselves and overcomes the disposition to provoke others; by lowliness of mind, or such modest views of ourselves, our position, attainments, ability or opinions, as excludes all pride and arrogance, and which prompts us to regard with respectful consideration the views, opinions and ability of others. By longsuffering, or the disposition which enables us to bear slights, insults and injuries without fiery resentment or a desire to revenge, but disposing us to hold the same kind, generous and loving tenor of our way, prompts us to seek to confer the largest amount of good upon those who have sought, and are seeking, to do us the greatest harm. By a spirit of loving forbearance, predisposing us to cast the mantle of charity over the faults and infirmities of our brethren from considerations of love; by forgiving one another, as we are wont to have others forgive us, we shall find, on a careful review of our Christian life, many things for which we can with difficulty forgive ourselves. Others doubtless find as much, or more, quite as difficult to forgive in us·

Let this mutual view of kindred offenses, arising from similar infirmities, so humble us as to prompt us as freely to forgive each other as we forgive ourselves, or hope to to be forgiven of the Lord. Let us frankly speak what we conscientiously believe to be the truth in reference to our brethren ; but in such manner, and under such circumstances, as will bring it within the category of "speaking the truth in love."

Much that tends to acrimony and strife, leading to discord and alienation among brethren, arises from misrepresentation ; either wilful, or the result of improper information. In our seeming haste to publish what we have heard, or at best know very imperfectly, we frequently indulge—however undesignedly—in gross misrepresentations seriously affecting each other's reputation. No possible loss, either to ourselves or community, could be sustained by a little delay in circulating what tends to the injury of a brother; and delay would, in many instaces, put us in possession of such facts in the case as would relieve the story of most, or all, of its injurious effects.

If the time, ability and research so carefully devoted to contentions about modes and ceremonial forms among denominations—to misrepresentations, or insidious efforts to inveigh character, among brethren, by innuendo, by a meaning smile, or by a manifestly false apology for one whose good name is being traduced, in which, by attempt-.ing a lame excuse, we admit the facts contained in the slander, although we do not believe them, and thus crystalize into truth what we might easily have branded and silenced as a falsehood.

If the time, effort and skill thus devoted to the interest of discord, were utilized in zealous efforts to cement more closely the ties of Christian brotherhood, what a vast amount of peace, prosperity and success would result to the Church: Infidelity and skepticism would be disarmed of their most formidable weapons, and Christ would, be gloriously enshrined in thousands of hearts, wherein Satan now presides in grim majesty.

Far more time and study are employed in attempts to belittle each other as Christians and as members of community, than is enlisted in battling against the common enemy, or in studied, honest and prayerful endeavor to establish the cause of Christ. "With what measure you mete the same shall be measured to you again," is a trite truism, that should serve to remind us that the thorn-seeds wilfully sown by us for the goading of others to-day, will be harvested and resown to-morrow, with the vast increase which the crop will yield, to recompense us for our toil with the largest interest by and by. The pupils before whom we recite a slander, a misrepresentation, or any belittling or depreciating lesson against our brother or sister to-day, are carefully appropriating our manner, our skill and our tact, to unite with their own, with which to recite a similar lesson against us to-morrow with all these damaging improvements. So that every effort of this character is throwing dust in the air, with the certainty that our own eyes will be filled with it, painfully, in the sequel.

It is not only, therefore, an unchristian course of conduct; but a wicked and costly folly.

Finally, if we would cultivate Christian unity and love

if we would encourage the diffident and strengthen the weak ; if we would counteract the sourness of spirit, which leads to alienation and estrangement; if we would contribute toward that oneness of heart which signalizes all the special and fuller manifestations of divine power and success in the Church of God, let us carefully avoid what we know to be reprehensible, and as carefully practice what we know is commendable.

Thus shall we foster that unity and harmony of spirit which infidelity cannot gainsay, the world cannot successfully resist, which Satan condemns and God approves.

This will embrace whatsoever is true, honest, just, pure and lovely ; and, if we would faithfully and successfully serve the cause of God and advance the interest of Zion, let us " think on these things."

And may God make our hearts one.

AN ADDRESS.

THE GOOD SAMARITAN.

BY BISHOP S. T. JONES, D. D.

Delivered before the Independent Order of Good Samaritans and Daughters of Samaria at Knoxville, Tenn.

"And Jesus answering said, A certain man went down from Jerusalem to Jericho, and fell among thieves, which stripped him of his raiment, and wounded him, and departed, leaving him half dead. And by chance there came down a certain priest that way; and when he saw him, he passed by on the other side. And likewise a Levite, when he was at the place, came and looked on him, and passed by on the other side. But a certain Samaritan, as he journeyed, came where he was; and when he saw him, he had compassion on him, and went to him, and bound up his wounds, pouring in oil and wine, and set him on his own beast, and brought him to an inn, and took care of him. And on the morrow when he departed, he took out two pence and gave them to the host and said unto him, Take care of him: and whatsoever thou spendest more, when I come again, I will repay thee. Which now of these three, thinkest thou, was neighbor unto him that fell among the thieves? And he said, He that shewed mercy on him. Then said Jesus unto him, Go, and do thou likewise."— Luke x, 30—37.

We have here briefly narrated an account of one of those attempts which are frequently put forth by the skeptical, to bring into disrepute and ridicule the loved doctrines of our holy religion, that they may substitute instead, their own peculiar views of right, however erroneous.

A lawyer—a man learned in the law—approaches the Saviour with all the seeming gravity which the subject demands, and inquires: "Master, what shall I do to inherit eternal life?" Notwithstanding the solemnity of the question, the sequel proves that this man, like thousands of others since his day, was far more anxious to justify his own course of conduct, right or wrong, than to learn what was the good and acceptable way of the Lord. For, in answer to the Saviour's questions, "What is written in the law? how readest thou?"—after answering very promptly and very correctly by repeating the two leading commandments embracing love to God and to man, comprehending piety and philanthropy, the soul of all true religion, the end of the law and the aim of the prophets—he shows either his ignorance or his disregard of the spirit of these commandments, or both, by asking, "Who is my neighbor?"

To cure at once his ignorance and narrowminded conceit, the Saviour puts the case in the strongest possible light, by giving either the historical facts or the striking parable of the unfortunate Jew, who, on his way from Jerusalem to Jericho, encountered a band of thieves, which, having stripped him of all he had, even to his raiment, and having beaten him unmercifully, left him wounded and bruised and half dead on the wayside. The lawyer is reluctantly forced to admit that, whoever came to the succor and salvation of this unfortunate man—whether an acquaintance or a stranger, a fellow-countryman or a foreigner, a former friend or foe, whether of kindred persuasion or different creed, whether clad in the sacred vestments of the sanctuary or in the tattered garments of the mendicant—proves himself to be neighbor to the sufferer, the friend of humanity, and therefore the friend of God.

First. I remark, that extensive endowments, vast powers of usefulness, the robes and sanction of the Church, are not to be relied upon as evidences of love to God. Nothing seems more evident than that the Saviour designs to teach us in this narration that there is a wide contrast between the mere forms and ceremonies of Christianity and the reality of it; the mere profession—however ostentatiously made, however loudly claimed—and that indwelling of the divine principle which is as certain to make its presence and influence known and felt by all who are within reach of that influence, as are the rays of the sun to effect, beneficially, every form and species of vegetable and animal existence and life with which they may come in contact.

He presents to us the mitered priest—the recognized leader of a Church founded in infinite tenderness and love for mankind by a Being who, in His remarkable self-forgetfulness and matchless devotion to the interest of those who had fallen among thieves and even been left helpless by the wayside, excites the astonishment and challenges the admiration of the universe—this high functionary who was to imitate the example of his divine Lord and Master by lifting the fallen, cheering the faint, and binding the broken-hearted—this distinguished representative of the High Priest of his profession nears the scene over which angels hover in deep sympathy;

but devoid of that tenderness of heart which weeps with
those who weep and mourns with those who mourn, un-
mindful of his solemn obligations and lost even to those patriotic impulses which should have prompted him to come
to the relief of one of his own countrymen and creed, he
gathers his priestly robes about him and passes on the
other side.   Doubtless we all would have been electrified
had we listened to the sermons and lectures of this divine,
in the temple of the synagogue; our sympathies would
have been aroused in the interest of suffering humanity,
as he discoursed with burning eloquence on that subject,
just as they are to-day, when we listen to the touching
appeals to those sympathies from the pulpit or read them
in the writings of distinguished men in the Church, who,
like this same priest, when practical sympathy—action,
and not words are required—almost invariably pass by
on the other side.

What a vast number of poor unfortunate beings, victims of injustice and wrong inflicted by those whom it is
unpopular to condemn, are passed by unassisted and un-
comforted.   Most of the evils which afflict mankind,
originating in man's inhumanity to man, might be effect-
ually remedied if the priesthood—the ministry of the
sanctuary—would take time to stop by the wayside and
have hearts to sympathize with God's poor unfortunate
ones who in one way or another have fallen among
thieves who have stripped them of rights and privileges
common to all men in this highway of life, and left them
friendless and comfortless.   These men will find time and
convenience too to stop to discuss the impropriety, the
crime, of plucking an ear of corn on the Sabbath day,

even if it be to meet the most pressing demands of nature; they can stop to defend the peculiar dogmas of their church, its rites and ceremonies; they will find time to stop to resent an insult, however slight, offered to some one of distinction or wealth, and raise their hands in holy horror at an injury inflicted upon these; but obscure humanity, suffering from whatever wrongs, burdened with whatever sorrow or cares, pleading with whatever pathos, is passed by on the other side. Matters of mint, anise and cummin—these formulas in religion are carefully looked after; but the weightier matters of the law, justice, judgment, humanity, mercy, are criminally neglected—passed by on the other side.

Thus it seems clear that the highest positions, the costliest robes and the most emphatic sanction of the church, do not necessarily prove the possession of Christianity, since he who practically denies his love to man, whatever may be his theory on that subject, ignores thereby all claim of saving love to God.

We come next to notice the conduct of the second personage whom the Saviour brings to view in this instructive narrative—the Levite, the attendant of the priest, the representative of that distinguished class in the Jewish church which in consequence of its loyalty to the divine government and its zeal for the divine worship were made the guardians of sacred things, the exponents of the law and the teachers of the people. It might be expected if the superior officer of the sanctuary had, like his predecessor Aaron at the foot of Mount Sinai, so far forgotten for the time his duty to God and humanity as to patronize this popular golden-calfship—if he, in his

character of one of the chief shepherds, had coldly passed
by this maimed and bleeding sheep of the fold rather
than provoke popular criticism by stepping to his relief—
this under-shepherd, this middle-man between the priest
and the flock, whose office and labors brought him into
more immediate contact with the people, and whose feelings and sympathies are consequently supposed to have
entered more fully into their wants, cares and burdens—
it might easily be expected, I repeat, that the imploring
look and sad and touching moans of this wounded man
of Israel would have been responded to by this Levite.
But he, too, following the cruel example of his superior,
passed by on the other side.

Second. This brings me to remark, that Church organizations, religious zeal and loud professions of charity,
are no proofs of christian character. As the priest represented the ministry, so the Levite may be taken as the
representative of the membership, the laity of the Church,
and we see in his conduct in this case a striking illustration of that trite scriptural phrase, "like priest like
people."

And thus we see it to day. Leading, wealthy, influen-
tial members of the Church are not wanting in ostentatious
exhibitions of so-called charity; interests wherein pomp and
display hold sway are patronized with lavish munificence,
while those which involve the well-being of the masses,
the poor, the unfortunate, the lowly sufferers of earth—
interests which do not provoke popular applause—are
passed by on the other side. True, there are exceptional
cases, but such is the rule.

There are but few evils of a general character but might

be cured, or at least checked, if the power and influence wielded by the Church were marshalled against them. But alas! for suffering humanity, the Church, divinely appointed to hear the cries and administer to the wants of the fallen and forlorn, has partaken of the popular frenzy, and the popular frenzy is to give prostrate humanity the go-by, unless it be distinguished humanity. The Church which eloquently proclaims a gospel which assures us that there is no respect of persons with God, emphasizes its faith in that gospel by practicing the most invidious distinction. In the privileges and immunities of government; in the necessities and comforts of life; in social intercourse; in tender sympathy; in its approach to the sacred altar of worship ; and even in death itself— in all these it leaves out the lowly and obscure, and passes by on the other side.

Evidently, church membership and religious observances and zeal are no warrant of eternal life.

Third. Finally, we notice that human kindness, acts of humanity impartially bestowed upon our fellow men, are the unmistakable outgoings of a heart imbued, influenced and controlled by the Divine Spirit, and are the unfailing signs of true piety.

In the person of this Samaritan we have a man who is on a journey, and therefore had but little time to wait on the way; he might have easily excused himself and silenced his conscience on this ground, and passed on; but he did not. In the next place, this traveler is a Samaritan, identified with a people who cherished a most inveterate hatred toward the Jews, and were equally despised by them. It was a marvel to the Samaritan

woman at the well, that even Christ, being a Jew after
the flesh, should be sufficiently civil even to ask her for a
drink of water. " How is it," said she, " that thou, being a
Jew, askest drink of me, which am a woman of Samaria?
for the Jews have no dealings with the Samaritans." From
the facts of history it is hardly possible to conceive of
anything much lower in the scale of humanity than the
Samaritans were held by the Jews; and as this hostility
was mutual, it required no ordinary degree of humanity,
large-heartedness, and love for man because he is a man,
to have induced this Samaritan traveler to perform the
kind offices he so generously bestows on the unfortunate
Jew. But he was equal to the emergency. His feelings
of humanity conquer all personal animosities, all race
pride, all religious differences, and proudly holds the
mastery. He does not plead immunity from duty on the
grounds that the priest and Levite, whose special duty it
was to look after this member of the Jewish Church, have
passed by. He does not hesitate to ask himself the question, will it be popular to relieve this Jew, or will I gain
notoriety in so doing, or will I be criticized damagingly
for my recognition of him, or will it in any way advance
my interests by eliciting the good opinion of the public
or the favorable comment of the chroniclers of events, or
will it expose me to the contemptuous scorn of my sect?
He does not even stop to contemplate the possible danger
to his own life and person on this lonely road, where at
any moment he might meet the same band of highway-
men which had perpetrated this foul deed of blood ; but,
forgetful of all else save the succor of a fellow mortal, he
approaches the ghastly form with a heart and purpose to

relieve him. He does not stop to ask him a number of needless questions as to his business, his politics, his nationality, his faith and order; he does not stop to lecture him about his tattered garments which still hung upon him, or his filthy appearance, or his want of prudent caution, and all this. No, he would first prove himself a *friend* by kind, generous, helpful treatment; then lecture him, if need be, when he had time and heart and strength to hear, comprehend and appreciate a lecture. But now, these gaping, bleeding wounds and painful bruises are to be bound up and mollified and soothed with ointment; strength is failing from loss of blood and from the agony of pain; the spirits are fast sinking, and the life of a fellow being is trembling in the balance. To meet these, the Samaritan at once addresses himself. He tenderly closes the gaps, binds up the wounds and pours on the soothing oil; thus he allays the pain. He next administers a cup of wine to the parching lips of the sufferer; this revives the sinking spirits. He then lifts him up and sets him on his own beast, and supporting him there, carries him to the next inn, places him in charge of proper attendants, orders him to be given every attention till fully recovered, pays down part of the expenses and promises to pay on his return, whatever additional expenses might have been incurred.

Such, my hearers, is the practical philanthropy which the religion of Christ infuses into the hearts of all who possess that religion ; such is the example of our divine Lord and Master, and such is the religion of the Bible. It matters little what is our creed, our office and standing, our gifts and qualifications, our nationality or complex-

ion, our church relations and religious zeal or our claims
to piety—it matters not by what name, order or association we are known—if we lack this practical humanity,
this genuine philanthrophy, this distinguishing mark of
Christian character, we are wanting in the most essential
element on which to base our claims to eternal life.

The founders and patrons of the order which I have
the honor to address at this time—"The Independent
Order of Good Samaritans and Daughters of Samaria "—
doubtless designed that the association, having the name
of the distinguished philanthropist whom we have been
considering, should also emulate his illustrious example.
Hence, your declaration of principles commits you to the
grand, ennobling and God-like work of hunting up the
outcast, the degraded and forlorn, and especially the ine-
briate; to relieve and to rescue them, to close up the gaps
and bind up the wounds which a wicked and profligate
course of life has inflicted, as well by your example as by
your precept, and to pour in the oil and wine of sympathy, material aid and spiritual consolation; to lift them
up by your personal efforts and influence as well as by
your prayers and tears, and, bearing them in the arms of
love and affection, bring them to the spiritual inn—the
Church of the living God—for final healing and full restoration to society and heaven.

See that the noble principles of your Order are supple-
mented and crystalized by the noble example of this
Good Samaritan; and, while your constitutional obligations make it your first duty to look after each other, let
the recollection of the common brotherhood of mankind

prompt you to extend your influence and aid to all within your reach, passing none by.

Remember your motto, " Love, Purity, Truth." Exemplify this beautiful and appropriate trio by love to God and to all mankind, by purity in principle and practice, and by truth in all things. Love the principles, rules and regulations of your Order ; see that they are observed in all their purity. Be true to each other, true to God, and true to humanity—then you will be true to yourselves. Finally, imitate, in all your intercourse with mankind, the example of the great prototype of the Good Samaritan—Jesus Christ—who never passes by, but stoops to lift up suffering humanity in every form and in every place, and your organization will prove a lasting blessing.

CPSIA information can be obtained
at www.ICGtesting.com
Printed in the USA
BVHW060038100920
588456BV00003B/83